Orchids, Rosebuds, *and* Sweet Flags

Also by the Author

Mexico in American and British Letters: A Bibliography of Fiction and Travel Books, Citing Original Editions. 1974.
American and British Writers in Mexico, 1556-1973. 1974.
Escritores norteamericanos y británicos en México, 1556-1973. Translated by Ernestina de Champourcin. 1977.
Arthur Rimbaud / Paul Verlaine: A Lover's Cock and Other Gay Poems. Translator with Jacques Murat. 1979. Revised edition, 1980.
Tennessee Williams: A Bibliography. 1980. Second edition. 1991.
The Gay Male Sleuth in Print and Film: A History and Annotated Bibliography. 2005. Second edition, 2012.
Ardennian Boy. Novel with William Maltese. 2007.
The Golden Age of Gay Fiction. Editor. 2009.
1960s Gay Pulp Fiction: The Misplaced Heritage. Co-editor with Jaime Harker. 2013.
Gay Novels of Britain, Ireland, and the Commonwealth, 1881-1981: A Reader's Guide. 2014.
Le garçon des Ardennes. Translated by Allie Vinsha and Jade Baiser. 2016.
Gay American Novels, 1870-1970: A Reader's Guide. 2016.
For the Gay Stage: A Guide to 456 Plays, Aristophanes to Peter Gill. 2017.

Orchids, Rosebuds, *and* Sweet Flags

Reflections on Gay Poetry

DREWEY WAYNE GUNN

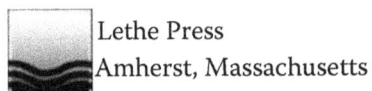

Lethe Press
Amherst, Massachusetts

ORCHIDS, ROSEBUDS, AND SWEET FLAGS: Reflections on Gay Poetry
Copyright © 2018 Drewey Wayne Gunn. ALL RIGHTS RESERVED. No part of this work may be reproduced or utilized in any form or by any means, electronic or mechanical, including photocopying, microfilm, and recording, or by any information storage and retrieval system, without permission in writing from the publisher.

Published in 2018 by Lethe Press, Inc.
6 University Drive • Suite 206 / PMB #223 • Amherst, MA 01002 USA
www.lethepressbooks.com • lethepress@aol.com
ISBN: 978-1-59021-691-0 / 1-59021-691-1

Set in Warnock, Jenson, and Hoefler Text.
Interior design: Alex Jeffers.
Cover design: TK.

LIBRARY OF CONGRESS CATALOGING-IN-PUBLICATION DATA
TK

Dedicated
to Ian Young,
whose bibliography has been indispensable to project after project;
and to my local health care givers,
Jerin Bryant and Timothy VanFrank,
and my radiant team at M. D. Anderson Cancer Center—
Kanwal Raghav, Armeen Mahvash, and Bruno Odisio
—who permitted me to finish this one.

Un orquídea, brasileña, lo sé ahora,
es el cuerpo que amo,
es tu boca buscando la mía sin miedos
en la oscuridad o a la luz de una vela.
                    —Jaime Manrique

    Es la rosa entreabierta
    de la que mana sombra,
    la rosa entraña
    que se pliega y expande
    evocada, invocada, abocada,
    es la rosa labial,
    la rosa herida.
                      —Xavier Villaurrutia

        Root of washed sweet-flag! Timorous pond-snipe!
        Nest of guarded duplicate eggs! It shall be you!
        Mixed tussled hay of head, beard, brawn, it shall be you!
        Trickling sap of maple! Fibre of manly wheat! it shall be you!
                      —Walt Whitman

Contents

Foreword	1
Reflections	7
Sîn-lēqi-unninni: *Gilgamesh* (Akkadian)	9
King David: Lament for Saul and Jonathan (Hebrew)	12
Homer: *The Iliad*, Books 9–11, 16–18, 23–24 (Greek)	14
Theocritus: Idylls (Greek)	16
Catullus: Epigrams & Invectives (Latin)	18
Virgil: *Eclogues* 2 & 3; *The Aeneid*, Books 5, 9 (Latin)	20
Horace: Odes (Latin)	22
Ovid: *Metamorphoses*, Book 10 (Latin)	24
Martial: Epigrams & Invectives (Latin)	25
Juvenal: Satires (Latin)	27
Strato of Sardis: Epigrams (Greek)	29
Abu Nuwas: Erotic Poems (Arabic)	31
Rumi: Love Poems (Persian)	33
Saʿdi: *The Rose Garden* (Persian)	35
Dante: *Inferno*, Canto 15; *Purgatorio*, Canto 26 (Italian)	37
Hafiz of Shiraz: Erotic Poems (Persian)	40
Pacifico Massimi: *Hecatelegium* (Latin)	41
Michelangelo: Sonnets to Tommaso de' Cavalieri (Italian)	44
Edmund Spenser: *The Shepherds' Calendar* (English)	46
Michael Drayton: *Piers Gaveston* (English)	49
Christopher Marlowe: *Hero and Leander* (English)	51
William Shakespeare: *Sonnets* (English)	53
Richard Barnfield: *The Affectionate Shepherd*; *Certain Sonnets* (English)	56
John Wilmot, Earl of Rochester: Bawdy Poems (English)	59
Lord Byron: Love Poems / Anonymous: *Don Leon* (English)	60
August von Platen: Love Sonnets (German)	67
Alfred, Lord Tennyson: *In Memoriam* (English)	69
Walt Whitman: *Leaves of Grass* (English)	70

John Addington Symonds: Poems in Various Keys (English)	74
Paul Verlaine: *Hombres*; Love Poems / Arthur Rimbaud: Bawdy Poems (French)	78
A. E. Housman: *A Shropshire Lad* (English)	84
C. P. Cavafy: "Days of…" (Greek)	87
Roger Casement: Love Poems (English)	90
John Henry Mackay: *On the Margin of Life* (German)	92
Lord Alfred Douglas: Early Poems (English)	93
Mikhail Kuzmin: Poetry Cycles (Russian)	96
Aleister Crowley: Two Pornographic Collections (English)	98
T. S. Eliot: *The Waste Land* (English)	101
Fernando Pessoa: *Antinoüs* / António Botto: *Songs* (Portuguese, English)	106
Wilfred Owen: Erotic Poems (English)	109
Federico García Lorca: *Ode to Walt Whitman*; *Sonnets of Dark Love* (Spanish)	111
Hart Crane: *White Buildings* (English)	116
Luis Cernuda: *Reality and Desire* (Spanish)	119
Xavier Villaurrutia: Nocturnes (Spanish)	122
Richard Bruce Nugent: "Smoke, Lilies, and Jade" (English)	125
Sandro Penna: Boy-Love Poems (Italian)	128
W. H. Auden: *The Platonic Blow*; Love Poems (English)	131
Jean Genet: Poems to Criminals (French)	136
Paul Goodman: *Hawkweed* (English)	139
Tennessee Williams: Erotic & Autobiographical Poems (English)	141
James Broughton: "Wondrous the Merge" (English)	145
Robert Friend: Narrative Poems (English)	148
Harold Norse: Poems about Various Subjects (English)	150
Robert Duncan: "The Torso" (English)	152
Rod McKuen: *Alone…* (English)	156
Allen Ginsberg: *Howl* (English)	158
James Merrill: *The Changing Light at Sandover* (English)	161
Frank O'Hara: "I do this I do that" (English)	164
Orlando Paris: 69 Flights of Fancy (English)	168
Jean Sénac: Corpoèmes (French)	170
Jaime Gil de Biedma: *Longing* (Spanish)	174
Thom Gunn: *Boss Cupid*; Earlier Poems (English)	177
Richard Howard: *Two-Part Inventions* (English)	180
Dinos Christianopoulos: *The Naked Piazza* (Greek)	183

Daryl Hine: *In and Out* (English)	186
E. A. Lacey: *Path of Snow* (English)	188
Mutsuo Takahashi: *Ode* (Japanese)	191
Joe Brainard: *I Remember* (English)	193
Jean-Paul Daoust: *Blue Ashes* (French)	195
Jaime Manrique: *My Body; Tarzan* (Spanish, English)	197
Tim Dlugos: *A Fast Life* / David Trinidad: *Notes on a Past Life* (English)	200
Vikram Seth: *The Golden Gate* (English)	203
Mark Doty: *Fire to Fire* (English)	206
Essex Hemphill: *Ceremonies* (English)	209
Brane Mozetič: *Banalities* (Slovene)	211
Jonathan Kemp: *26* (English)	213
Justin Chin: Poems Selected by Friends (English)	215
Hal Duncan: Poems of a Sodomite (English)	217
Slava Mogutin: *Food Chain* (Russian)	219
Stephen S. Mills: Two Collections (English)	221
Some Last Thoughts	**225**
A Note on Translation	**227**
General References	**233**
Index	**237**
About the Author	**241**

Foreword

Throughout history, poetry has been both a very public and a most personal form of recreation/re-creation. Publicly, it is designed to be read or recited aloud to an audience of one or of hundreds. It is drama without the fourth wall. It serves to unite, to affirm family and tribal loyalties. It may be sung in harmony, spoken with force, or whispered in intimacy. Personally, it reaffirms self. It unlocks one's private emotions. As Faulkner said in his Nobel address, "The poet's, the writer's, duty…his privilege [is] to help man endure by lifting his heart, by reminding him of the courage and honor and hope and pride and compassion and pity and sacrifice which have been the glory of his past. The poet's voice need not merely be the record of man, it can be one of the props, the pillars to help him endure and prevail." It always amuses me to hear someone say, "I don't like poetry," and then see him walk away with his pods in his ear, listening to lyrics.

To some extent I blame my profession for making students dislike poetry. My department used to use Laurence Perrine's *Sound and Sense* to teach poetry. There was much to admire about the textbook, but two sections increasingly jarred me. One was something like "Good Poetry and Bad Poetry" (I may have the adjectives wrong, but that was the idea), and the other was "Good Poetry and Great Poetry." Why should I tell a student that a poem he likes is a bad poem? It might be by Perrine's standards; it might be by mine. But to criticize a person's taste is to criticize the person. I stopped teaching both sections. I notice the text is now in its 14th edition with new authors. The two sections are now disguised as "Evaluating Poetry 1: Sentimental, Rhetorical, Didactic Verse" and "Evaluating Poetry 2: Poetic Excellence." The publisher takes pride in their existence; its advertising copy informs the prospective teacher: "Unique chapters on evaluating poetry speak directly to students with straightforward answers to questions most introduction to poetry books ignore: 'Is some literature better?' and 'How can it be evaluated?'" I am tired of cultural mandarins determining our reading. I try to be democratic; my own taste is pretty catholic. *The Waste Land* had a major impact on my life, but I also enjoy pulling down Walter Cooper's *Briefs* from my bookshelf. I remind myself that my taste is based on my experiences. They have predisposed me to like certain poems and to dislike others. Your taste may concur with mine; it well may diverge.

I do love friends to pass on poems that mean a lot to them. I read the poems then through both my eyes and theirs. As I type this, it strikes me that that is exactly the kind of gift my ninth-grade substitute English teacher gave her students. She loved poetry. She would sit on the teacher's desk, cross her shapely legs, and read us poem after poem. Since she was only a few years older than we and a bleached blonde to boot (I'm writing this from a 1954 perspective), enormous numbers of the adolescent boys in the class suddenly discovered that they too loved poetry, and the baseball coach was no longer able to beg the loan of players during English class to attend to the ball field. And once a poem gets under the skin, it survives and takes on a life of its own. I remember a UNC graduate school alumnus returning to campus for a visit. He had been a POW during the Korean conflict. He thanked his English professors for having led him to love poetry. Validating Faulkner's observation, he had kept his fellow POWs' morale high by teaching them the poems he recalled from his student days.

No doubt memorability in part explains my personal bias towards poems that rhyme or observe a strict metrical pattern. Like jingles and songs, they enter the memory without one even being aware they are doing so. I memorized such different poems as "Stopping by Woods on a Snowy Evening" and "Everything Happens That Can't Be Done" before I realized I had done so. A genuine question: can or does anyone memorize a typical Robert Duncan poem? (After reading too much Duncan, I jotted down a reaction: "I'm tired of seeing typography / Passed off as poetry.") Could a POW teach a bill bissett poem to his fellow prisoners? I am also partial to poems that present at least a hint of a narrative. David Trinidad uses a line from Ted Hughes as an epigraph to his collection *Dear Prudence*. The British poet wrote, "Without a story there is no poem. Not even a writer." My head is filled with such poems: nursery rhymes and Cummings's playfulness, Frost's wry observations and Langston Hughes's jubilant and sometimes angry lyrics, Dickinson's musings and Whitman's outpourings, Eliot's Prufrock as well as his Waste Land,

FitzGerald's Rubaiyat and Dylan Thomas's lyricism, Stephen Crane's pills and Housman's potions. There are lots of individual poems I have stored away too, from Marvell's Mistress to Burgess's Purple Cow. The older I get the more I hear Yeats's "Sailing to Byzantium" ("That is no country for old men"). A number of these poets were gay, but it is singular how few gay poems I knew.

The past fifteen years I have dedicated to exploring gay mysteries, gay pulps, gay fiction, gay drama. Clearly, it was time to explore gay poetry, as my colleague Susan Roberson pointed out. Gregory Woods at the beginning of his *History of Gay Literature* (1) asserts, "The relationship between poetry and homosexual advocacy has a long history. After all, in Greek myth, the most prominent candidate for the honour of having been the first mortal man to love his own sex was the poet Orpheus.... Another of the men reputed to have been the first homosexual mortal, Thamyris, was also a wonderful poet." So, Woods continues, "If we are to speak of a continuous, or even intermittent 'gay tradition' in literature,…it would be a tradition not of novels but mainly of verse." Woods, however, does not address a fundamental question: What is gay poetry? Is it, as some wag asked, poems that want to sleep with other poems? Actually, I discovered, to some extent it is. Early on there is a sense that poets of the epic tradition were implicitly referencing each other. By the time of the Romans the references start becoming explicit. As a gay canon builds, it becomes apparent that poets are quite aware of both their predecessors and their contemporaries. Verlaine basked in the idea,

> We count an illustrative lineage
> Of princes and sages,
> Of heroes and demigods,
> At all times, in all ages.

The label *gay*, of course, is a present-day tag. The earliest poems are gay for readers today; at the time they would have been labeled with other tags. Foucault's strictures about nomenclature are valid, but they are of little concern to me in these readings.

As with my previous excursions I focus on exploring my identity as a gay male, leaving my ties to the larger queer community in the background. Alberto Mira, in his introduction to Ángel Sahuquillo's study of Lorca (6), points out that insisting on examining a writer's homosexuality is not, per se, a carnal matter: "The feeling of rejection, fear of the law, doubts, the lack of an authorized language to wrap emotions into words, the awareness of disgust around the individual, the need to accept marginality to find sexual or emotional satisfaction, the feeling of difference, the importance of a close circle of friends…are far more important aspects of homosexual experience than the actual sex act, and have a stronger influence on any artist's work." I first overheard the word *homosexual* at age nine as a result of the discussions attending publication of Kinsey's *Sexual Behavior in the Human Male* and somehow knew it described me. I never felt confused about my sexuality, just confused about what to do with it and where I fit in. It never once crossed my mind to seek psychological counseling. As an adult, if I never flaunted my relationship with Jacques, I never hid it either. In most ways I think I was fairly typical of my generation and my culture. No doubt that background colors my encounters with these poems.

To come up with my reading list I turned to gay and GLBT anthologies, histories, encyclopedias, and dictionaries. The only criticism I used has been that which looks at these poets from a sexual perspective. Throughout the period of my formal academic training, so-called New Criticism reigned. *Merriam-Webster's Encyclopedia of Literature* in its succinct definition observes, "New Critics insisted on the intrinsic value of a work of art and focused attention on the work alone as an independent unit of meaning; they were opposed to the critical practice of bringing historical or biographical data to bear on interpretation." I took their strictures so to heart that I virtually ignored *all* criticism, including that of the New Critics themselves. Of my cohort at UNC I was probably the most widely read in the primary literature and absolutely the most ignorant of critical thought. I did read biography. Reasoning that one gets a sense of the writer from his or her work, I saw no reason not to explore the real person, and that interest has continued. Via Northrop Frye, I also discovered Joseph Campbell and thence Carl Jung. I remain fascinated by the heroic quest. I read far more poets than the ones represented here. These are the ones who spoke to me personally or who seemed historically too important not to pay homage to them, whether I clutched them to my heart or not. All the poets felt an attraction to other males (though the case of Tennyson is definitely murky) or were at least gay-friendly (Dante, despite assertions to the contrary).

I embarked upon the journey chronologically. It begins appropriately with a quest, the oldest gay poem now known to exist, followed by two other narratives from the Heroic Age and a Greek pastoral reaction against such exploits. Next come a series of Roman poets, mostly Latin-speaking but a very comical Greek also. The Middle Ages take us into Italy, with another great quest that has all sorts of gay implications, and into the Middle East, where god, sex, and wine intertwine to provide ecstasy. The Renaissance opens in Italy and flowers in Elizabethan England with some of the greatest stars of the gay pantheon. Poetic voices seem not so loud during the Enlightenment (clearly a topic to explore: is my assertion valid?), but the nineteenth century sees the beginnings of the push for gay liberation fought by greater and lesser voices, sometimes in relatively open ways. The twentieth century seems dominated by American voices. Is this an illusion created by my failure to find relevant non-American voices or a reflection of the actuality that in some ways "gay literature" comes across as an American invention? (Were Gide and Proust, who have had so much influence on gay letters, aware of themselves as gay writers the way Americans are and have been?) The post-WWII periods has provided the most revelations for me personally. Its richness is so great that I ended up, sometimes almost arbitrarily, eliminating some very interesting poets from the finished record so as not to write a tome.

When I first began reflecting on gay poetry, I was pretty much taking a guide-book approach, similar to the one I had used with novels and drama. This survey, however, was conceived while I was at M. D. Anderson in Houston, and it took a decided turn upon a return visit there. Facing my own mortality, I gradually became more forthcoming about my personal relations with the poems. And when I reached the second half of the twentieth century, I increasingly allowed my own taste to determine which poets I wanted to explore. I read poets who are habitually anthologized, but I also searched out poets who have received short shrift. I am sure that some of my choices will seem quirky, as I have included poets not usually admitted to academic discussion. While I was drawing up my list, I anticipated liking such recognized poets as Frank Bidart, J. D. McClatchy and Rafael Campos, but we failed to connect. At the other extreme, though I enjoy the saucy insolence of poets like Gavin Geoffrey Dillard, Sky Gilbert, and Trebor Healey, upon rereading them and then closing the book, I found I remembered little of their verse. No POW material there for me. Throughout I have quoted samplings of the poets' works. I would like to have quoted more, but the fair use rules for poetry are far less clear than those for prose. I have let the Center for Social Media's *Code of Best Practices in Fair Use for Poetry* guide me in determining how much I could offer. My hope is that the following pages will come across as one friend sharing poems with another friend.

Friends have accompanied me on this quest. Though I seldom take his advice (he hates the title I have chosen, for instance), I consider Ron Hamm to be my golden editor. While walking our dogs, Glenna Cannon and Monica Simoncelli allowed me to muse aloud about what I was discovering. I spent a delightful afternoon with John Morgan checking my understanding of two Spanish poets. Steve Delaney and David Lennon have cheered me along since the inception of the idea. Alex Amador and Will Parish, Cathy Downs and Mike Hess have put up with my babbling about my most recent find while sharing meals. As always I am indebted to Aggie Gonzalez of the interlibrary loan department at the Jernigan Library (Texas A&M University–Kingsville). Each new book I publish becomes my favorite, but I think I have genuinely enjoyed writing this one the most, perhaps because I have been more willing to open up in ways I never had before.

Reflections

Sîn-lēqi-unninni: *Gilgamesh* (Akkadian)

Whether it is an example of homosexuality, bromance, male bonding, comradery, or symbolic male doubling, the Gilgamesh legend remains the oldest surviving story whose plot builds on male intimacy. Probably based on a historic third millennium bce king, the earliest known version, *Shūtur eli sharrī* (Surpassing All Other Kings), is an Akkadian reworking of older Sumerian texts (where the king's name appears as Bilgames). The standard version has become the one ascribed to the priest Sîn-lēqi-unninni (13th–11th c. bce): *Sha naqba īmuru* (He Who Saw the Abyss). All these texts were written in cuneiform on clay tablets. Sîn-lēqi-unninni's poem was written on twelve, with six columns each. Fragments of the tablets containing the poem were not discovered until 1853, and translation did not begin in earnest until 1872. Unfortunately, not a single tablet found so far is complete, and some tablets are almost altogether missing. Thus, scholars have had to piece together the narrative from fragments from various sites, other similar Akkadian and Sumerian stories, and educated guesses.

A number of themes, most prominently the nature of heroism, mortality, and love, and repeated images, such as the city, unify the various episodes that make up the plot. To heighten the drama it uses such poetic devices as parallelism, repetition (with variations), symbolism, allusion, and word play. Novelist John Gardner and English Professor John Maier in their translation tried to preserve these features, all the while respecting "the integrity of the poetic line" (5). For many reasons I prefer their translation, though several versions, in both poetry and prose, are available. Even though it is now a quarter of a century old (and new discoveries have been made since), Gardner and Maier's preserves the fragmentary state of the text, using notes to bring in evidence from other sources. Thus the reader actively participates in the reconstruction of the poem. For those who want a more conventional reading experience, I recommend poet Stephen Mitchell's version. Both Maier's and Mitchell's introductions, each clearly influenced by Joseph Campbell's concept of the monomyth, are illuminating.

The ancients referred to the work as a series rather than an epic (a Greek term). It opens with a prologue in the poet's own voice introducing King Gilgamesh, two-thirds divine, one third human: "The one who saw the abyss I will make the land know; / of him who knew all, let me tell the whole story." In his beginnings the king oppressed his subjects to the point that the gods decided to create his equal to tame him. Thus Enkidu comes into existence, an uncivilized creature of the forests until he is seduced by a temple prostitute. Their sexual union (very explicitly described) humanizes him. Stirring his heart, she reveals that the gods have ordained he will become Gilgamesh's companion. Meanwhile, Gilgamesh has two dreams that foretell Enkidu's coming: one of a meteorite and the other of an axe, both of which he embraces as a wife. Reinforcing a gay reading, Anne Kilmer notes that the names of both objects may embody word plays on terms used for male prostitutes (George, 452; Greenberg, 113).

In Tablet 2 the two heroes meet and clash as Gilgamesh is on his way to deflower yet another bride. Gilgamesh subdues Enkidu, but the two instantly embrace and become inseparable friends. With Enkidu beside him, Gilgamesh embarks on the hero's journey. His first challenge is to destroy Humbaba, a guardian-demon of the cedar forest. The rest of Tablet 2 through Tablet 5 describes the two men's preparations for the battle, their departure, and their encounter with and destruction of the demon. In a comic interlude Tablet 6 records how a goddess renowned for her capriciousness becomes enamored of Gilgamesh and proposes that they become lovers. He angrily spurns her advances. She thereupon pleads with the head god to avenge her by sending the Bull of Heaven to punish him. The two heroes vanquish the Bull, and Enkidu physically insults the goddess. As a result she demands his life, and in Tablet 7 Enkidu dies. Tablet 8 opens with Gilgamesh's moving eulogy for his lost friend in which he says even nature mourns his passing. At the end Gilgamesh covers Enkidu's face "like a bride's."

Now keenly aware of his own mortality, Gilgamesh, in Tablet 9, decides to seek out the one man who has never died: Utnapishtim, a survivor of the great flood which the gods sent to punish humans. He undertakes an arduous journey through darkness and over the waters of death to the Underworld (Tablet 10). In Tablet 11 Utnapishtim recounts his ordeal, which transformed him into a godlike being. He challenges Gilgamesh to a test to see if he is worthy of similarly petitioning the gods. The king is to remain awake for six days and seven nights. Gilgamesh does not last even a day. At the urging of Utnapishtim's wife, he is given a second chance: Utnapishtim reveals the existence of a plant that will confer eternal life. But once it is in his possession, Gilgamesh becomes distracted, and a serpent steals the flower. Gilgamesh must accept that, like all men, he will die. He returns to his city, and the poem ends with images that recall its opening lines.

Sîn-lēqi-unninni's poem is finished. His reasons, therefore, for appending Tablet 12 to the work are much debated. It is a close translation of a Sumerian original in which Enkidu is still alive at the beginning. He offers to go to the Underworld to retrieve two objects (whose exact nature remains uncertain). Told how to conduct himself, he does just the opposite and is seized by death. Gilgamesh searches for a god who can bring Enkidu back to life. For a moment Enkidu's ghost appears, and the two men attempt to embrace and kiss one another but cannot. Enkidu recounts what happens in the Underworld to all humans. Column 4 is particularly tantalizing for a gay reader. A potentially telling set of four lines is broken and has a word whose meaning is uncertain. For certain, Enkidu is describing what has happened to his physical body, saying that that which gave Gilgamesh so much pleasure is now decayed. Taking his cue from similar Sumerian contexts, Babylonian specialist Andrew George (733) proposes the reading

My friend, the penis that you touched so your heart rejoiced,
grubs devour it…like an old garment.
My friend, the crotch that you touched so your heart rejoiced,
it is filled with dust like a crack in the ground.

Curiously, though George revised his Penguin edition of the epic the same year he published his scholarly Oxford edition, he left intact his earlier reading of the first line as "the one whom you touched." George, however, does have the man and the ghost actually hug and kiss.

Maier (29) stresses that one lesson the poem teaches is that "death is inevitable and terrifying, but life…is precious." *Carpe diem.* Mitchell (56) writes, "Experiencing intimacy seems to be for Gilgamesh what experiencing sex is for Enkidu: an initiation into human vulnerability." Yet the prologue suggests that Gilgamesh is aware that at least his heroic name and the record of the exploits undertaken by him and his friend to the doors of death itself can survive in legend:

Find the copper tablet-box,

slip loose the ring-bolt made of bronze,
Open the mouth to its secrets,
Draw out the tablet of lapis lazuli and read it aloud.

    Until Enkidu came into his life, Gilgamesh seems to have had little purpose or direction, but, as Raymond-Jean Frontain argues, "By wrestling with and finally embracing the wild man Enkidu, Gilgamesh is able to contain his own dangerously lawless heterosexual impulses and channel his superhuman energies in heroic endeavors, his love for Enkidu allowing him a psychological completeness unavailable in any other relationship" (Summers, 330). United, the friends transcend their limitations and leave their distinctive mark on human history. In Maier's words (42), "Nowhere else is the identification between lover and loved so strong as in Gilgamesh's attempt to become Enkidu.... In *Gilgamesh*, the pain of love and loss is the defining feature of humanity." The epic provides a stirring beginning for a journey through gay poetry. Even its fragmentary state seems appropriate since gays have had to piece together their history from all sorts of clues.

TEXT: John Gardner & John Maier, trans., *Gilgamesh: Translated from the Sîn-leqi-unninnī Version*, with Richard A. Henshaw (Knopf, 1984). SUPPLEMENT: Stephen Mitchell, *Gilgamesh: A New English Version* (Free, 2004). REFERENCE: A. R. George, ed., *The Babylonian Gilgamesh Epic: Introduction, Critical Edition, and Cuneiform Texts*, 2 vols. (Oxford, 2003).

King David: Lament for Saul and Jonathan (Hebrew)

Before the advent of Lord Douglas's "Two Loves," the most quoted homoerotic lines in English letters were probably 2 Samuel 1:26 (KJV): "thy love to me was wonderful, / passing the love of women." For a long time it would be the one indication for isolated gays that they were not alone. The familiar story of David and Jonathan is recounted in 1 Samuel. David (c. 1040–c. 970 BCE) becomes King Saul's harp player; his music soothes the often tormented king. One day David hears the repeated challenge that the Philistine giant Goliath tauntingly throws out to Israelite warriors. He offers to take on the giant, successfully kills him with his slingshot, and severs the giant's head. Prince Jonathan sees the youth and binds his soul to David's, to Saul's disgust (or perhaps jealousy). Daniel Helminiak (124) draws a parallel between their relationship and that of Gilgamesh and Enkidu: "their relationship fits the model of noble military lovers, common throughout the societies of the ancient mid-East." He amasses evidence that their friendship was sexual as well as emotional and spiritual. (Helminiak also brings together clues that Saul and Saul's daughter equally vied for David's affection.) Saul's behavior becomes increasingly erratic as he grows more and more envious of David's successes with his people.

In this tense situation David departs to battle the Amalekites. While he is away Saul and his sons engage in another battle with the Philistines; Jonathan and his brothers are killed, and Saul commits suicide. When David returns and hears the news, he composes an eulogy and orders it to be taught to the people he now rules. He laments the deaths of both Saul and Jonathan in some thirty lines unified through the use of metaphorical language, repetition, parallelism, and symmetry (as well as a system of stresses in the original Hebrew). The King James Version for long was the standard. But the New International Version brings out the homoeroticism of the original more clearly. It begins by describing Jonathan as a gazelle, a time-honored Mid-Eastern metaphor for a lovely youth. The only ones who will rejoice over his death are "the daughters of the uncircumcised." The lament finishes with the famous lines rendered thus:

I grieve for you, Jonathan my brother;
    you were very dear to me.
Your love for me was wonderful,
    more wonderful than that of women.

It has been rewarding rereading the story sandwiched between two epics. I don't remember it having any effect on me as a youth. Probably it was glossed over in Sunday school, and I can't imagine any minister in Mom and Dad's church using it as a text. Rather it was the story of David and Bathsheba that was considered fit for a sermon (and for a Cecil B. DeMille movie).

TEXT: 2 Samuel 1:19–27, *Holy Bible* (Zondervan, 2011). REFERENCE: Daniel A. Helminiak, *What the Bible Really Says about Homosexuality*, 2nd ed. (Alamo Square, 2000), 123–26.

Homer: *The Iliad*, Books 9–11, 16–18, 23–24 (Greek)

I first read *The Iliad* (8th/7th c. BCE) in a prose translation while still a teenager. I hated it. After encountering Shakespeare's *Troilus and Cressida*, I tried again, this time with a verse translation, and felt as if I had been transported in space and time. If translation is betrayal (*tradurre = tradire*), a prose translation of a poem is plain murder (*assassinare*). I reread the relevant passages in Robert Fagles's 1990 translation because it is the one currently on my shelf, though it was the one by Richmond Lattimore, 1951, that first reached me. *The Iliad* recounts the last weeks of the Greeks' siege of Troy (Ilium). The stories of many heroes on both sides are interwoven into the plot, but the opening line, "Rage—Goddess, sing the rage of Peleus' son Achilles," emphasizes the importance of this particular warrior. His companion Patroclus is also mentioned early on, but nothing is made of their special relationship until the latter's death. Achilles and King Agamemnon fall out over a woman, the spoils of war, and Achilles sulks when he does not get his way. He calls upon his divine mother to convince Zeus to let the Trojans prevail in order to make Agamemnon understand his dependence upon Achilles to win the war and get back his wife, Helen. It takes until Book 9 for Agamemnon to concede the point, but Achilles is still not ready to listen to his ambassador. Patroclus, however, is moved and in Book 16 begs Achilles to lend him his armor so he may join battle under his guise. Achilles warns Patroclus not to proceed to the very walls of the citadel, but Patroclus does not heed his advice and is killed by Hector.

When Achilles hears the news in Book 18, he mourns "Patroclus—the man I loved beyond all other comrades, / loved as my own life." He returns to battle, not to aid Agamemnon but to avenge Patroclus. Having vanquished Hector, in Book 23 Achilles gives "his dear comrade" a solemn funeral. Soon afterwards, while he sleeps, he is visited by Patroclus's ghost (much as Gilgamesh is visited by Enkidu's). It requests that Achilles not permit the two men to be separated when death comes, but to have their bones "lie together." Achilles "stretched his loving arms" to grasp Patroclus, but the ghost disappears. Achilles lays the body on a funeral pyre with a lock of his own hair. Afterwards he places the burnt bones "in a golden urn" to await his own. Achilles continues to grieve: "he longed for

Patroclus' manhood, his gallant heart" (Book 24). When Hector's father begs for the return of his son's body, though Achilles weeps once again for Patroclus, he is moved to relinquish Hector's corpse. With Hector's funeral the epic ends. The original Greek consists of 15,693 lines written in dactylic hexameter, arranged in twenty-four books (which may correspond to the need for twenty-four scrolls to contain the poem). Fagles uses strong five- or six-stressed lines to render the Greek hexameters.

Bernard Sergent (250) reminds us, "That there was a sexual aspect to the friendship between Achilles and Patroclus has been a commonplace since the fifth century B.C." It was read thus from Plato through Plutarch, with Aeschylus making such a connection between the two men quite explicit in a lost play of his, *The Myrmidons*. There is also at least one suggestive vase painting. Such a reading was revived during the Renaissance. Shakespeare's portrayal of Patroclus is so strong that I found myself looking this time for lines in Homer that actually are in Shakespeare. It seems, however, that modern scholars have become so fixated on the idea that the Greeks practiced only *paiderastia* that most reject the idea of anything sexual between the two heroes, and even Sergent strangely waffles.

David Greenberg (113) in looking at a larger context points out, "Parallels to the Gilgamesh-Enkidu relationship have often been seen in the biblical story of David and Jonathan and in the devotion of Achilles and Patroclus for one another in the *Iliad*." Is it significant, or merely coincidental, that the gay poetic tradition begins with stories from three different cultures (though all three in the same general area) about warrior heroes who form, at the very least, intense homoerotic bonds? And what are we to make of the fact that the more subordinate member of each couple dies and goes to a stygian underworld (from whence two return as ghosts)?

TEXT: Homer, *The Iliad*, trans. Robert Fagles (Viking, 1990). REFERENCE: Bernard Sergent, *Homosexuality in Greek Myth*, trans. Arthur Goldhammer (Beacon, 1986), 250–58.

Theocritus: Idylls (Greek)

Standing in stark contrast with the heroic world of Homer are the idylls of Theocritus (c. 308–c. 240 BCE). With him begins the tradition of bucolic poetry (from the Greek for cowherd), or the pastoral (from the Latin for shepherd). Though clearly aimed at urban readers (he himself spent much time in Alexandria, then the cultural center of the Greek world), his idylls are peopled with simple folks working in the outdoors and filled with rich descriptions of nature, probably recalled from childhood memories of rural life around Syracuse. Of the thirty idylls ascribed to him (only twenty-two are thought genuine), some eight (including one spurious example) address, to a greater or lesser degree, an attraction between males. Raymond-Jean Frontain writes, "With the biblical Song of Songs, Theocritus' *Idylls* provided a model that allows for the configuration of the male body with the natural landscape, Nature herself permitting the unleashing of homoerotic desire." As a result, "His *Idylls* are the source of a homoerotic pastoral tradition that includes Virgil's second eclogue, Spenser's *Shepherd's Calendar*, and Barnfield's *Affectionate Shepherd*, as well as anticipates the homoerotic confusion in the Forest of Arden in Shakespeare's *As You Like It*, Milton's 'Lycidas,' and possibly even Whitman's *Calamus* poems" (Summers, 700). Perhaps he could have added the second act of Wilde's *Importance of Being Earnest*? (Wilde wrote a villanelle to Theocritus.) *Idyll*, a term never used by the Greek, merely means a short poem. They work as mini-narratives.

Three of the gay idylls are in the form of dialogues interspersed with songs. Idyll 5 recounts a humorous meeting between the straight (or bisexual) goat herder Comatas and the gay shepherd Lacon. Each accuses the other of having stolen something from him; both deny the allegation. As their exchange becomes heated, the taunts turn sexual. Comatas tells Lacon, "When I buggered you I taught you to moan and groan." Lacon casts aspersions on the size of Comatas's penis. Lacon challenges Comatas to a singing match, to be judged by a nearby woodcutter. This contest takes the form of alternating verses, Comatas setting forth a subject and Lacon trying to top him (both speaking in the third person). When Comatas, in song, brags how his girl Clearista helps him, Lacon replies how he "Pulls his boy down among flowers and does what he pleases." They describe gifts they will give their respective lovers. Comatas returns to the time he buggered Lacon; Lacon remembers the day he tied Comatas up so his master could chastise him with whips. Then in an abrupt switch Comatas recalls a gift he gave another girl but got no kiss in return, while Lacon succeeded with his gift of pipes (the same that he accused Comatas of stealing?) to another boy. For no clear reason the woodcutter stops the contest at this point and awards the prize to Comatas.

Idyll 6 presents a friendlier contest between two barely adolescent shepherds. They engage in a song about a flirtation between the sea nymph Galatea and the cyclops Polyphemus. When they finish, they kiss: "There was no winning or losing where both played best." In Idyll 7, set on the Island of Cos (where Theocritus lived for a time), his alter-ego Simichidas describes a pilgrimage he and two friends are undertaking to the shrine to Demeter, when he runs into the goatherd Lycidas. To pass the time they engage in a singing contest. Lycidas begins with an elaborate lyric expressing his wish that his lover will have smooth sailing on a voyage and imagining the pleasures they may receive. Simichidas sings of the love of his best friend for a boy. He lists the punishments he would want to see inflicted upon the lad if he does not return his friend's love. In face of such ferocity, Lycidas awards the prize to Simichidas.

Very different in tone and approach, four idylls use the poet's voice alone to celebrate the power of love. They all reflect the Greek tradition of *paiderastia* in which a man, the *erastês*, functions as the lover, protector, and educator of a male youth, the *erômenos* (the pattern already seen in Idyll 7). In the very short Idyll 12 the poet salutes the reappearance of a beloved lad, missing for three days. With obvious relief, he sets forth for the youth the beauties of mutual love. He cites how such may lead to the two of them becoming celebrated in song long after they are dead, the same way that a legendary hero who died for his friend is now celebrated by a kissing contest. Idyll 13 retells the story of the overwhelming grief that Hercules suffered upon the death of the boy Hylas. The poet makes it personal by opening the poem with the observation to his *erômenos*,

> When Love, the foundling god, came into our lives
> We believed that he existed for us alone.
> But, Nicias, how could we think the discovery ours,
> Of our day only? We are not the first or last.

In Idyll 29 the poet moans that a boy does not return his love the way he deserves. He warns the lad that, instead of flirting with any man who flatters him, he should seek to discern true love when offered. The poet envisions that then, as the boy ages, they will be given the same esteem offered Achilles and Patroclus. But if the boy disdains his love, then he should be prepared to find, "Should we meet / And you call out, I will not cross the street." The collection ends with Idyll 30. The poet records how helplessly in love he is with a boy, one not beautiful but nonetheless beguiling. He berates himself for behaving so irrationally at his advanced age. But he claims he has no free will: he is under the command of the same god who maddened even other gods, including Zeus himself (a veiled allusion to Ganymede).

The simplicity and charm of Theocritus's poems still provide pleasure for modern readers. Of the three translations I read, that by Robert Wells is for me the most satisfying. Anthony Verity's has its moments, and the précis provided for it by Richard Hunter are useful. Anthony Holden's translation can sometimes be curious ("you *raped* me *blissfully* against the oak"; my italics), but his version of the songs in Idyll 7 is by far the most felicitous. Also he is the only one to translate Idyll 23, whose authenticity modern scholars question. It recounts the obsession of a man for a heartless boy. Driven to despair, the man hangs himself. Feeling neither remorse nor pity, the boy blithely goes to a bathing pool over which a statue of Eros presides. When the boy plunges in, the statue dives on top of him, killing him. Certainly the stark narrative seems at odds with the canonical idylls, and it ends with a most un-Theocritus-like moral.

TEXT: Theocritus, *The Idylls*, trans. Robert Wells (Penguin, 1989). SUPPLEMENT: Anthony Holden, trans., *Greek Pastoral Poetry* (Penguin, 1974).

Catullus: Epigrams & Invectives (Latin)

Judging by the number of translations of the poems of Gaius Valerius Catullus (c. 84–c. 54 BCE) available, he must speak to the modern ear as vigorously as any Roman poet. In part he owes his popularity, as does Martial from a century later, to a reputation for salaciousness. This was true even in his own day, as Catullus was aware. He poses a rhetorical question in poem 16: "So you dare conclude / Because my verse is wanton that I'm lewd?" The bawdy actually makes up only a small part of his 116 poems that survived into the Middle Ages by grace of one sole manuscript. The poems in it are arranged by meters; the reader therefore skips from topic to topic so that tender verse appears side by side with scurrilous attacks. Actually for a long time Catullus's modern reputation rested on poems about his relationship with the married Lesbia. Theirs was a troubled and ultimately unsatisfactory romance which ended in separation. These poems, however, make up only about an eighth of his total output. The others deal with literature, politics, human follies, friends and enemies. The poet anticipates Martial in several of his jibes. He makes fun of the still living Julius Caesar for his fondness of sex with men (Poems 29, 57). He chastises the otherwise unknown Vibennius for being a bath-house thief and his son for being "as grasping with his anus" (Poem 33). He makes fun of one Naso who does his "best to please / Any man—on [his] hands and knees" (Poem 112). In seven poems (Poems 74, 80, 88–90, 116) the poet snickers about the way someone named Gellius relishes incest, having sex with his mother, sister, and uncle, as well as a slave boy, both passively and actively. The poet concludes that Gellius could not be "more obscene" even if he sucked himself off.

Only some twenty or so of the poems could actually be labeled gay. At least four (Poems 24, 48, 99, 103) refer by name to the boy Juventius, whom he was wooing; he is called simply his boy in three others (Poems 15, 21, 81) in which the poet warns his sexually active friends Aurelius and Furius that they had better not try any hanky-panky with him. These two men show up in three other poems (Poems 16, 23, 26). The series illustrate the non-thematic way the poems are assembled. In Poem 16 he asks these friends, "Do you think that just because you read of 'lips' / And 'a thousand kisses' I'm no man?" It is not until Poem 48, however, that the poet says of Juventius's "honey-steeped / Eyes, I should kiss them all day till / I'd reached three hundred thousand," and still later, in Poem 99, that he talks about kissing Juventius on the lips. By then we have already discovered in Poem 81 that the affair has ended because of Juventius's infidelity. As for Aurelius and Furius, the exact nature of their relationship with the poet is difficult to judge. Are the three such good friends that they get pleasure out of verbal jousting with each other? Or do they actually have a falling out? In Poem 16 the poet threatens to take one anally and the other orally in response to a perceived insult. The poet, however, makes it clear that he too has experienced being buggered. In one of three poems (9, 28, 47) to his friends Veranius and Fabullus, apparently a couple, he commiserates with them, imagining that they are being screwed by the provincial governor Memmius's huge penis the same way the poet was when he was part of Memmius's retinue. Still other friendships with men are important. Hearing about two youths in Verona (Catullus's hometown) who fell in love, one with the sister, the other with her brother, the poet wishes the latter the most luck, recalling his "True friendship, tried and tested in the fire / When my wild passion burnt me to the bone" (Poem 100). Yet he acknowledges a wife's rights: in an unexpected moment for contemporary readers, as part of an epithalamium (Poem 61), a groom who apparently does not want to give up his sexual hijinks with men is admonished.

Having so many different translations of his poems available illustrates how tricky it is to find an acceptable English equivalent of this very Latin genre. On the whole, I find James Michie's renderings superior (though the notes to his text, supplied by Robert Rowland, are inadequate). Jacob Rabinowitz, however, is also worthwhile since his edition has the advantage of grouping poems by subject matter rather than following the hodgepodge order of the manuscript tradition.

TEXT: Catullus, *The Poems...A Bilingual Edition*, trans. James Michie (Random House, 1969). REFERENCE: Jacob Rabinowitz, trans., *Gaius Valerius Catullus's Complete Poetic Works* (Spring, 1991).

Virgil: *Eclogues 2 & 3*; *The Aeneid*, Books 5, 9 (Latin)

Known in English as both Virgil and Vergil, Publius Vergilius Maro (70–19 BCE) has maintained his high reputation from his own time through the Middle Ages and the Renaissance (think Dante) on to the present. He has one of the most anthologized gay poems. Inspired by Theocritus, he wrote his own series of ten bucolics, 39/38 BCE. They later became known as eclogues or pastorals. Two in particular appeal to gay readers. Eclogue 3 was obviously influenced by Theocritus's Idyll 5. Two herders, the gay Menalcas and the straight Damoetas, meet up and engage in banter. Damoetas accuses Menalcas of having committed some impropriety in a shrine that shocked even his billy goats and caused the nymphs to giggle.

When they engage in a singing contest, while Damoetas celebrates women, Damoetas praises his Amyntas ("my flame, and never coy"). Both sing of Gaius Asinius Pollio, who was Virgil's patron and a friend of Horace; Menalcas contrasts him with two bad poets, whose admirers would stoop to "milk he-goats that have no titties." (Presumably the image means exactly what it says.) The judge of the contest avows both deserve the prize.

But it is Eclogue 2 that has become, in Louis Crompton's words, "the most famous poem on male love in Latin literature" (Summers, 717). Its hero, Corydon (a name found in Theocritus's Idyll 4), voices his hopeless love for the handsome Alexis. He asks how Alexis can ignore his "sad airs," the riches that he has to offer him. In a close echo of the Cyclops's words in Theocritus's Idyll 6, Corydon speaks of his own good looks glimpsed in his reflection in the sea. He envisions what a good life he and Alexis could have together, piping in harmony. In his mind he offers Alexis yet other gifts before he draws himself up short and admits that his dream will never come true. He consoles himself that, though he has been scorched by love, there is always another man awaiting him. However, when Corydon returns in Eclogue 7, he admits he is not yet over Alexis. The eclogue apparently had personal significance for Virgil. A fourth-century commentary by Aelius Donatus asserts that Virgil's "sexual desire was more inclined to boys, among whom he especially loved [his slaves] Cebes and Alexander, whom he names 'Alexis' in the *Second Eclogue*. Alexander was the gift of Asinius Pollio" (Hubbard, 372). Throughout the Middle Ages, Virgil was widely believed also to have also contributed to the scurrilous verses to Priapus that were collected as the *Priapea*. Writing of Eclogue 2's influence on later writers, Gregory Woods (History, 39) reminds us, "Both Richard Barnfield and Christopher Marlowe were enchanted imitators of it, and their imitations were imitated in turn. Traces of Virgil's poem can be found throughout the English elegiac tradition…. In the ultimate homage, André Gide gave his Socratic dialogue on male homosexuality the Virgilian title *Corydon*." The anonymous author of *Don Leon*, supposedly Lord Byron's account of his sexual life, has the poet ask, "When young Alexis claimed a Virgil's sigh, / He told the world his choice, and may not I?"

Virgil's epic of the founding of Rome, *The Aeneid*, 19 BCE, was modeled after Homer's *Iliad*. Therefore, it is not surprising to find two warriors who reflect the relationship between Achilles and Patroclus. However, Nisus and Euryalus, two who are "one in love," have a relatively minor role in the poem, appearing only in Books 5 and 9 (of twelve). We first meet them participating in ceremonial games: "Euryalus outstanding in beauty and bloom of youth, / Nisus renowned for his pure love of his friend." The latter, with the crowd's approval, deliberately fouls a runner to help his friend win a race. When next we meet the pair, Nisus is hatching a plan to raid the enemy for spoils of war. He tries to dissuade Euryalus from joining him, but the youth is obstinate. Successful, they make their retreat, but Euryalus is betrayed by the moonlight glinting off an enemy helmet that he has unthinkingly donned. When Nisus realizes that his lover has been captured and killed, he returns to meet his own death. Virgil concludes the episode: "Ah, fortunate pair! If my poetry has any influence, / Time in its passing shall never obliterate your memory." Crompton cites the importance of the two men for Lord Byron "in search of literature that would validate his own youthful homosexual feelings." While still a teenager, Byron wrote *The Episode of Nisus and Euryalus.* Crompton also notes that the episodes influenced Jeremy Bentham's thought (Summers, 719). There are almost too many modern translations of Virgil to choose from. C. Day Lewis's not only are pleasing but have the advantage of being available in one volume.

TEXT: Virgil, *The Eclogues, Georgics and Aeneid*, trans. C. Day Lewis (Oxford, 1966). SUPPLEMENT: W. H. Parker, trans., *Priapea: Poems for a Phallic God* (Croom Helm, 1988).

Horace: Odes (Latin)

Quintus Horatius Flaccus (65–8 BCE) was a good friend of Virgil's; in Ode 1.3 he calls him "half my soul." Like him, Horace never married. He was also very close to the flamboyant bisexual Maecenas, to whom he addressed Ode 2.20 and next to whose grave he was buried. Horace published three books of odes in 23 BCE, with a fourth book in 13 BCE—103 poems in all, written in deliberate imitation of Greek lyrics. Odes 4.1 and 4.10 are the ones most often found in gay anthologies. In the first, the poet faces that he is too old to find love with either a boy or a woman, yet he still dreams nightly of indifferent Ligurinus. In the second he warns Ligurinus that one day he will lose his boyish charm when his beard begins to grow, and then he will regret his "debonaire insouciance." Many of the poems are marked by this sense of passing time and the need to enjoy life while you can. Ode 2.9 urges Valgius to give up mourning the dead Mystes and take pleasure in the moment. Ode 1.4 reminds Sestius that he will not be able to gaze on Lycidas forever. Ode 4.7 ends with the reminder, "Passionate Theseus was, yet could not shatter the chains Death / Forged for his Pirithous." Even such a humorous poem as Ode 3.20 warns us to enjoy what is actually available to us: it makes fun of Pyrrhus for thinking he can seduce Nearchus away from his female lover. While the two are fighting over him, Nearchus will have walked out on the both of them. The often quoted Ode 1.11 sums up Horace's philosophy in two words: *carpe diem.*

Brad Walton stresses how "Horace's treatment of friendship inspired homosexuals in later ages" (Summers, 370). Louis Compton more specifically writes, "In the eleventh century, Norman clerical poets, writing medieval Latin verse, harked back to Horace, referring pointedly to his love poems to boys. In a later age, Byron used Latin phrases from Horace's poems to communicate his own homosexual interests in letters to knowledgeable friends and made the adjective 'Horatian' a code word for 'bisexual'" (Summers, 596). Walton emphasizes how "A. E. Housman, when he translated Ode 4.7 (*More Poems* 5), interpreted Horace's mention of the love between Theseus and Pirithous as homoerotic" (Summers, 370). Horace's poems, however, no longer seem to be an important part of our gay heritage. Anthologies by Carpenter, Fone, and Hubbard omit him altogether. I never before bothered to read him, I blush to say. I now regret the fact. Certainly, heterosexual poems dominate Horace's oeuvre, but the odes have not lost their ability to move gay readers. Of the many translations available, English poet James Michie's is the one to have. It would be hard to better the ingenuity of his rhymes and verse forms.

TEXT: Horace, *The Odes...with the Latin Text*, trans. James Michie (Orion, 1963).

Ovid: *Metamorphoses*, Book 10 (Latin)

Though Publius Ovidius Naso (43 BCE–18 CE) seems to have been at ease with Roman bisexuality, he himself was apparently heterosexual and barely treated gay themes. However, his retelling of the story of Orpheus in his *Metamorphoses* influenced later writers from the time of the Renaissance, beginning with the Italian poet and playwright Poliziano, on to modern times, including Tennessee Williams. Thus we cannot ignore him. Ovid announces his strategy for choosing his stories in the opening lines of the poem: "My intention is to tell of bodies changed / to different forms." He does not get to Orpheus until Book 10. He first recounts the familiar story of the death of Eurydice, Orpheus's wife, his attempt to bring her out of Hades, and her "second" death when he looks back at her too soon. Ovid then continues the singer's story with details (never taught to me in high school) that were set forth by the fourth-century Greek poet Phanocles in his poem about Orpheus's love for Calais, the son of the North Wind. Phanocles asserts that "first among the Thracians he showed the love / Of males and never praised desire for women" (Hubbard, 287). Ovid puts it thus: "His love was given / To young boys only, and he told the Thracians / That was the better way: *enjoy the springtime, / Take those first flowers!*"

Orpheus finds his way to a grove of trees. Spellbound by his music, the very trees uproot themselves and encircle him to listen. Among them is the cypress, formerly the boy Cyparissus, beloved by Apollo, who turned the youth into the tree in pity for the excessive grief he felt upon accidentally killing his pet deer. In this setting, Orpheus announces his theme: " I would sing of boys / Loved by gods, and girls inflamed by love / To things forbidden." He begins with a brief reminder of a theme set forth by the sixth-century Greek poet Theognis, that love of boys has been a delight ever since Zeus fell for Ganymede and, in the form of an eagle, took him to the home of the gods to serve as his cup-bearer (Hubbard, 45). This brief prologue is followed by the story of Apollo and Hyacinthus: how the god accidentally killed the boy while they were playing with a discus. In rue, Apollo turned Hyacinthus's corpse into the flower that bears his name. Hard on this story come the ones about "girls inflamed by love." His song finished, Orpheus, at the beginning of Book 11, is attacked by crazed women belonging to a cult and killed, releasing his ghost to be with Eurydice. Neither Phanocles nor Ovid makes a point that the women were jealous of those boys, but such has become a general interpretation. The reader has many translations to choose from. Rolfe Humphries's blank verse retains its pleasure.

TEXT: Ovid, *Metamorphoses*, trans. Rolfe Humphries (Indiana, 1983).

Martial: Epigrams & Invectives (Latin)

Marcus Valerius Martialis (c. 40–104) was Rome's bad boy. The satirist defended himself. He argues, "My poetry is filthy—but not I" (Epigram 1.4). In Epigram 1.67 he twits someone, "I grant you there is foul stuff in my book. / But why? You're in it—take a look." A native of Spain, he spent some thirty years in the imperial city. There he gained his reputation by attacking sham and hypocrisy of every type, often in language so crude that some of the poems were not translated in print until the twentieth century. At the same time, if you accept that the poems' first-person narrators may be equated to the poet, he does not try to cover up his own shortcomings. His witty observations, 1172 poems gathered in twelve books, quite frequently focus on sexual peccadillos. Translator Garry Wills (9–10) sums up the poet's approach: "His poems are bisexual in the accepted way of his time, praising pliable boys and frisky women, but he upholds classical misogyny and the view that the only decent homosexual relation is that of an active male adult and a passive boy. Other relationships, including any between women and women, are treated as shameful—as are all forms of oral sex (fellatio as well as cunnilingus, whether performed by males or females)." Thus, Martial mocks Decianus (all the names are made up, but presumably mask recognizable persons or at least common types) for his putting on noble airs, his only claim to such status coming from being "a highborn noble's-bride" (1.24). He mocks Amillus for screwing handsome boys in the open in order to deflect the fact of "what's *done* to you" (7.62). He laughs at the obvious implications that it is Phoebus's slave boy who always "has the hard-on / While your poor prick must ask for pardon" (3.73). Tongue in cheek, he mocks where Apicius's tongue apparently goes (3.80). But the poet admits that he himself puts up with Zoilus, even though he is a miserly host, "Because he sucks us off" (3.82). He may be something of a size queen too; at least he remarks on the fact that one can always know when Maro shows up at the baths because of the round of applause one hears (9.33).

Were Martial alive today, you would not be able to count on him to be a supporter of gay rights. Here's what he has to say about same-sex marriage in Epigram 12.42 as translated by Richard E. Prior (Fone, 83):

> Bearded Callistratus wedded rugged Afer
> In the way a young woman usually weds a man.
> The torches glowed, the veil covered his face
> Nor were you, Thalassus [god of marriage], short on words.
> There was even a dowry. Well, Rome, is this enough for you?
> Or are you waiting for him to give birth too?

Martial himself never married. In one epigram (2.49) the poet says, tongue in cheek,

> Make her my wife? But only if she toys
> With specially delicious sexy boys.
> If screwing in her bed I catch the two,
> As husband, legally, I can him screw.

In another (11.43) his persona claims to have a wife who offers up her anus when she catches him *in flagrante delicto* with a young boy; after listing all the Greek gods and heroes with wives who still preferred boys, he counters that all she really has are "two twats."

Even if bisexuality was for him the norm, he leans to boys. After cataloguing ways young males can be maddening, he concludes, "The richest wife could not replace 'em" (12.75). He begs one boy, "Kiss hard and often as you might" (6.34). Scattered among the jibes, the reader finds lyrics that pay tribute to young males in such glowing terms that their tone clashes with the scurrilous tenor of the rest. He holds that the effect a boy can have on him is equivalent to the effect Ganymede had on Jupiter (11.26). Both Epigrams 3.65 and 11.8 employ a whole series of sensual metaphors to describe the effect of a boy's embrace. The poet sets out in Epigram 4.42 to "describe my perfect boy." After discussing appearance, sexual willingness, disdain for women, and desire to continue to serve as a boy even when he reaches manhood, he ends by asserting that he has described "the very boy I've found." Several other poems (7.89, 10.32) celebrate male friendship with such tenderness that they still resonate. But the majority of the epigrams are smutty jokes aimed at types that remain recognizable. There is no complete verse translation. Of selections there seems no end. I settled on Garry Wills's both for its ingenuous wit and the greater number of gay epigrams that it contains.

TEXT: *Martial's Epigrams: A Selection*, trans. Garry Wills (Viking, 2007).
SUPPLEMENT: J. P. Sullivan & A. J. Boyle, eds., *Martial in English* (Penguin, 1996).

Juvenal: Satires (Latin)

In Epigram 12.18 Martial invites his fellow satirist Decimus Iunius Iuvenalis (c. 55–c. 130) to visit him in Spain. Martial promises Juvenal that there he will find all sorts of rural pleasures, not least the delights of being with a young huntsman in the woods. This seems surprising since Juvenal comes across as being so negative about homosexuality in his own satires. His scorn, however, actually may be for excess of any kind. At least this is the way one translator, Peter Green (xxv), sees it: "insofar as the satirist is castigating sexual perversion *per se* (rather than hypocrisy, avarice, meanness, or breach of class protocol), what excites his anger and contempt—a highly conventional reaction—is the adult invert, the transvestite queen, the middle-aged or elderly *fellator*, above all the habitually sodomized." Warren Johansson reminds us, "Juvenal was a convinced misogynist; he detested and despised not the women of his own corrupt age, but women in general. However, there are favorable references to boys as love objects, which would imply that his own preferences were those of a pederast" (Dynes, 652). Thus, for example, in Satire 6, his lengthy attack on women (his longest poem), the poet pauses long enough to ask, "don't you think it better to sleep with a pretty boy?" For Green (xxxi) Juvenal is someone of "intense political conservatism, with a corresponding fear of change and revolution, …a tendency to see all problems…in over-simplified moral terms, with the application of right conduct to existing authority as a kind of panacea for all ills." In other words, a puritan despite an itch to take huntsmen into the woods. Juvenal wrote his sixteen satires, collected in five books, in his late years. Almost nothing is known of the poet, neither his private nor his public life.

His portrait of gay life in the capital in Satire 2, despite his strictures against homosexual behavior, is so detailed and so vivid that it makes fascinating reading. The poem is a stream of conscious survey of the subject at hand, ideas linked through association rather than by any logical progression. The poet lashes out at two-faced men, judges and legislators, who come across as ultra-moralists when in reality they are passing laws that would condemn themselves were the truth known. He prefers the effeminate Peribomius to the ones who affect extreme masculinity as a coverup; he at least is honest. He also argues that Peribomius is the way he is because of fate, not choice, and therefore deserves "pity" and "indulgence." The poet goes on to comment on the way one masculine-looking lawgiver douses himself in perfume, the ways others dally with athletes and still others take up feminine tasks. He digresses to comment on how Hister's wife was richly bribed by her husband to keep silent that an ex-slave was sharing his bed. Thinking of mixed roles leads the poet to heap scorn on a prosecutor who dresses in chiffon to argue his cases. The poet claims such fashions are as catching as a disease. This leads him to allege that "secret torchlight orgies" occur in which men dress like women. He recalls an emperor who admired himself in the mirror before battle. (William Barr in his notes tells us that men did not habitually use mirrors.) All this must remind him of Martial's Epigram 12.42, and he gives his own description of a same-sex wedding between a soldier and a musician: "Such things, before we're very much older, / Will be done in public—in *public*, and will want to appear in the papers!" He takes comfort in the fact that such brides can have no babies. Somehow, this leads the poet to imagine how gays will be received by the heroes in Hades and how they are being perceived by the people the Romans are conquering. This last thought stirs up his innate xenophobia and causes him to fulminate about an Armenian immigrant who has become the boy toy of a tribune and will return home tainted by Rome's immature morals. With this last jibe, our satirist runs out of steam, and the poem ends abruptly. One can only marvel how contemporary all this sounds in an age of Trumpery.

Satire 9 often makes its way into gay anthologies, though its subject, an aging male prostitute, is bisexual. The poet encounters Naevolus and asks why he is so downhearted. The hustler responds that if the stars do not favor a man, even a super-huge penis counts for nothing. Virro (perhaps an ironic pun on *virile*), who woos him with love letters, has proven to be miserly. Naevolus wails, "Do you think it's nice and easy to thrust a proper-sized penis / into a person's guts, encountering yesterday's dinner?" Why can his john not at least remember him in his will? To demonstrate why he deserves more gratitude, Naevolus goes on to confide that he rescued Virro's wife from remaining a virgin and thus saved their marriage. In fact, Naevolus claims to be the actual father of Virro's two children. And now the man is looking for another man to satisfy his desires. Then, feeling he has gone too far, Naevolus begs the poet not to let out what he has said, citing fear for his life if the secret is known. With an allusion to Virgil's second eclogue, the poet reminds Naevolus that in Rome it is impossible to keep any secret. Naevolus admits the truth of the observation and asks what he should do. The poet bids him to take courage; as long as Rome lasts he will never be without some member of the gay underworld to take care of him. However, the poet goes on to say that it would be better for Naevolus to seek out a rich old woman. The hustler repeats that fate is against him, that all he can hope for is that his penis will provide enough for him to get by. It is not always easy to identify who is speaking in the poem or to whom; *you* is used sometimes in speeches in which Naevolus is simply imagining what he would say were the other person present. Presumably, in recitation the speaker could distinguish what is actually going on through change of voice.

TEXT: Juvenal, *The Satires*, trans. Nial Rudd, 2nd ed. (Oxford, 2000). REFERENCE: Peter Green, trans., *The Sixteen Satires* (Penguin, 1999).

Strato of Sardis: Epigrams (Greek)

During the reign of Emperor Hadrian, Straton of Sardis (2nd c.), better known by his Latin name Strato, assembled a collection of his epigrams. Appropriate to the age, given the emperor's love and deification of young Antinous, they deal almost exclusively with the attractions of male youths on the brink of puberty. During the Middle Ages, Strato's collection became the basis for the twelfth book of *The Greek Anthology*, the so-called *Mousa Paidike*. Epigrams by other Greek poets (particularly fifty-nine by Meleager of Gadara [c. 140–c. 70 BCE], considered by many to be the best of the Greek epigrammatists) were interspersed with his ninety-five poems to bring the total to 258. Read just by themselves, undiluted with the other poets' offerings, Strato's prove to be stronger than they first appear. He begins with an announcement of his themes (12.1–2). He defines the kind of boys who beguiles him and warns, "if you fall for older fellows, that / Suggests child's play no more but tit-for-tat" (12.4). He explains that he does not like girls because "They've nothing for a groping hand to hold" (12.7). Later he contrasts girls and boys and says, "No, give me boys all sweaty from the gym, / Glistening with oil on every limb, / I like sex unembellished" (12.192). For the bulk of the poems, he describes his experiences with individual boys—though in his last poem (12.258) he becomes coy about just how autobiographical his poetry is, informing us that many of the epigrams were commissioned by other boy lovers. In some the poems he demonstrates that he does not have the aversion to pubic hair found in classic *paiderastia* (12.10, 12.178), but in others he rues the day "the killjoy hairs begin to sprout" (12.21, 12.191) and the boy's penis becomes man-size (12.242). He enjoys the chase (12.200) and puts down one ever-ready boy (12.184). He deplores how some youths have become prostitutes (12.6, 12.207), but he also reminds us that many of the lads he plays with are slaves (12.247). In one the poet does seem to take his role as mentor seriously, humorously commenting on the difficulties of teaching a boy whose voice is changing to sing (12.187), and he faults teachers who take advantage of their charges (12.222).

The poems poke fun at sex in general. He laments how sometimes one's penis simply will not obey one's will (12.11, 12.216) and bemoans the day he will be so old that, "Though I know how, I can no longer screw" (12.240). Unexpectedly, he often defies both the Greek and the Roman strictures against taking a passive role, seeing nothing disgraceful in switching positions. He snarls at a lover who has announced he has taken a vow of celibacy and then is caught not only with another man, but demanding money (12.237). One of his riddles so tickled the fourth-century Roman poet Ausonius that he recast it: how can there be only three men in a bed when two are screwing and two are being screwed? (12.210). Strato undermines any argument that homosexuality is a crime against nature: "Dumb brutes only fuck; we clever human / Beings, in this superior at least, / Invented buggery" (12.245). The Greek's wittiness is at the opposite pole to the sentimentality of the nineteenth-century Uranian poets who addressed their poems to boys. I think this goes a long way towards explaining why his poems are still such fun to read despite their subject matter.

TEXT: Daryl Hine, trans., *Puerilities: Erotic Epigrams of The Greek Anthology* (Princeton, 2001). SUPPLEMENT: Peter Jay, ed., *The Greek Anthology and Other Ancient Epigrams: A Selection in Modern Verse Translation* (Penguin, 1981).

Abu Nuwas: Erotic Poems (Arabic)

Abu Nuwas (Al-Hasan ibn Hani al-Hakami, c. 756–c. 814) was an Arab poet living in Baghdad during the reigns of the the caliph Harun al-Rashid and his libertine son Muhammad al-Amin. He gained his nickname because of the two locks of long curly hair that he sported. Edward Lacey (24) writes that even during his lifetime he was "singled out as *the* rebel and *the* homosexual poet...partly because he obviously, in his life and by his dogmatic, doctrinaire poetic assertions, deliberately sought out and cultivated such a role." For a time he was the lover of his cousin, another poet, Abu Usama Waliba, but according to the poet and anecdotalist Ahmad al-Tifashi (137), writing some four centuries later, Waliba broke off the relationship when Abu Nuwas improvised a quatrain during the sexual act itself—

    Oh, what a pretty picture!
    a poet of world renown
    caught in the act of being fucked
    by Waliba, al-Hubab's son!

—and "realized how dangerous to his reputation Abu Nuwas's unbridled tongue was."

Abu Nuwas was associated with the caliph's court, becoming, in Lacey's words (21), "a palace favorite, a sort of combined poet laureate and court jester." He appears in such a capacity in several stories in *The Arabian Nights*, most notably "Harun al-Rashid, the Slave Girl, and Abu Nuwas," the bawdy "Abu Nuwas and the Three Boys," and "Harun al-Rashid and the Three Poets." Several poems attributed to him are inserted within the tales. Still other poems are included in the stories gathered by al-Tifashi for his miscellany *The Delight of Hearts*. After supporting Harun al-Rashid's chief minister when the two had a falling out, Abu Nuwas prudently self-exiled himself to Cairo. He returned after Harun al-Rashid's death and became court poet anew. Unfortunately, al-Amin was killed in a civil war with his homophobic half-brother, and shortly thereafter Abu Nuwas died—"in prison, according to some accounts; in a tavern, according to others; murdered, because of a satirical poem he had written, according to still others" (Lacey, 22).

In his introduction to his slim selection of poems (viii), Jaafar Abu Tarab notes similarities between Abu Nuwas and the poets of *The Greek Anthology*, citing their celebration of "wine, the erotic love of males, and pleasure." He goes on to say (xi) that the Arab poet, in addition, "frequently develops the theme of atheism." Or, as he translates one poem:

O, I'll take the lads, and leave the lasses to you!
For you, sparkling water! For me, wine will do.
The True Path is yours! To the False Path I'll hew.
You can quest for the Holy, while I seek the Taboo!

To achieve his sexual goals, he even quotes the Quran to suit his purposes. Unlike most of the poets in the *Mousa Paidike*, however, Abu Nuwas celebrates not only boys but also men. When one youth refuses any longer to kiss, on the grounds that he is growing a beard and adults don't kiss, the poet counters that he's "old enough now to play / The Real Game!" With that, he grabs the youth "Until we were hugging hard, and at last / My prick was plunged up right in his ass!" Yet much of his praise is for young lads, "entrancing gazelles."

He is very much the urban poet, rejecting all the folderol about the nobleness of desert life. He luxuriates in the pleasures of the tavern with its male server "With a beautiful butt, and a handsome cock / Flexing inside his pants as he walks"; the joys of being "In the bathhouse [where] the mysteries concealed by trousers / Are revealed to you"; and the sensuality of nights spent "in complete lechery / Ingloriously pulling the tails of debauchery!" Like the epigrammatists, he can also be quite biting (as in this poem saved by Al-Tifashi, 220):

Where have you hidden
your majesty and pride?
Maybe in your asshole,
that everyone can ride?

Considered one of the greatest of Arab language poets, Abu Nuwas not only mastered all the existing forms but created whole new ones. He had an enormous influence on subsequent poets, especially the Sufi poets Rumi and Hafiz, as well as Omar Khayyam and Sa'di, all of whom leave ambiguous whether they are describing sexual union with a boy or with Allah, whether they are intoxicated by wine or by divine love. According to Lacey some 1500 extant poems have been credited to Abu Nuwas. It is incredible, therefore, how little attention his poetry has received in the English-speaking world. Unfortunately, even then many of the collections are relatively expensive and/or hard to obtain. Jaafar Abu Tarab's translation of seventeen gay poems is the most readily available at the moment. Abu Tarab also provides a direct prose translation of each in an appendix, plus, for one, a sample of the original Arabic in transliteration.

TEXT: Abu Nuwas, *Carousing with Gazelles: Homoerotic Songs of Old Bagdad*, trans. Jaafar Abu Tarab (iUniverse, 2005). SUPPLEMENTS: Ahmad al-Tifashi, *The Delight of Hearts, or What You Will Not Find in Any Book*, trans. Edward A. Lacey, ed. Winston Leyland (Gay Sunshine, 1988). Malcolm C. Lyons & Ursula Lyons, trans., *The Arabian Nights: Tales of 1001 Nights*, Vol. 2 (Penguin, 2010).

Rumi: Love Poems (Persian)

Persian pronouns do not indicate gender. As a result, unless the gender is specified via a noun, the reader is left to decide whether the object of love is male or female or even God. Take one of the most famous quatrains to come out of Persian poetry into English from Edward FitzGerald's translation of the *rubai* of Omar Khayyam (1048–1131):
    A Book of Verses underneath the Bough,
    A Jug of Wine, a Loaf of Bread—and Thou
        Beside me singing in the Wilderness—
    Oh, Wilderness were Paradise enow!
The person being addressed must be a young male, but most readers (and the illustrator of the volume I own) probably take him to be a young woman. This transfiguration of meaningless existence into something di-

vine through the invocation of worldly experiences, including intoxication caused by the vision of a beardless youth, was intrinsic to Sufism, the Islamic quest to experience God directly. Maarten Schild clarifies, "Love and wine both led to drunkenness, to loss of reason, to an absolute indifference to the world, and ultimately to a loss of self. The cupbearer (*saki*), often a beautiful youth, symbolized the spiritual guide, who helped the lover on his way by making him drunk with love" (Dynes, 1262).

The Anatolian poet Maulana Jalal al-Din Rumi (1207–1273) becomes a principal example of this practice of spiritual intoxication. But unlike the vague youths you find in Khayyam's poetry, Rumi's is firmly grounded in the very real friendships he held with three men. Those men and their importance to his emotional life are mentioned openly in his poems, making his work a natural for inclusion in anthologies of gay poetry. The first of the three was Shams e-Tabrīzī, some twenty years older than he. Schild writes, "The relationship between Rumi and Shams was unique because it was not the usual adoration for Divine Beauty in the form of a beautiful youth, as in Sufism, but a love between two older mystics of great personal strength and character" (Dynes, 1133). Their short-lived relationship, 1244–48, was so intense and so exclusive that it created tensions between Rumi and his students and within his family. Shams disappeared, probably murdered with the tacit consent of Rumi's own son. But his name is evoked in Rumi's poetry for the rest of his life:

Start walking toward Shams. Your legs will get heavy
and tired. Then comes a moment
of feeling the wings you've grown,
lifting.

After Shams's death, a goldsmith named Salah al-Din Zarkub took his place: "Saladin is how the soul looks. Rub your eyes, / and look again with love at love." Upon his death, the scribe Husam Chelebi became Rumi's companion: "Husam is the sun." Pretty clearly Rumi presents a case of a man who falls in love with other men, whether that love is expressed sexually or not. As a consequence, readers are free to interpret such a poem as the following on whatever level they need:

When I am with you, we stay up all night.
When you're not here, I can't go to sleep.
Praise God for these two insomnias!
And the difference between them.

Coleman Barks, to his own amusement, has cornered the American market on Rumi. His interpretations have been criticized; he has never learned Persian and relies on others to provide him with the texts from which he creates the poems. He has been faulted with combining poems, and he himself has mentioned how he has taken "the tastiest lines" out of context. You receive no clear sense of the appearance of the original poems, nor of their biographical or historical progression. (Some of the same criticisms, it must be said, can be leveled at FitzGerald, though the latter did learn Persian.) Barks has been accused of turning Rumi into a New Age sage. But his translations are the ones most readers will find. In 2003 he brought out a smaller selection, *Rumi: The Book of Love*, in which he notes, "Gay lovers hear Rumi's poetry as gay. I don't agree." The negative seems a most un-Rumi moment for the translator. Coleman and I, by the way, were fellow students at Chapel Hill; he was the one I turned to when I wanted to know which contemporary poets I should be reading.

TEXT: Rumi, *The Essential Rumi*, trans. Coleman Barks (QPBC, 1998).
SUPPLEMENT: Omar Khayyám, *Rubáiyát*, trans. Edward FitzGerald (Random House, 1947).

Sa'di: *The Rose Garden* (Persian)

Sa'di (Abu-Muhammad Muslih al-Din bin Abdallah Shirazi, 1213–1292) created two major works: *Bustan* (The Orchard, 1257) and *Gulistan* (The Rose Garden, 1258). In addition, he wrote any number of odes and lyrics. Maarten Schild asserts, "An important theme in the works of Sa'di is the love for beautiful young boys, which he describes in all its facets, ranging from purely platonic and spiritual in the mystical love poems to obscene and lustful in what can be called his 'pornographic' works" (Dynes, 1142). We are still waiting for an adequate inexpensive rendition of his verse into English. Edward Rehatsek's translation of the *Gulistan* was done in 1888. For the section "Love and Youth," he allowed the pederastic nature of many of the verses to be plain, but sometimes he gave in to the Victorian subterfuge of allowing the lack of gender specificity in Persian to turn males into females. He opens the last poem in this section thus: "A virtuous and beauteous youth / Was pledged to a chaste maiden." Edward Carpenter in his 1906 anthology *Ioläus* follows a German translation in providing this instead: "A youth there was of golden heart and nature, / Who loved a friend, his like in every feature." Rehatsek ends the poem,

> Because Sa'di is of the ways and means of love affairs
> Well aware in the Arabian city of Baghdad.
> Tie your heart to the heart-charmer you possess
> And shut your eye to all the rest of the world,

followed by two more lines not given by Carpenter. The latter has,

> For Sadi knows full well the lover's part,
> And Bagdad understands the Arab heart.
> More than all else thy loved one shalt thou prize,
> Else is the whole world hidden from thine eyes.

The Rose Garden is made up of anecdotes interspersed with poems. These are divided into eight sections (plus introductory and concluding matter), the fifth of which is dedicated to "Love and Youth." Of the twenty-one stories, some are indeed heterosexual, but most are (or would be, if translated correctly) gay, conflating as usual in Persian poetry carnality and spirituality. Themes are familiar to anyone who knows Greek pederastic poetry. We have again the tyranny the youth has over the adult lover, the desire for intimacy of some sort, the distaste for the youth once he has grown a beard, with the accompanying admonishment that boys should seize the opportunity while it is theirs. The twentieth story, as given by Rehatsek, is the most overt. There a judge is caught, intoxicated by both wine and the boy he holds to his breast. There follows a series of exchanges between the judge and his ruler, in which he finally makes the ruler laugh and forgive him for violating his trust. These tantalizing glances make it maddening that we have no reliable translation in English.

FLAWED TEXT: Sa'di, *The Gulistan, or Rose Garden*, trans. Edward Rehatsek, ed. David Rosenbaum (Omphaloskepsis, 2010).

Dante: *Inferno*, Canto 15; *Purgatorio*, Canto 26 (Italian)

Until I found John Ciardi's verse translation, I could not abide Dante. I thought he was an arrogant prick, too full of himself. I was taken aback to read T. E. Eliot's pronouncement, in his essay on Dante, that "Dante and Shakespeare divide the modern world between them.... Shakespeare gives the greatest width of human passion; Dante the greatest altitude and greatest depth." In retrospect, I think I was projecting my distaste for the wooden translations that I was reading onto the poet, though it certainly did not help to find him nonchalantly assigning all those gays to hell. But when I found Ciardi, I could not stop reading; he was for me what Chapman had been for Keats with Homer. The pleasure Ciardi provided with his adroit handling of terza rima, the inclusion of illuminating diagrams, and the general usefulness of his notes propelled me from the *Inferno* into the *Purgatorio* and swept me onwards through the magnificent *Paradiso*. Those who think they know Dante Alighieri (1265–1321) after reading only the *Inferno* have no idea what they are missing. There are many other translations now available, but Ciardi is my Dante.

The *Commedia*, 1314–20, which is all its author ever called his allegorical poem, consists of one hundred cantos, thirty-three to each section plus the opening canto. It recounts the poet's heroic quest, the soul's journey to God, through hell, purgatory, and heaven. Thus reenacting Joseph Campbell's monomyth, the poet is accompanied at each stage by a guide, the Roman poet Virgil through the depths of Hell and up most of Mount Purgatory (to be joined there by the Roman poet Statius), where he is turned over to Beatrice, Dante's romantic ideal, for the final ascent to Heaven. His last guide, just before he has his final vision of the mystic rose, is St. Bernard. Along the way the poet meets those souls consigned, according to their nature, to appropriate places. So it is not surprising to find gay men consigned to the seventh circle of Hell, ring three, prepared for those who were "violent against...Nature." Ciardi (71) describes it as "a great *Plain of Burning Sand* upon which there descends an eternal slow *Rain of Fire*." He holds, "The symbolism of the burning plain is obviously centered in sterility (the desert image) and wrath (the fire image)." The poet and his guide encounter the damned gays in Canto 15, where they eternally walk in a circle. When the dead see the two men, they cannot resist cruising them: "They stared at us / as men at evening by the new moon's light // stare at one another when they pass by / on a dark road." (One wonders just how Dante came by his knowledge.) There the poet meets one of his former teachers, Brunetto Latino. Presumably the appearance of his name would have shocked Dante's first readers, for here we have, in Joseph Pequigney's words "the first—and the classic—instance of 'outing'" (Summers, 187). Brunetto speaks of the wide moral range of homosexuals: "Of some who share this walk / it is good to know; of the rest let us say nothing," and sums up: "In brief, we all were clerks and men of worth, / great men of letters, scholars of renown; / all by the one same crime defiled on earth." Brunetto points out other condemned souls by name, before he turns away from them, "like one of those who run // for the green cloth at Verona; and of those / more like the one who wins, than those who lose." Clearly, the poet finds his emotions are mixed about these men.

Moreover, there is the presence of Virgil as the poet's guide. The Roman has been condemned to Hell, along with all the other virtuous but unbaptized souls who died "before the age of the Christian mysteries, / and so…did not worship God's Trinity" (Canto 4). These condemned thus are in the outermost circle of Hell, the farthest away from Satan, who is imprisoned at the bottom of the pit. To Dante's contemporaries, Virgil would have seemed most fitting for his role on the basis of his fourth eclogue, by which he came across to them as a proto-Christian. This is the one written about 42 BCE in which Virgil prophesies the birth of a boy who will become divine and save the world. When Statius shows up in purgatory, Dante will credit the latter's reading of this eclogue as the Latin poet's inspiration to convert to Christianity (a claim not backed by historical sources). Yet Dante would also have known the second eclogue and probably Donatus's identification of Virgil as gay as well. Moreover, Dante may have known of Statius's tribute to a dead slave, much loved by his master, in *Silvae* 2.6 (Hubbard, 427–28).

Thus, we have a counterweight to arguments that Dante was anti-gay provided by the fact that he was guided across Hell and Purgatory first by one and then by two homosexual Roman poets. Consequently, it is hardly surprising to find gays also in Purgatory (Canto 26)—not only that, but on the seventh cornice, that dedicated to purifying the lustful, the last circle just before arriving at the earthly paradise that caps the mountain. Pequigney emphasizes that in Dante's eyes there is nothing "unnatural" about their love; rather it is the excessive nature of it that needs purging

(Summers, 186). Whereas the fire in Hell is torturing, that in Purgatory is purifying. One of the straights occupying the same cornice describes the gay penitents thus:

> Those souls you saw......
>   grew stained in that for which triumphant Caesar
>   heard his own legions call him 'Queen' one day.
> Therefore their band, at parting from us, cries
>   'Sodom!'—as you have heard—that by their shame
>   they aid the fire that makes them fit to rise.

None is identified by name.

If then homosexuality is not an unforgivable sin but one that can be purified in Purgatory, logically there must be men who were formerly gay in Heaven. As James Wilhelm (265) argues, "if one can make any rung of Purgatory, then the way is ultimately open to Paradise." It would follow that gays should be in the third sphere under the influence of Venus, but now chaste and therefore not readily identifiable. One possibility that strikes me is Charles Martel, who appears in Canto 8. A contemporary of Dante's, the two men briefly knew each other, and Martel had recognized the poet's genius. Now he says, "You loved me much, and you had reason to, / for had I stayed below, you would have seen / more than the green leaves of my love for you." No exegesis I have encountered has hazarded a possibility that the married prince might have been bisexual. But that reference to *green* intrigued me, even more so when coupled with that "green cloth at Verona" mentioned in the *Inferno*. Graham Robb (151) reminds us that "green had been a gay colour for centuries. Effeminate men in Ancient Rome were called *galbinati* because of their fondness for the colour green." I remember well being teased in high school in the 1950s for wearing green on Thursday. There turns out to be only one problem with my ingenious reading: "green" was Ciardi's addition to "leaves" for the sake of scansion; it does not occur in the Italian. Nevertheless, this does not alter the fact that, for Dante, gays can go to Heaven.

TEXT: Dante Alighieri, *The Divine Comedy*, trans. John Ciardi (Norton, 1977).

Hafiz of Shiraz: Erotic Poems (Persian)

The *ghazals* of Sams al-Din Muhammad Hafiz (1325/6–1389/90) became influential among early nineteenth-century German writers, their homosocial quality intact because of Joseph von Hammer's faithful prose translations. Goethe was inspired by Hafiz, as was Count von Platen, whose friend Friedrich Rückert also translated the Persian poet. Save for Emerson's admiration, via Goethe, Hafiz has not fared so well in English. FitzGerald considered him too difficult to translate, and he could interest no other to make the attempt. The 1952 translation of scholar Peter Avery and poet John Heath-Stubbs remains the most accessible and inexpensive avenue we have to the poet who is perhaps the most revered in Persian literature. They preserve the couplet but eschew the rhyme. Fidelity yields a certain flatness as a result. Whatever faults FitzGerald's translation of the Persian may have, at least his lines are memorable. Much as I try to admire "Boy, bring the cup, and circulate the wine: / How easy at first love seemed, but now the snags begin" (Poem 1)—Avery and Heath-Stubbs's opening couplet (and one actually using slant rhyme)—it just does not remain in my mind once I close the book. (Contrast FitzGerald's "Come, fill the Cup, and in the Fire of Spring," etc.). How one longs for something more striking to be made of the lines "I can't trust those who sneer at us drinking down the lees: / That is the kind of thing which gets a bad name for religion" (Poem 7).

As with the other Persian poets, the sacred and the profane, the spiritual and the physical, may be the same. The poet pays occasional tribute to the physical charms of boys—the scent of musk from "the bright twist of black curls" (Poem 1), "the Indian-black mole on his cheek" (Poem 8)—but mostly it is roses, "the image of Beauty," and nightingales, "Love" (Poem 528). Some of the verses seem to move to the carnal, such as Poem 44, in which a drunken boy comes to Hafiz's bed. I have no idea how I should read Poem 80, where something genital seems to be going on—or am I inventing my own pornography? I give Edward Carpenter (*Ioläus*, 109–10) the final word: "The extraordinary way in which, following the method of the Sufis, and of Plato, [Persian poets] identify the mortal and the divine love, and see in their beloved an image or revelation of God himself, makes their poems difficult of comprehension to the Western mind."

TEXT: Hafiz of Shiraz, *Thirty Poems*, trans. Peter Avery & John Heath-Stubbs (Handsel, 2003).

Pacifico Massimi: *Hecatelegium* (Latin)

In the General Prologue to *The Canterbury Tales* Geoffrey Chaucer (c. 1343–1400) sketches what is probably the best-known same-sex couple in literature between Achilles and Patroclus on one side and Edward II and Gaveston on the other: a Summoner and a Pardoner. The Summoner is described as "hot" and "lecherous as a sparrow. He has scabby black brows and a thin beard." He is a drunkard, having low morals and easy tastes. The Pardoner rides beside him to share a song, "Come hither, Love, to me." He has thin hair, no beard, and a high-pitched voice, leading Chaucer to conclude that "he were a gelding or a mare." Clearly, there's something about lots of hair equaling manliness in Chaucer's mind. But nothing further is made of the pair's relationship in the tales, and though the Miller's tale is certainly queer, nothing homosexual occurs in any of them.

Chaucer's intent is satiric, but the pair's song was far from being unusual during the Middle Ages. Helen Waddell (*Medieval Latin Lyrics*, 1948), John Boswell (*Christianity, Social Tolerance, and Homosexuality*, 1980), and Thomas Stehling (*Medieval Latin Poems of Male Love and Friendship*, 1984) have translated a surprising number of ecclesiastical same-sex love poems that have survived. All three stop with the fourteenth century, but the tradition of using Latin to celebrate same-sex relationships persisted. We have two book-length cycles from two fifteenth-century Italians. Curiously *The Hermaphrodite* by Antonio Beccadelli (1394–1471, also known as Antonio Panormita), though far less interesting, has received two recent translations (one by Eugene O'Connor, 2001; another by Holt Parker, 2010). A series of smutty jokes about cock and cunt (hence the title), it is scatological both in the sense of being obscene and in bringing excrement into poetry's domain. Far more interesting and personal is the *Hecatelegium* by Pacifico Massimi (1400–c. 1500).

His volume of often personal revelations was published in 1489. The ten poems and parts of two more translated by James Wilhelm whet the appetite for more. Unfortunately, for the time being that means either reading the original Medieval Latin or finding the French translations that exist. American inattention to the poems seems mysterious: in Wilhelm's translations the poems come across as quite modern in tone and outlook. Giovanni Dall'Orto lays the neglect to the poet's frankness: "What other Renaissance poet dared to admit openly that he had practiced passive sodomy? Massimi's uncompromising verses condemned him to ostracism by literary historians" (Aldrich & Wotherspoon, 301). Even in the limited sampling Wilhelm provides us, we find a rich cross-section of gay life in fifteenth-century Italy. Massimi cheerfully admits, "I have only one thing I care about: my penis" (Book 4.2). The whole of Book 9.2 is an ode to this penis and its relentless demands. He says,

I foolishly used to think you'd get satiated or tired,
   That you wouldn't be able to keep lifting your head.
You're not ashamed of your past; in fact, you desire worse things
   So that you can heap one dirty deed on another.

And if no other person presents himself to relieve the aching need, "Then I'll spit on you and polish you off with a hand!" In Book 5.4, he says he is so horny he is indifferent whether he finds a boy or a girl: all he needs "is simply a pussy or a prick." He entertains the thoughts of a general orgy. At the end he resigns himself again: "As usual, the right hand ends the job."

But some of the poems are true love songs. Book 5.8 is the most moving. It is a long tribute to his boyfriend. He relishes moments of their being joined together outside in nature; at such times, "I possess everything; my mind wishes nothing more, / Except what I hold and will always enjoy." He will keep quiet about his happiness, however: "A man who gabs about his joys in love is a damned fool." Book 10.2 of the *Hecatelegium* describes a pair of twins whom he is in love with. He thinks, "If I could embrace the two of you together in my loving arms," it would be perfect bliss. There are also rough patches. Book 2.10 is addressed to one Marcus. The youth, the "cause and cure for my desires," makes the poet's life miserable by holding himself aloof. If he would but yield, the poet says, "No one would consider Jove a greater being than I."

The poet, drawing on his own experiences, offers advice to younger men. Book I.9 urges one Paulinus to shun vice. He confesses that he himself was sullied by a tutor, "the king of the pederasts." From him, "O yes, I learned a lot of things I'd have preferred not to. / I learned a lot about using my mouth—and my asshole." He fears Paulinus's present company is leading him down a similar path, and soon people will start talking. Book 9.3 seems to hearken back to Greek mores. The poet accuses a young man of continuing to act like the wanton child even though he is now cursed with "a noxious beard" and no longer so desirable. He seem both to sympathize with and to be annoyed by the youth's refusal to change his ways. In Book 5.6 he advises a hustler that "it is wrong to sell anything that Nature freely grants. / It is shameful to offer for silver what has been given as a gift." The poet does not seem altogether altruistic in his advice, however, for when the hustler turns a deaf ear to his hints, the poet begins to attack not only his profession but also his character and his appearance. In the end, however, he good-naturedly says, "O hell! Go ahead! May your asshole make you a millionaire!" Book 9.6 puts down another hustler who persists even though the poet is not at all interested. He admits that it is his fault: "I have the reputation of being kind to tender gay boys / So now he's after anything he can get." And in a moment of candor, he acknowledges that, were the youth better looking, he probably would not be pursuing the poet so adamantly. But he avows, "well, if he / Wants to be browned, he's going to have to pay *me*!"

Dall'Orto writes, "Homosexual themes also appear in some twenty unpublished epigrams and verse letters." He goes on to say that "Massimi was notorious as a sodomite during his own life, admitting that when he walked in the streets, boys touched their ear in a gesture—still used today—to indicate a 'poof'" (Aldrich & Wotherspoon, 302). Such a life must have nourished him: he lived to be at least eighty, and perhaps even was a centenarian at his death.

⁂

TEXT: James J. Wilhelm, ed., *Gay and Lesbian Poetry: An Anthology from Sappho to Michelangelo* (Garland, 1995), 290–302. SUPPLEMENT: Geoffrey Chaucer, "General Prologue," *The Canterbury Tales*, trans. Nevill Coghill (Cresset, 1992).

Michelangelo: Sonnets to Tommaso de' Cavalieri (Italian)

In 1532 Michelangelo Buonarroti (1475–1564) met the young Roman Tommaso dei Cavalieri, half the artist's age. James Saslow (16) writes, "Cavalieri was for him what Ganymede was to Jupiter or Alcibiades to Socrates—younger, beautiful, and a spur to the most intense emotional rapture of his often solitary life." He was acutely aware of the age difference and often rued his advancing years. It made no difference, of course, since unfortunately for him the young Tommaso was straight. That did not prevent Michelangelo from penning some thirty-five sonnets and madrigals (Poems 58–62, 72–84, 87–98, 105–09), all essentially love letters, including some of his best poems, to him. He refers directly to the young man punningly by name in Poem 98 (italics mine): "If being bested and bound is my delight, / no wonder I'm made a prisoner, nude, alone, / as a *cavalier* in armor turns the key." The intensity of his feelings for Cavalieri is so clear that, as Saslow continues, "Beginning with the artist's grandnephew, critics uncomfortable with the specter of homosexuality have attempted to deny or minimize this possibility by allegorizing Michelangelo's obvious male references or asserting that his talk of 'desire' and 'sin' is simply a rhetorical flourish applied to a commonplace spiritual affection." Some translators in the past went so far so to blithely erase any hint of "impropriety" by changing the pronouns to the feminine.

The poems are not given to fast perusal. They are dense, sometimes convoluted, and rather abstract. For an artist who so glorified the flesh in his sculptures and paintings, the young man's body, save his eyes, is scarcely visible. Poem 82 begins,

> Not even, in dreams sent soaring, can I imagine
> a form, nude apparition or flesh and bone,
> who'd so win over my will I'd dare disown
> for such acquaintance the beauty I see in you.

But instead of concrete examples of that beauty, the poet gives us images of the sun, of flames, of the phoenix and talk of beauty, of the soul, and of heaven. At times, as in Poem 87, it is hard to know whether he is speaking of his lord or of his Lord. Is the fire that is consuming him passion or the divine spirit—or both? Is it hellish, purgatorial, or heavenly—or all of these? Only in Poem 75 do we sense a real Italian male flaunting his physicality. Whatever the effect in Italian, English versions of the poems seem more exercises in language than heartfelt ardor.

Michelangelo's literary masters included Dante (the subject of two sonnets), Petrarch, and the gay classics scholar Angelo Poliziano. He knew Latin and Greek poets only second hand. He was influenced by the resurgence of interest in Neoplationism fostered by such gay Florentine thinkers as Marsilio Ficino (whom Michelangelo undoubtedly knew in person). Through them he would know of Plato's *Symposium* as well as Greek myths such as Ganymede. (He made his celebrated drawing of the boy's abduction for Cavalieri, and in Poem 89 he imagined himself as Ganymede being born aloft by Cavalieri.) For an artist so long associated with the Sistine Chapel, the Bible seems to have had no influence on his poetry. The biographical record leaves behind no hint of any sexually intimate relationship between the artist and another human. In Poem 82 the poet goes on to say, "Love unmans me quite / of the vigor it gave." In Poem 260 in crediting love for preparing a soul for heaven, the poet explicitly excludes passion for women from the sort of love he is describing. He himself, however, gave into convention and sometimes changed masculine pronouns to feminine ones in his poems. Others, particularly with "you," remain ambiguous: is the person being addressed a woman or a man? Cavalieri went on to marry and father children, but he remained friends with Michelangelo and was present when the aged artist died.

Saslow (17) sums up, "Michelangelo's statements about love and desire leave little doubt that he conceived of intimate relationships in what would now be considered fundamentally homosexual terms." He also remarks that the artist seems to have felt profound guilt about his lustful desires. This "sense of sin and fear of vengeance" (Saslow, 13) shows up early, in a series of poems written 1522–24 (Poems 18, 22, 27, 32, 36), before Cavalieri, which may reflect the passion he felt for the young Florentine Gherardo Perini. Personally speaking, I find Poem 22, in which he faces his mortality and his frustrations head on, to be the most moving of all the poems that Michelangelo wrote for men. Some of the artist's repressed ardor also spills over into two sonnets (Poems 99–100) for a young man named Febo di Poggio, whom he met briefly in 1535. Perhaps he sublimated his physical desires into the magnificent male forms he sculpted and painted. The statue of David, the ceiling of the Sistine Chapel, the Christs at St. Peter's and Santa Maria, and the slaves at the Louvre remain vivid in my memory. Through the years I have tried to come to grips with the sonnets. But for me his poetry inspires none of the awe his art does.

The American poet John Frederick Nims has tackled the entire corpus. His is probably the book to choose for his fidelity not only to the Italian forms but to the meanings. To my ear, however, the translations by the gay English poet J. A. Symonds are more memorable, perhaps because he poured his own passion into turning the Italian into English. Regardless of choice, the edition by James Saslow, even though his translations do not aspire to poetry, is indispensable for its introduction, notes, and illustrations.

TEXT: Michelangelo Buonarroti, *The Complete Poems*, trans. John Frederick Nims (Chicago, 1998). REFERENCE: James M. Saslow, ed., *The Poetry of Michelangelo: An Annotated Translation* (Yale, 1991).

Edmund Spenser: *The Shepherds' Calendar* (English)

Allegory has always appealed to me. It is not surprising that I fell in love with Edmund Spenser's (c. 1552–1599) *Faerie Queene* upon being introduced to it in my sophomore year at Wake Forest by the late William Harris, the English professor who influenced me the most. I waited until graduate school at UNC before I read all 35,000 lines, but then I devoured them. Britomart is simply one of the greatest female characters of all time, an unheralded queer model for us all. On the other hand, *The Shepheardes Calender, Conteyning Twelve Æglogues Proportionable to the Twelve Monethes*, 1579, left me cold. I now realize that I did not give it a chance, made no attempt to work out its intricacies, particularly the triangle that exists at its core: Hobbinol loves Colin Cloute; Colin loves Rosalind; Rosalind loves another (or at least does not love Colin back). Their story threads itself through six of the months that make up the calendar.

We open in January with Colin's complaint: "It is not Hobbinol wherefore I 'plain, / All be my love he seek with daily suit: / His clownish gifts and courtesies I disdain." And then, speaking in the third person, Colin insultingly explains, "Ah, foolish Hobbinol! thy gifts be vain: / Colin them gives to Rosalind again." But receiving no encouragement from her, her mocking his gifts indeed, in despair Colin breaks his shepherd's pipes and renounces song. April gives us Hobbinol's pain: "Nor this, nor that, so much does make me mourn, / But for the lad whom long I loved so dear / Now loves a lass that all his love does scorn." At the request of another shepherd Hobbinol sings one of of Colin's lays, an ode to Queen Elizabeth. In June the two shepherds meet. Hobbinol begs Colin to cease his fruitless pursuit and regain his love of song. But Colin only nurses his hurt, now doubled because another has seized Rosalind's affection.

In September Hobbinol listens to another shepherd's harangue against "popish prelates," with only a mention of his constant affection for Colin. He does try to temper the irate outburst, giving gay scholar Rictor Norton (165) occasion to comment on how basically good Hobbinol is and how he, rather than Colin, functions as "the central *human* focus" of the eclogues. November returns to Colin. Another shepherd tempts him to sing, and he chooses a mournful lay about the tragic queen Dido. In December Colin reviews his fruitless pursuit of Rosalind. His concluding lines bid, "Adieu, good Hobbinol, that was so true: / Tell Rosalind her Colin bids her adieu." Norton sums up: "Only Hobbinol remains true to Colin, and most of the positive elements in the *Calendar* focus upon him. Hobbinol's love for Colin is referred to in the first and last lines of the entire *Calendar*, and his constancy is contrasted with the faithlessness of Rosalind. Just as Rosalind and winter form the negative framework, so Hobbinol's love forms the positive framework."

The Calendar was presented to the public as having an editor, one E.K., who provides a summary of each eclogue, a gloss, sometimes a commentary, and a description of the accompanying woodcut illustration for each month. Just who E.K. was is still debated. Some have advocated Spenser's Cambridge friend (lover?) Gabriel Harvey, of whom E.K. writes in his gloss for September: "Now I think no man doubts but by Colin is ever meant the author [him]self: whose special good friend Hobbinoll says he is, or more rightly Master Gabriel Harvey." Whoever E.K. may have been, the relationship between Hobbinol and Colin made him nervous. He opens with a preemptive strike in his gloss for January. Without referring back to Theocritus and Virgil, whom he mentions in his introduction, E.K. writes, "In this place seems to be some savor of disorderly love, which the learned call *pæderasty*: but it is gathered beside [its] meaning. For who that has read Plato's dialogue called *Alcibiades*...may easily perceive that such love is much to be allowed and liked of, especially so meant as Socrates used it...much to be preferred before *gynerasticy*, that is the love which inflames men with lust toward womankind. But yet let no man think that herein I stand with Lucian, or his devilish disciple Unico Aretino [Bernardo Accolti], in defense of execrable and horrible sins of forbidden and unlawful fleshliness. Whose abominable error is fully confuted of [Joachim] Perionius and others." Thus, by raising the issue to dismiss it, he makes sure the reader is aware that something more than romantic friendship may be in play. As Norton remarks (169), "In the *Calender* itself there is no explicit condemnation or praise of amorous love between males."

Spenser goes on to drop allusions to mythological and historical male figures associated with same-sex love in *The Fairy Queen*, 1590, 1596. Book 3.6.45, mentions in passing "Fresh Hyacinthus, Phoebus's paramour / And dear love, / Foolish Narcissus," as well as "the winged boy," who "laying his sad darts / Aside, with fair Adonis plays his wanton parts." In Book 3.12.7, the poet imagines a masque of Cupid in which Ganymede and Hylas both appear. Book 4,10, takes one of the Queen's knights to the Temple of Venus. There he witnesses a "thousand pairs of lovers," all unnamed:

> But far away from these, another sort
> Of lovers linked in true hearts' consent;
> Which loved not as these, for like intent
> But on chaste virtue grounded their desire,
> Far from all fraud, or feigned blandishment;
> Which, in their spirits kindling zealous fire,
>   Brave thoughts and noble deeds did evermore aspire.

Having thus apparently sided with E.K. that this love is chaste, the poet names

> ......great Hercules and Hylas dear,
> True Jonathan and David trusty tried,
> Stout Theseus and Pirithous his fear,
> Pylades and Orestes by his side,
> Mild Titus and Gesippus without pride,
> Damon and Pythias, whom death could not sever:
> All these and all that ever had been tied
> In bands of friendship, there did live forever,
>   Whose lives although decayed, yet loves decayed never (4.10.25–27).

Spenser chose deliberately to write in an archaic English. Though editors have felt compelled to acknowledge the changing alphabet, most have used this fact to avoid otherwise updating the spelling. There are a few editions, most notably the Longman edition of the shorter poems, with modernized spelling. For convenience, I used the volume of the complete poems, which I have lugged around for now fifty-seven years, but I have modernized the spelling in the excerpts I have quoted.

TEXT: Edmund Spenser, *The Complete Poetical Works*, ed. R. E. Neil Dodge (Houghton Mifflin, 1936).

Michael Drayton: *Piers Gaveston* (English)

Inspired by the tragedy of King Edward II as recounted in Raphael Holinshed's *Chronicles of Britain* (2nd edition, 1587), Michael Drayton (1563–1631) published his narrative poem *Peirs Gaueston, Earle of Cornwall: His Life, Death, and Fortune* around the same time Christopher Marlowe was staging *Edward II*. Their titles announce their different focuses. Drayton's poem is narrated by Gaveston himself. He emerges from Hades/Hell (typically, Greek and Christian iconography are fused) to recount his downfall. He begins his story with his birth and his assignment by King Edward I to serve as the prince's page. Piers's beauty so captivates young Edward that he becomes enthralled to this "Ganymede" and grants Piers's every wish. The poet leaves no doubt that the relationship is physical: "What act so vile that we attempted not… // …wandering in the labyrinth of lust." Denounced to the king, Piers is exiled. Prince Edward is distraught and laments his loss of "my sweetest Gaveston." As soon as his father dies, the new king summons Gaveston back to court and again succumbs to his capricious desires: "By birth my sovereign, but by love my thrall, / King Edward's idol all men did me call." To seal their relationship Edward offers his niece as wife to Gaveston. He himself takes Isabel of France as his consort. But upon her arrival in England, Gaveston outshines her in the ceremonies and the two men reveal "that his queen, … / Though she his wife, yet I alone his love."

The relationship between the two men not only upsets hierarchy but threatens the kingdom's treasury. The barons cannot accept this state of affairs. To protect Gaveston from their wrath, Edward devises his lover's removal to Ireland. Piers likens the king's ensuing grief to that Alcides felt when he lost Hylas. Edward continues to send wealth and tokens of affection to the exiled lord and finally cajoles the barons to let Gaveston return. Neither man has learned from their experience, and again they indulge in hedonistic pleasures:

> Now wandering in a labyrinth of error,
> Lost in my pride, no hope of my return,
> Of sin and shame my life a perfect mirror,
> No spark of virtue once is seen to burn.
> Nothing there was could be discerned in me
> But beastly lust and sensuality.

The barons react predictably, and for a third time Gaveston departs, this time in self-exile to the Continent. He returns to England prepared to fight, but after bloody battle he is captured and beheaded. The king, nearly mad with grief, delivers an emotional eulogy. And now the ghost of Gaveston seeks to preserve his story in verse.

Whole sections of the poem, particularly the battle scenes, retain power. Paul Hammond (*Love*, 56–57) writes, "The reader's imagination is engaged by erotic descriptions of masculine beauty and homosexual embraces, evocations of intense sensual pleasure and of profound spiritual union; and interwoven with this extraordinarily intense narrative is an acknowledgment of the power of lust and ambition which destroyed the two lovers and tore apart the kingdom. It is thus a story with a clear moral content, but the homosexual character of the relationship is not denounced *per se*." As Hammond notes a page earlier (55), "What is striking about this presentation of mutual homosexual desire is that nowhere does Drayton use language which he would not have used about some illicit heterosexual affair." However, he did revise it when James I came to the throne, perhaps, as Hammond (*Figuring*, 122) suggests, out of fear that "the poem might be read as a critique of James and his entourage." The reader thus loses passages describing the king's emotions. The poem has been overshadowed by Marlowe's drama; Hammond is almost alone in taking it seriously (Gregory Woods, for example, relegates it to a footnote). Unfortunately, the only available text retains the original orthography (including its spelling of the protagonist's name as Peirs, though the editor did convert *v* to *u* and *i* to *j* when necessary and made such changes as *vv* to *w* and *ſ* to *s*). Thus, the reader is forced to make mental readjustments the entire course of the poem as he encounters such spellings as "Now wandring in a Laborinth of error, / ...beastly lust, and censualitie." The work more than merits the effort.

TEXT: Michael Drayton, *The Works*, ed. J. William Hebel (Shakespeare Head, 1961).

Christopher Marlowe: *Hero and Leander* (English)

Christopher Marlowe (1564–1593) comes across as a central figure in the loose coterie of London writers who were attracted to homoerotic themes at the time. They allude to him, quote from his works, and cultivate directions he explores. As a result of a record one Richard Baines left accusing Marlowe of being a blasphemer, some of the playwright's alleged sayings have become notorious, notably his quip: "That all they that love not tobacco and boys were fools." It is worthy of being turned into a Martial-like epigram. The opening scene of his play *Dido, Queen of Carthage*, c. 1584, presents a dialogue between the gods, with Ganymede ("a female wanton boy," Venus calls him) sitting on Jupiter's knee. Marlowe's play *The Troublesome Reign and Lamentable Death of Edward the Second, King of England, with the Tragical Fall of Proud Mortimer*, c. 1592, is his great manifestation of the wonders and dangers of gay desire. Written in the blank verse that he made his own, it was likewise inspired by Holinshed's *Chronicles of Britain*. A history play, it is also a romantic tragedy in which the king's affection for Gaveston leads to his alienation from his queen; as a result Isabella begins an adulterous relationship with young Mortimer. The outcome is the death of all three men and her banishment to the Tower.

Though Marlowe left us translations of Ovid's elegies and Lucan's *Pharsalia*, only two original poems have come down to us. His pastoral "The Passionate Shepherd to His Love" on its surface seems to be a completely heterosexual poem, but its obvious indebtedness to Virgil's second eclogue can lead one to read the famous opening invitation quite otherwise: "Come live with me, and be my love, / And we will all the pleasures prove." True, the appearance of "a kirtle" and later a "gown" suggests to modern ears a lass more than a lad, but a visit to the dictionary dispels the notion that these garments are gender-specific. Even if they were, it is not difficult to imagine a boy-actor from one of Marlowe's plays dressed to perform the part. The poem was first published posthumously in 1599, but it was well known before Marlowe's untimely death; Richard Barnfield, for one, quoted lines from it in his own pastoral.

The second poem is an epyllion in rhyming couplets, *Hero and Leander*, 1593. Ostensibly about Leander's hopeless infatuation for Hero, a woman despite her name, the poem takes on a homoerotic hue almost at once. It begins with a description of Hero, focusing on her *dress*, then turns to a highly sensual portrayal of Leander's *body*. The poet alludes indirectly to Ganymede ("Jove might have sipped out nectar from his hand") and Narcissus, and directly to the supposed misogynist Hippolytus. (Somewhat later Marlowe mentions Ganymede again, along with Cyparissus.) He conjures up who knows what in the hearer's mind when he says, "Even as delicious meat is to the taste, / So was his neck in touching." He concludes his description by stressing Leander's androgyny: "Some swore he was a maid in man's attire, / For in his looks were all that men desire." Leander's first view of Hero inspires Marlowe's often quoted line, "Whoever loved that loved not at first sight?" (It was quoted by Shakespeare in his homoerotic play *As You Like It*.) Leander instantly begins a siege on her virginity in terms not likely to appeal to feminists. But he suffers just as vigorous an attack on his own purity in his swim across the Hellespont (the lovers live on opposite sides of the strait). Naked in the water, he encounters Neptune. Mistaking the youth for Ganymede, "The lusty god embraced him, called him love, / And swore he never should return to Jove." When he sees his mistake, he is not deterred. He swims under the youth so he can "pry / Upon his breast, his thighs, and every limb." When Leander cries, "You are deceived, I am no woman, I," the god merely smiles and recites a pastoral about a shepherd and a lad. Leander finally escapes and makes his way to shore to cajole Hero into joining him in nakedness. But as Bruce Smith (134) notes tartly, "What was graphic and passionate with Neptune and Leander becomes figurative and ridiculous with Leander and Hero. Neptune pulls Leander down to the splendors of the sea-bottom; out of bed and on the floor is where Hero lands."

The unfinished poem was not published until 1598, but clearly it was also known to Marlowe's peers earlier; again Barnfield echoes lines from it in his own poetry. Over two centuries later the poem still impacted Byron so much that in 1810 the twenty-two year old recreated the swim and penned a witty bit of verse afterwards: "Written after Swimming from Sestos to Abydos." There is no record of Marlowe's having had any relationship with a woman. He moved in an exclusively male world from the time he left his home for Cambridge until his murder in the outskirts of London. He was roommates with the playwright Thomas Kyd and the spy Richard Baines, among others. And he was almost certainly Sir Thomas Walsingham's lover. His biographer Park Honan (290–91) writes, "Critical to his late artistic development was his honesty with himself, and a painful understanding of sexual desire, sexual obsession, infatuation, and perhaps buggery. He willingly may have yielded to impulse...in the process of coming to terms with himself." Honan continues (299–300), "Little that Marlowe did was unrelated to his need for comradeship and the male gang; ...and there is no reason to think he was particularly chaste at Cambridge or later on."

TEXT: Christopher Marlowe, *Complete Plays and Poems*, ed. E. D. Pendry (Dent, 1976). REFERENCE: Park Honan, *Christopher Marlowe, Poet & Spy* (Oxford, 2005).

William Shakespeare: *Sonnets* (English)

The most famous sonnet sequence from the English Renaissance is, of course, that by William Shakespeare (1564–1616). Reading the poems for what they obviously say, you can prick out (to use a Shakespearean verb) a sort of narrative line. There are three principal characters: the poet (explicitly named Will at one point), a younger man (whose name may also be Will), and the poet's mistress. Before the series is over they will find themselves in a triangular relationship, bisexual on the part of the two men. Consisting of 152 poems, the first 126 are addressed to the unknown youth that the poet has fallen in love with. The sequence begins, Sonnets 1–17, as a series of varying conceits, with the poet begging the youth to have children, at least a son, so that his beauty may live on. He urges him not to waste his sperm in empty masturbation (Sonnet 4). He has trouble accepting the fact that "thou art beloved of many, / But that thou none lovest is most evident" (Sonnet 10). Beginning at Sonnet 14, the poet begins to play with the idea that the youth's beauty may at least live on through his poetry, climaxing with the oft-quoted Sonnet 18 ("Shall I compare thee to a summer's day"), which ends by saying, "So long as men can breathe or eyes can see, / So long lives this, and this gives life to thee."

Seemingly, the idea that his poetry could preserve the youth's memory causes him to look at the man with new eyes. In Sonnet 20 he realizes that the only thing that differentiates the youth from a woman in his estimation is his penis. His ardor for the youth increases and seems to be reciprocated. In Sonnet 22, speaking of their hearts, he says, "Thou gavest me thine not to give back again." In Sonnets 23–32 (including the famous "When in disgrace with fortune and men's eyes"), he exults in their love, becomes possessive of it, cannot stop thinking about it. There are even hints that their affair becomes sexual (Sonnet 31). But, as Lysander says (*A Midsummer Night's Dream*), "The course of…love never did run smooth." The demands of their lives often occasion their physical separation. Beginning with Sonnets 33–40 the poet becomes aware of his overpossessiveness and admits the youth's rights as an individual. Another poet becomes a rival and briefly entices the youth to him. But out poet is forgiving: "No more be grieved at that which thou hast done: / Roses have thorns, and silver fountains mud" (Sonnet 35). He feels greater chagrin when, in Sonnets 40–42, he learns that his mistress has also become enamored of the youth, and the feeling may be mutual.

In the following sonnets his mind darts in different directions, trying out one conceit after another, repeating ideas he has presented earlier, all trying to come to terms with the emotions he feels. Repeatedly he takes comfort that "Not marble nor the gilded monuments / Of princes shall outlive this powerful rhyme… // You live in this, and dwell in lovers' eyes" (Sonnet 55). He admits again that he is besotted: "So true a fool is love that in your Will, / Though you do anything, he thinks no ill" (Sonnet 57). Or again, "I love you so / That I in your sweet thoughts would be forgot / If thinking on me then should make you woe" (Sonnet 71). As so often in sonnet sequences, the poet begins thinking of his own mortality (Sonnets 73–74). The rival returns (or another shows up) and troubles the poet throughout Sonnets 79–99; he feels "Like a deceived husband" (Sonnet 93). Once again he turns for comfort to the poems he is writing, before asserting again his privilege—"thou mine, I thine, / Even as when first I hallowed thy fair name" (Sonnet 108)—and affirming his constancy (Sonnet 110). This builds to the famous Sonnet 116:

> Let me not to the marriage of true minds
> Admit impediments. Love is not love
> Which alters when it alteration finds,
> Or bends with the remover to remove.

And so the poet can say—374 years before Albin made "I Am What I Am" a gay anthem in *La Cage aux Folles*—"I am that I am" (Sonnet 121).

Beginning with Sonnet 127 the poet addresses the so-called dark lady. But the youth retains his greater importance. The poet chides her for the "deep wound" she has inflicted on "my friend and me" and moans, "Of him, myself, and thee I am forsaken— / A torment thrice threefold thus to be crossed" (Sonnet 133). Immediately following, he surrenders—"So, now I have confessed that he is thine"—and blames himself: "So him I lose through my unkind abuse. / Him have I lost; thou hast both him and me; / He pays the whole, and yet am I not free" (Sonnet 134). (Notice the possible pun on *whole* / *hole*.) In Sonnet 144 he sums up:

> Two loves I have, of comfort and despair,
> Which like two spirits do suggest me still.
> The better angel is a man right fair,
> The worser spirit a woman coloured ill.

One is thus taken aback to discover in Sonnet 151 that our poet is actually torn between the two of them. Though the youth remains his greater love, whenever he is with the woman he cannot help having an erection. And so the sequence concludes, Sonnet 152, with his forgiving her, acknowledging, "But why of two oaths' breach do I accuse thee / When I break twenty?" Two additional sonnets to Cupid are tacked onto the sequence; they seemingly have nothing to do with the rest of the poems.

It is Sonnet 135 that suggests the poet and the youth may share first names. The poet says to the woman, "thou hast thy Will, / And Will to boot, and Will in overplus." This and other such word plays led Oscar Wilde, who undertook a close reading of the sonnets in 1889, to deduce that the youth was a boy actor named Willie Hughes. (The idea was actually first proposed in the eighteenth century. The dedication to the first printing of the *Sonnets*, 1609, was "To the only begetter of these ensuing sonnets, Mr W.H., all happiness and that eternity promised by our ever-living poet.") A reader has many texts to choose from. I would counsel you to select one with modernized spelling and no footnotes to distract from the poems.

Many of Shakespeare's plays, all written for the greater part in blank verse, also lend themselves to gay interpretations. Such involve gender-bending (made easier by the convention that women's roles were played by boy actors), homoerotic subtexts, male bonding, and outright same-sex attractions. Two Antonios in particular allow for homosexual readings, even if the relationship is unrequited. Antonio, the title character of *The Merchant of Venice*, 1598, is willing to give everything he has, including his life, to make his friend Bassanio happy, knowing that success means losing Bassanio to marriage with a wealthy heiress. Another Antonio, a shipwrecked captain in *Twelfth Night*, 1602, likewise is willing to risk his life out of love for the intriguingly named Sebastian, but loses him to a countess. Shakespeare's dark take on the chaotic world of the Trojan War, *Troilus and Cressida*, presents two characters who are explicitly described in terms we would today label as homosexual: Achilles and Patroclus. There are still other plays by Shakespeare whose characters can easily be played as gays: the king in *Richard II*, Mercutio in *Romeo and Juliet*, Slender in *The Merry Wives of Windsor*, Don John in *Much Ado about Nothing*, Iago in *Othello*, Coriolanus and Aufidius in *Coriolanus*, and Arcite and Palamon in *The Two Noble Kinsmen*. Stanley Wells (67) justifies such interpretations: "If the plays are open to gay readings then those readings have their own kind of validity."

TEXT: William Shakespeare, *The Complete Works*, ed. Stanley Wells & Gary Taylor, 2nd ed. (Clarendon, 2005). REFERENCE: Stanley Wells, *Looking for Sex in Shakespeare* (Cambridge, 2004), 38–65.

Richard Barnfield: *The Affectionate Shepherd; Certain Sonnets* (English)

The dedication to *The Affectionate Shepheard, Containing the Complaint of Daphnis for the Love of Ganymede*, 1594, identifies the author as Daphnis, the legendary founder of pastoral poetry celebrated by Theocritus and later Virgil. The full title of the poem is given inside the volume as "The

Teares of an Affectionate Shepheard Sicke for Love, or The Complaint of Daphnis for the Love of Ganimede." (The Elizabethans' indifference to spelling, as indicated in the two renderings of *Ganymede*, makes it all the harder to understand why modern editions will not modernize the spelling. I have in all my quotations.) A long pastoral poem in two parts, written in six-line stanzas rhyming *ababcc*, it recounts one shepherd's wooing of another. The first part is immediately followed by "The Second Dayes Lamentation of the Affectionate Shepheard," in which, after trying once more to seduce the lad, he resigns himself and offers him counsel instead. Bruce Smith (99) identifies the two parts as "the most explicitly homosexual poems of the entire English Renaissance." Paul Hammond (*Love*, 38) agrees, saying, "What is unambiguously clear about this work...is that it voices an adult male's sexual passion for a beautiful young man, urges him to reciprocate, and seeks physical consummation." The reader must be alert for all sorts of sly innuendos and double entendres: "Then shouldest thou suck my sweet and my fair flower"; "Thou suckest the flower till all the sweet be gone / And lovest me for my coin till I have none"; " suck that sweet, which many have desired." Changing from oral to anal imagery, Daphnis says, "I would thy hive, and thou my honeybee." and later, "yet meat thou shall not lack, / I'll hang a bag and a bottle at thy back."

There are allusions to rabbits, goats, throstle cocks, and sparrows, notorious for their supposed lechery. Smith (101–02) concludes, "The birding blandishments come to a climax when Daphnis promises Ganymede 'a pleasant noted Nightingale'...'Kept in 'a cage of bone' that sounds very much like a codpiece, this 'noted' bird was won 'with singing of *Philemon*' (whatever happened to female Philomel?) and is 'as white as Whale.'" Daphnis begs Ganymede to "be my boy, or else my bride." He laments, "Thou art my love, and I must be thy thrall." Unfortunately for Daphnis, a double triangle exists: Daphnis loves Ganymede; Ganymede loves Gwendolyn; Gwendolyn loves "a lusty youth / That now was dead"; she is now pursued by an "Old-Man." Editor George Klawitter (30–32) unveils the names behind the pseudonyms. Read for the above: Richard Barnfield loves Charles Blount, a very good-looking and "much-liked figure in Elizabeth's court"; Blount has taken Lady Penelope Rich, to whom Barnfield dedicates the volume, to be his mistress; she still mourns the loss of her lover Sir Philip Sidney; her husband is the highly disliked Robert Rich. Barnfield stands no chance in this intrigue.

The volume is followed by *Cynthia, with Certaine Sonnets, and the Legend of Cassandra,* 1595. In its dedication Barnfield (1574–1620) admits that he is the author of the former volume. He follows with a note defending its homoeroticism as "nothing else but an imitation of Virgil in the second eclogue of Alexis." Then he brazenly includes twenty sonnets that continue the same themes. By then the English Renaissance had established sonnet sequences as a genre with its own conventions; thus these poems by Barnfield are more moderate, less audacious, in their imagery than "The Affectionate Shepherd." As in heterosexual sonnets, we hear talk of the lover's eyes. The kisses seem more sanctioned, less sexual, though the poet does say in Sonnet 8, "Sometimes I wish that I his pillow were, / So might I steal a kiss." When the youth demands to know why the poet is in such pain and asks what girl has brought him low, the poet tells him to look into a mirror to see "The perfect form of my felicity." The names Daphnis and Ganymede are still used for the principal characters, but now more as allusions than as true names. The mythological names of Achilles, Hyacinth, Cyparissus, Narcissus, among others associated with male/male love, also show up. Again Barnfield is quite open about the object of his sexual desire. But he is forced to face the fact that his beloved "loves to be beloved, but not to love." Mourning his own mortality (the poet would then have been scarcely twenty), he admits defeat.

In a following Ode he sums up,

> Love I did the fairest boy
> That these fields did e'er enjoy.
> Love I did, fair Ganymede
> (Venus's darling, beauty's bed):
> His I thought the fairest creature;
> Him the quintessence of Nature;
> But yet, alas, I was deceived
> (Love of reason is bereaved).

Whereupon, he goes on to announce that he has fallen for a "lass," only to leave the impression that *she* is none other than Queen Elizabeth. Hammond (*Love,* 43) reads this development thus: "Thus we have an ending which is not an ending, for although the shepherd dies broken-hearted, it is not through despair of Ganymede; Ganymede is displaced from the shepherd's affections, but not by a woman who can reciprocate sexually. This form of closure may leave desire unsatisfied on a narrative level, but it leaves intact the world of homoerotic play in a perpetual present which the reader has helped to construct." There is no evidence Barnfield ever married. For a long while it was thought that he died in 1627 with children, but recent discoveries have identified the death as his father's.

TEXT: Richard Barnfield, *The Complete Poems*, ed. George Klawitter (Susquehanna, 1990).

John Wilmot, Earl of Rochester: Bawdy Poems (English)

The image of John Wilmot, Earl of Rochester (1647–1680), as the quintessential Restoration libertine is probably as important as his writings. Only a few of his poems, in fact, fit into gay anthologies. A song beginning "Love a woman? You're an ass!" renounces the gender. The poet says he would rather spend the evening drinking with a "lewd well-natured friend." And if the sexual impulse should present itself, "There's a sweet, soft page of mine / Does the trick worth forty wenches." The persona of Rochester's witty "The Disabled Debauchee" imagines himself past his prime, unmanned "by pox and wine's unlucky chance." He maintains, "Past joys have more than paid what I endure." Among other joys he remembers "love-fits" with his mistress, "When each the well-looked linkboy strove t'enjoy, / And the best kiss was the deciding lot / Whether the boy fucked you, or I the boy." There is mention of "buggery" in "A Ramble in St. James's Park," and a description of "two lovely boys" whose "limbs in amorous folds entwine" in "Upon His Drinking a Bowl." In "The Imperfect Enjoyment," a poem about his unruly penis that will not rise to a second occasion after a premature ejaculation all over a woman, he rages about his "dart of love, whose piercing point" has always in the past "Stiffly resolved, 'twould carelessly invade / Woman or man, nor ought its fury stayed: / Where'er it pierced, a cunt it found or made."

Homoerotic allusions run through Rochester's adaptation of John Fletcher's play Valentinian. A piece of dialogue (II.1) in which a character asserts "the kind tender Naked Boy is Love" is found in some gay anthologies as if it were a separate poem. Rochester's most notorious drama was his closet play in rhyming couplets, *Sodom, or The Quintessence of Debauchery*. A satire on the libertine court of Charles II, the work is basically one extended smutty joke. Paul Hammond (*Figuring*, 251–52) sums up well how "homosexual sex is never included within a grammar of love, or a syntax of subjectivity; it belongs to epigram rather than narrative, and the isolated moments which present it do not take on that extra dimension of existential contemplation which we find associated with reflection on erotic experience in Rochester's finest poems."

"The Debauchee," a poem about using a page sexually, is often ascribed to Rochester. His editor David Vieth (227–28) attributes it, however, to his close friend Charles Sackville, Sixth Earl of Dorset (1638–1706). This is the poem that begins

    I rise at eleven, I dine about two,
    I get drunk before sev'n; and the next thing I do,
    I send for my whore, when for fear of a clap,
    I spend in her hand, and I spew in her lap;
    Then we quarrel and scold, 'till I fall fast asleep,

and concludes

    If by chance then I wake, hotheaded and drunk,
    What a coil do I make for the loss of my punk?
    I storm and I roar, and I fall in a rage,
    And missing my whore, I bugger my page.
    Then, crop-sick all morning, I rail at my men,
    And in bed I lie yawning 'till eleven again.

Dorset's editor, Brice Harris, however, denies that it is his. It is really too much fun to be left so in limbo, but there it seems to have fallen.

TEXT: John Wilmot, Earl of Rochester, *The Complete Poems*, ed. David M. Vieth (Yale, 2002). SUPPLEMENT: John Wilmot, Earl of Rochester, *Sodom, or The Quintessence of Debauchery* (Brandon House, 1966); attrib., "The Debauchee" (online).

Lord Byron: Love Poems / Anonymous: *Don Leon* (English)

As Louis Crompton has amply documented, George Gordon Byron, Sixth Baron Byron (1788–1824), lived during one of the most virulently homophobic periods in British history. England during the first three decades of the nineteenth century, out of step with the Continent and even puritan American, hanged sixty men for sodomy, plus another score under its naval regulations. Thus the bravery of the bisexual poet in alluding to same-sex male attraction is all the more startling; the discretion with which he veiled his poems, particularly his *cris de cœur*, is only too understandable. Byron's first sexual experience with a male probably occurred when he was fourteen, with a young lord who was ten years older. By then Byron had already matriculated at Harrow (at age twelve) with all its opportunities for schoolboy experimentation. He refers to the school in his poems as Ida, the mountain from which Zeus abducted Ganymede. There, as he writes in "On a Distant View…of Harrow," "friendships were form'd, too romantic to last." Recalling them in "Childish Recollections," he feels nostalgic about the time when one did not question the rightness of such

> Friendship, the dear peculiar bond of youth,
> When every artless bosom throbs with truth,
> Untaught by worldly wisdom how to feign
> And check each impulse with prudential rein.

Between 1802 and 1807 he wrote poems about his classmates of such maturity that I have to keep reminding myself that he was still a teenager at the time. The verses are relatively conventional, however, and few make much impression on me. One exception is a poem he wrote "To the Duke of Dorset." He was Byron's ten-year-old fag—i.e., the junior boy assigned to him to do menial work. Byron's biographer Fiona MacCarthy (38) says, "Byron, in a letter to a friend, denied that…Dorset had ever been 'a Friend' of his: 'I *petted* the *child*, but did not make him a *Friend*.'" But the poem opens,

> Dorset! Whose early steps with mine have stray'd,
> Exploring every path of Ida's glade;
> Whom still affection taught me to defend,
> And made me less a tyrant than a friend.

And it builds toward a conclusion—"Still, if the wishes of a heart untaught / To veil those feelings which perchance it ought"—when it breaks off abruptly, as if the poet fears he is about to go too far.

Byron enrolled in Cambridge at age sixteen. Many of his Harrow friends had gone to Oxford, so he formed a largely new coterie. Now he definitely moved in a homosexual circle. His most intimate friends included William Bankes, Charles Skinner Matthews, and John Cam Hobhouse. MacCarthy (58, 67) asserts that, while Bankes "indoctrinated" Byron into a "thriving subculture of sodomy, with its own rituals and codes" at Cambridge, "in matters sodomitical he depended upon Matthews as his 'guide, philosopher and friend.'" About this time Byron wrote a poem called "My Character." Published in 1807 as "Damætas," it begins, "In law an infant and in years a boy, / In mind a slave to every vicious joy; / From every sense of shame and virtue wean'd," and goes on to say, "Old in the world, though scarcely broke from school; / Damætas ran through all the maze of sin, / And found the goal when others just begin." By now Byron was fully aware how he was heir to a gay tradition of long standing. In his mock epic *Don Juan*, 1819, Canto 1, stanzas 42–43, he displays his knowledge of Greek and Roman poets with whom, no doubt, he identified. He begins his list,

>Ovid's a rake, as half his verses show him,
>   Anacreon's morals are a still worse sample,
> Catullus scarcely has a decent poem,

then moves on,

> But Virgil's songs are pure, except that horrid one
> Beginning with *Formosum Pastor Corydon*,

to conclude:

> I can't help thinking Juvenal was wrong,
>   Although no doubt his real intent was good,
> For speaking out so plainly in his song,
>   So much indeed as to be downright rude;
> And then what proper person can be partial
> To all those nauseous epigrams of Martial?

Missing from his list is Horace, a curious omission since *Horatian* became a code term for bisexuality among Byron's university clique.

Byron also imitated Latin originals. He translated Catullus's Poem 48 but disguised that the person whose kisses the speaker desired is a male by dedicating it "To Ellen." He was bolder with his "Episode of Nisus and Euryalus: A Paraphrase from the *Æneid*, Lib. IX." Presumably the story of the two warriors who "burn with one pure flame of generous love" was regarded so firmly at the time as an example of romantic friendship that Byron was not fearful of anyone reading too much into his rhyming couplets:

> Thus Nisus all his fond affection proved—

Dying, revenged the fate of him he loved;
Then on his bosom sought his wonted place,
And death was heavenly in his friend's embrace.

However, he dismissed the whole pastoral tradition in "The First Kiss of Love" as "a region of dreams" whose "fantastic themes" would be exposed for the "tissues of falsehood" they are by a true physical passion.

The great love of Byron's life at Cambridge was John Edleston (or Edlestone). He was fifteen and Byron seventeen when they met. Edleston was a chorister and, in class-ridden England, distinctly below Byron in rank. But the two were soon inseparable. It was with hesitation that the youth offered Byron "a gold ring mounted with a gleaming pale pink stone in the shape of a heart...poignantly small" (MacCarthy, 59). Byron responded with a poem, "The Cornelian," in which he proclaims, "the simple gift I prize,— / For I am sure the giver loved me." The ring still exists. "Pignus Amoris" (Pledge of Love), which recasts the same sentiments into a longer poem, was not published until nearly seventy-five years after Byron's death. Theirs was a short relationship. By July 1807 Edleston's voice had changed, and he left Cambridge to become a clerk in a London investment firm. The poem "Stanzas to Jessy" may commemorate this parting, with John concealed behind Jessy. In a letter to a female friend about this time, Byron expressed his hope that the two boys would forge a true partnership in which they would "put *Lady E. Butler*, & Miss *Ponsonby* to the *Blush, Pylades* & *Orestes* out of countenance, & want nothing but a *Catastrophe* like *Nisus* & *Euryalus*, to give *Jonathan* & *David* the 'go by'" (Crompton, 102). Byron received his M.A. in 1808. He first resided in London and Brighton and then, in 1809, embarked on the tour of Mediterranean countries that would provide the basis for *Childe Harold's Pilgrimage*. His letters to Hobhouse indicate that he plunged into the sexual possibilities now open to him with abandon. None of the boys that he took up occasioned a poem, however, and, curiously, Edleston seems to disappear from Byron's emotional life until 1811. Then, news of his unexpected death occasioned a flurry of poems in which the choirboy was once again metamorphosed into a woman, Thyrza. In "To Thyrza" he remembers

Ours too the glance none saw beside,
  The smile none else might understand;
The whisper'd thought of hearts allied,
  The pressure of the thrilling hand;

> The kiss, so guiltless and refined
>   That Love each warmer wish forbore;
> Those eyes proclaim'd so pure a mind,
>   Even passion blush'd to plead for more.

This was followed by six more poems: "Away, Away, Ye Notes of Woe," "One Struggle More, and I Am Free," "And Thou Art Dead, as Young and Fair," "If Sometimes in the Haunts of Men," "On a Cornelian Heart Which Was Broken," and an uncollected poem in Latin—the only one using a masculine gender—headed "Edleston Edleston Edleston." By now Byron was leaning more to his heterosexual side, but I get the impression (particularly with the Latin poem) that the dead Edleston began to assume the role that Jean Verdenal would for Eliot or Jimmy Trimble for Gore Vidal—a matchless ideal rather than a real person.

For more than a decade Byron's attraction to other men seems to have lain dormant. These were the years he was penning his masterpiece, *Don Juan*. Then in 1823 he became involved in the Greek struggle for independence from the Ottoman Empire. He was joined by fifteen-year-old Lukas Chalandrutsanos. The passion that the youth awakened in the poet, twenty years his elder, occasioned a return to the lyric. Three poems are tributes to Lukas. "On This Day I Complete My Thirty-Sixth Year" reveals the poet's awareness that his emotions are not returned in kind. In "Last Words on Greece" Byron announces, "I am a fool of passion," and goes on to record how even a frown from Lukas depresses him: "So strong thy magic or so weak am I." He reviews their brief life together in "Love and Death" and again acknowledges:

> ......yet thou lov'st me not,
>   And never wilt! Love dwells not in our will.
> Nor can I blame thee, though it be my lot
>   To strongly, wrongly, vainly love thee still.

There may have been one more poem to Lukas that Hobhouse destroyed (MacCarthy, 505); the protectiveness of Byron's friends erected major barriers to any exploration of the poet's sexuality. He died in April 1824. Lukas's fate remains unknown. In a final note MacCarthy (571–74) reveals that when Byron's vault was opened in 1938, his "body was still in an excellent state of preservation." That permitted the discovery that our poet was apparently well-hung, or as the official report put it, "his sexual organ showed 'quite abnormal development.'"

Don Leon: A Poem by the Late Lord Byron, Author of Childe Harold, Don Juan, &c., &c., and Forming Part of the Private Journal of His Lordship, Supposed to Have Been Entirely Destroyed by Thos. Moore was published in London in 1866 by William Dugdale, though there is evidence that there may have been an earlier printing. Fortune Press reprinted the poem in 1934, but the British government condemned the book as obscene, and all copies were ordered destroyed. One that escaped was reprinted in facsimile in 1975 by Arno Press as part of its Homosexuality series. Peter Cochran included it in his anthology *Byron and Women (and Men)*, 2010, but it is easier (and cheaper) to read on his website. John Lauritsen brought out his edition in 2017. Though the poet made mistakes and was clearly ignorant about parts of Byron's life, the story of Don Leon is essentially Byron's rendered in heroic couplets. The real Byron and the invented Leon are so close, in fact, that critics (Crompton, for one) are prone to call the poem's hero "Byron," especially since it is written in the first person. It is, however, more than an exposé. The poem is also an attack on the government's (and the church's) barbaric treatment of sodomites, a manifesto calling for the end of capital punishment. The question of nature v. laws is raised almost at once. The 1866 text was provided with copious footnotes; the opening scene is therein identified as the hanging of Captain Henry Nicholas Nicholls in August 1833. Later in the poem, via another footnote, the case of Byron's friend Bankes, who was arrested in June 1833 for importuning, is recorded at some length, including his second arrest in 1841 and subsequent disappearance from society. The poem's author is unknown. Candidates include George Colman the Younger (1762–1836), William Bankes (1786–1855) himself, and John Hobhouse (1786–1869), but none quite fits. Lauritsen suggests it may have been a collaboration.

Don Leon begins his history with an account of his love for [Robert] Ruston (Byron's young servant who accompanied him partway on his grand tour) and "Eddlestone" [*sic*]. These are examples, Leon admits, of "illicit love .../ But what prompts nature then to set the trap?" Moreover, since such relations are "harming no one, wherefore call them wrong?" Thereupon, he quotes the Golden Rule. He goes on to allude to Plato, Socrates, Bion, Plutarch, Virgil, Horace, and Ovid, follows them with examples of popes, priests, kings, scholars, jurists, poets, and captains who "Have found their solace in a minion's arms," and caps them with the example of Shakespeare. At one point he wittily observes about himself, "I plough no fields in other men's domain; / And where I delve no seed shall spring again." The poem records Leon's experiences at Harrow, where he meets Eddlestone (Byron knew Edleston at Cambridge); next at an unnamed college; then on the grand tour, accompanied by a friend (Hobhouse in real life), all the while with "Love, love, clandestine love...still my dream." Finally, he finds a Greek youth who partakes, in looks, of both genders. With him

......anon, like some Artesian fount
Would oozings foul e'en from my entrails mount,
Salacious, and in murky current wet
The urn beneath with interrupted jet.

There are still other Greek boys, including [Niccolò] Giraud, who satisfied "the wish, long cherished, long denied."

The poem at this point abruptly veers into an argument that sodomy serves as a solution to Thomas Malthus's concerns about the effects of uncontrolled population growth: "In sterile furrows why not sow his seed? / Why follow not the strict Malthusian creed?" This contention is immediately followed, rather bizarrely, with a description of other acts that violate sexual codes: indecent exposure, pederasty, cunnilingus, caning, fellatio, voyeurism, incest, cross-dressing, mutual masturbation, and institutional sodomy, along with acts that I am simply too ignorant to identify. Above all, the poet is angry with the "hypocritic cant" that he hears "the bench disdain, the pulpit rant." After this long interlude the poem returns to Leon's life, now to his relationship with his wife Annabella. Her being great with child, he talks her into allowing him to take her anally. The act leads to a long digression about anal intercourse, including the need for cleanliness lifted right out of Juvenal's Satire 9. That is followed by an appeal to Byron's friend Thomas Moore to "paint me as I am; / Abate no sin I had, no virtue sham." The poem ends with a paean to the anus. Structurally it is something of a mess. And in truth the poet does not always remember that Leon, and not Byron, is his hero. But it is rollicking fun to read, no matter how much or how little one know about Byron.

᛭

TEXTS: George Gordon, Lord Byron, *The Complete Poetical Works*, ed. Paul Elmer More (Houghton Mifflin, 1933). "Lord Byron," *Don Leon & Leon to Annabella*, ed. John Lauritsen (Pagan, 2017). REFERENCES: Peter

Cochran, ed., *Don Leon* (online). Louis Crompton, *Byron and Greek Love: Homophobia in 19th-Century England* (California, 1985). Fiona MacCarthy, *Byron: Life and Legend* (Farrar, Straus & Giroux, 2002).

August von Platen: Love Sonnets (German)

The case of August von Platen (Karl August Georg Maximilian, Graf von Platen-Hallermünde, 1796–1835) is a strange one. Almost every gay encyclopedia provides the poet an entry, yet his poetry is ignored by gay anthologists. Stephen Coote is the only one to have represented him to any degree. Reginald Cooke's translations of the sonnets, 1919–23, remain the only extensive collection of his poetry in English. Platen's candid diary, published in two volumes, 1896 and 1900, is yet untranslated. Edward Prime Stevenson (566) has summarized its contents. According to him, Platen himself saw the work as "the mirror of...what he thought was an uncommon kind of nature and sexual life." Platen's attraction to men was well-known by his peers; it was blatantly exposed by fellow poet Heinrich Heine in retaliation for antisemitic remarks Platen made about him. Platen, in fact, was troubled by his physical urges and never found the lasting sexual and spiritual partner he was searching for ("that true comrade of my need")—a search that took him from Germany into Italy, where he died.

Most of the sonnets were written between 1817 and 1826 to friends and potential lovers. There are eight poems written 1822–23 to Justus Liebig (the founder of organic chemistry), another eight written during the same period to "Cardenio" (a law student named Hoffmann?), and still another twenty-three composed in 1826 for Karl Theodor German. In addition, Cooke translates fifteen sonnets, 1817–24, addressed to six other men, including Eduard Schmidtlein, Herman von Rotenhan, Otto von Bulow, and Friedrich von Brandenstein. It was Platen's lot to continually fall in love with the wrong person and then to be hurt. Schmidtlein is a perfect example. Prime Stevenson tells us that Schmidtlein dominates over 300 pages of the diary (roughly fifteen percent). In the three sonnets for Schmidtlein that Cooke gives us, Platen records in the first how he became the young man's "slave." Then he begins to doubt the wisdom of having revealed himself so nakedly: "Thou dost lament our love's degeneracy, / And thy desires too bold and sinful deem." Yet still the poet yearns to lie "Cheek against cheek, at dusk beneath the trees, / Breast pressing close to breast and thigh to thigh," as the elms "whisper soft, sweet bridal melodies." But finally, in the third sonnet, he accuses Schmidtlein:

> Yet in thy glowing glance but ruin lies.
> Now well I know, awakened from delight,
> Which all too truly dazzled every sense,
> Thou hast a heart as black as thy black eyes!

The poems are not particularly memorable. They are filled with abstractions, the few images mostly external to the lovers and, even then, acting more as symbols than concrete description. In his first sonnet to Brandenstein he wrote, "No later image dims mine imagery / Of thee," but when we finish the fourteen lines we have no inkling what that image might be. Verifying that this vagueness is present in the original, Edward Carpenter's translation of the same sonnet (in *Ioläus*) is equally abstract. Upon closing Cooke's selection, the fourth sonnet to Cardenio is one of the few that remain in my mind. The octave reads:

> Well I recall that bitter winter's night,
> More exquisite than any night in spring,
> When I, my friend, could watch thee carrying
> A torch, so to direct me by its light
> Upon our solitary path. How bright
> And beautiful the myriad sparks would fling
> Abroad their radiant showers, as, in a ring,
> Thou whirl'dst the fiery fagots left and right.

The sestet then personifies the stars, having them look down in envy. It ends with an unanswered question about the nature of the two men's thoughts. Otherwise, the poems are a blur.

·⁜·

TEXT: August von Platen, *The Sonnets*, trans. Reginald Bancroft Cooke (Richard G. Badger, 1923). REFERENCE: Xavier Mayne (Edward Prime Stevenson), *The Intersexes: History of Similisexualism as a Problem in Social Life* (Arno, 1975), 563–620.

Alfred, Lord Tennyson: *In Memoriam* (English)

Alfred Tennyson (latter the first Baron Tennyson, 1809–1892) met eighteen-year-old Arthur Henry Hallam in the spring of 1829 at Cambridge. They were both students at Trinity College and members of the Apostles, a group eventually to gain a certain gay notoriety. Their friendship led to Hallam's courting Tennyson's younger sister, but Hallam's father forbade any contact between the two as long as Hallam was in his minority. When he came of age in 1832, the two renewed their romance, and Hallam began working in London to earn enough money to marry. In the fall of 1833, however, while on a tour of the Continent with his father, he died of a stroke. Tennyson was devastated. Soon he began the series of lyrics that form *In Memoriam*. It is the journal of a distressed soul seeking consolation. Tennyson added to it constantly over the next years. It was finally published in 1850, first in a limited and then in a public edition; later revisions brought the total number of lyrics—written in iambic tetrameter, rhyming abba—to 131, plus a prologue and an epilogue. Its success was immense and led directly to his being appointed Poet Laureate. Even so, many readers were disquieted by both the language and the intensity of the emotion displayed. A heterosexual poet had managed to write what seems to be one of the gayest poems in the English anthology. I remember my delight when I discovered that the often-quoted lines "'Tis better to have loved and lost / Than never to have loved at all" (Poems 27, 85) were written by one man about another.

Watching sexually insecure scholars wriggling to explain away such statements provides amusement of its own kind. I conclude on rereading it, however, that they really need not bother. Despite the gender-transferred language (ex., Poem 59), fleeting allusions to the pastoral tradition (Poem 23), Urania (Poem 37), Shakespeare's sonnets (Poem 61), Michelangelo (Poem 87), and "some Socratic dream" (Poem 89), and Tennyson's uneasiness about two lines in Poem 95 that seemed perhaps too erotic, in the end it is hard to believe that "Arthur" was anything more than an abstraction for the poet. We finish all those many stanzas with no idea what he looked like, what his speech sounded like, how he dressed, what his facial expressions were. The sequence of poems is all about Love and Grief and Sorrow and Death, about Nature and Soul and Shadow, those capitalized generalizations that produce no image. No wonder the mind seizes upon such lyrics as "Old Yew" (Poem 2), "Dark House" (Poem 7), and "Wild Bells" (Poem 106) with their concrete references. Even his evocation of the grass that grows on Hallam's grave (Poem 21) has none of the impact of Whitman's grassy graves. One understands why Queen Victoria found Tennyson's poem comforting. Eliot, in a comment that takes on significance in an examination of his own poetry, wrote: "It happens now and then that a poet by some strange accident expresses the mood of his generation, at the same time that he is expressing a mood of his own which is quite remote from that of his generation" (Gray, 136).

Nonetheless, we must not discount the impact that the sequence had on later gay poets. Paul Hammond (*Love*, 148) writes: "Whether or not Tennyson wrote these poems as ways of exploring a love for Hallam which included sexual desire, there is no doubt that they provide an imagined space in which poet and reader can own those lyrical utterances and unconsummated narratives which enact desire for a man who is indifferent to, or who has even rebuffed and forsaken, the speaker." To see which lyrics come across as gayest, I collated the ones that were included in five anthologies (Carpenter, Sutherland & Anderson, Reade, Coote, and Fone). These 24 poems appear in one or more: Poems 1, 4–7, 9, 12–13, 18, 22–23, 25, 27, 37, 41, 43, 50, 61, 70, 79, 91, 126, 129–130.

TEXT: Alfred, Lord Tennyson, *In Memoriam*, ed. Erik Gray (Norton, 2004).

Walt Whitman: *Leaves of Grass* (English)

It appeared on July 4, 1855. Quarto-sized. Ninety-five pages. A green cover embossed with darker green foliage, the title in gold leaf with roots and leaves springing out of the words *Leaves of Grass*. Inside, an engraving of a handsome bearded man in work clothes: open collar, hat tilted at a jaunty angle; one hand resting on the hip, the other stuck in a pocket. Opposite the engraving, the page with the title and "Brooklyn, New York: 1855." No author's name, although the copyright page yields "Walter Whitman." Twelve pages of prose set in double columns, its opening word "America." Then eighty-three pages of unrhymed verse set in irregular lines. Twelve poems. The first six all titled "Leaves of Grass," the opening poem alone covering pages 13–56. It contains the lines "Walt Whitman, an American, one of the roughs, a kosmos, / Disorderly fleshy and sensual." The second six poems are all short, untitled. Poetry would never be the same again. Gay literature in one day became "before Whitman" and "after Whitman." His name itself would, for over a century, be a code word for "gay," much as Wilde, Gide, and Proust would later serve. A smaller-sized and fatter edition, expanded now to thirty-two poems, all titled, came out the next year. Then in 1860 a new edition with 146 new poems began shaping the work into the form we presently know. This decisive turn included a section called Calamus, forty-five poems that explored what Whitman called *adhesiveness*: the attraction of one man for another. There would be six more editions in which he would fold in new poems, revise or discard old ones, and regroup sequences to arrive at the last, so-called deathbed edition of 1892.

Although Whitman (1819–1892) was guarded about his life, he had a string of boyfriends, Peter Doyle being the best-known. His home became a mecca for gay visitors, including Thoreau, 1856; Edward Carpenter, 1877; Wilde, 1882; Bram Stoker, 1884; the painter Thomas Eakins, 1887. Eakins painted a famous portrait, 1887–88, and may have taken a series of unidentified nude photographs of the poet. Carpenter (1844–1929) paid Whitman the ultimate compliment: imitation. Lines from *Towards Democracy*, published in four parts 1883–1922, are at times so indebted to Whitman's verse that it is difficult to read Carpenter on his own terms. Recently it has been argued that Whitman influenced Stoker's depiction of Dracula. Those who could not come wrote: Charles Warren Stoddard, 1869; J. A. Symonds, 1871. All but Thoreau would have read him in a later edition of *Leaves*. But from the beginning only the most innocent could escape understanding what was being described in such a passage as

> I mind how we lay in June, such a transparent summer morning;
> You settled your head athwart my hips and gently turned over upon me,
> And parted the shirt from my bosom-bone, and plunged your tongue to
>   my barestript heart,
> And reached till you felt my beard, and reached till you held my feet.

Even as naïve as I was as a teenager, I understood the line "Root of washed sweet-flag, timorous pond-snipe, nest of guarded duplicate eggs." And those twenty-eight young men swimming naked while the hidden young woman imagines being with them I found sexually as arousing as anything I read in *Peyton Place*. Indeed, "Through me forbidden voices, / Voices of sexes and lusts, voices veil'd and I remove the veil, / Voices indecent by me clarified and transfigur'd."

All these lines come from the poem that came to be called "Song of Myself." They were changed very little in later editions ("in June" did disappear). Just as erotic was the fourth poem, which came to be known as "The Sleepers." In an almost surrealistic way, the poet moves in his imagination among various people, sharing their beds and their dreams. Personification and realistic description merge and pronouns escape their references:

> My truant lover has come and it is dark.
> Double yourself and receive me darkness,
> Receive me and my lover too…he will not let me go without him.
> I roll myself upon you as upon a bed…I resign myself to the dusk.
> He whom I call answers me and takes the place of my lover,
> He rises with me silently from the bed.
> Darkness you are gentler than my lover…his flesh was sweaty and
>   panting,
> I feel the hot moisture yet that he left me.

There follow lines cut from later editions telling how the dreamer's clothes are stolen, and he must ponder where to hide his nakedness, until he sees the piers, a traditional cruising area.

> The cloth laps a first sweet eating and drinking,
> Laps life-swelling yolks…laps ear of rose-corn, milky and just ripened:
> The white teeth stay, and the boss-tooth advances in darkness,
> And liquor is spilled on lips and bosoms by touching glasses, and the
>   best liquor afterwards.

Addressing Lucifer (in lines cut from the revised poem), Whitman comes closer than usual to confronting evil, the dark aspects of his own ego. Day brings back his usual overflowing optimism.

The 1860 Calamus poems were not so shocking to antebellum Americans as was the section Enfans d'Adam (later titled more naturally Children of Adam), a set of fifteen heterosexual poems created to balance the Calamus ones—sometimes, as we learned from manuscripts, by deliberately changing the original male gender. Gay readers though immediately saw the importance of the Calamus section. The calamus plant takes its name from a Greek legend. Calamus, *reed*, the son of a river god, falls in love with Carpus, *fruit*. Carpus drowns while swimming with Calamus;

grieved, Calamus withers away to become the rustling reed, which sports a phallic-like flower stem. Also known as sweet flag, it was likewise a favorite of Thoreau. The section was eventually reduced to thirty-nine poems. In the opening poem, as it appears in the 1860 edition, Whitman forthrightly announces that he has "Escaped from the life that exhibits itself, / From all the standards hitherto publish'd." He makes clear that "the Soul of the man I speak for, feeds, rejoices only in comrades," and goes on to say that he feels "No longer abashed—for in this secluded spot I can respond as I would not dare elsewhere, / Strong upon me the life that does not exhibit itself, yet contains all the rest, / Resolved to sing no songs today but those of manly attachments."

Like Shakespeare before him, in the ninth poem he accepts "I am what I am." And in the next poem he stands proud to say: "Publish my name and hang up my picture as that of the tenderest lover." He remembers a happy night spent with his lover's arm around him (Calamus 11) and admits that he himself is "burning for his love whom I love" (Calamus 14). He envisions a "brotherhood of lovers" (Calamus 28) who will eventually create a city where their "robust love" can express itself freely (Calamus 33). He records a contact made in a bar (Calamus 29) and describes cruising the streets, where "I perceive one picking me out by secret and divine signs." Returning to the mystical experience described in "Song of Myself," he muses, "Doubtless I could not have perceived the universe, or written one of my poems, if I had not freely given myself to comrades, to love" (Calamus 39). He sums up (Calamus 44), "Here I shade down and hide my thoughts—I do not expose them, / And yet they expose me more than all my other poems." Whitman is our gay poet. He is also our universal poet. Though perhaps lacking their sense of the dark and tragic, he is America's Shakespeare, its Hugo, its Pushkin. "I am large...I contain multitudes," he writes. And indeed he does.

TEXTS: Walt Whitman, *Leaves of Grass: An Exact Copy of the First Edition 1855* (Eakins, 1966); *Leaves of Grass...Facsimile Edition of the 1860 Text* (Cornell, 1961). SUPPLEMENT: Harold W. Blodgett & Sculley Bradley, eds., *Leaves of Grass: Comprehensive Reader's Edition* (New York, 1965). REFERENCE: David S. Reynolds, *Walt Whitman's America: A Cultural Biography* (Knopf, 1995).

John Addington Symonds: Poems in Various Keys (English)

No collected edition of John Addington Symonds's (1840–1893) poetry exists. For that matter, there is no selected edition either: only the individual volumes that he published during his lifetime, most now available as cheap reprints. Given what Amber Regis, the editor of his *Memoirs* tells us about copyright laws (16), a collected poems will not appear until the status of poems that Symonds privately printed is resolved. Meanwhile, we have to make do by piecing together what we have from various sources. Symonds's verse seldom soars into the truly memorable, but he is a master of the easy line that flows unhesitatingly from rhyme to rhyme, and some of his images startle. His translation of Michelangelo's sonnets remains quite readable (not to mention the credit he deserves for having clearly identified the ones written to Cavalieri).

Early (and unconsummated) infatuations produced poems saved mostly in his memoirs. At Harrow, age eighteen, he fell in love with a fifteen-year-old chorister, Willie Dyer. Two poems that he inspired are available on scholar Rictor Norton's website. A chorister at Oxford, Alfred Brooke, sixteen, had a major impact on Symonds's emotional life at age twenty-two. The memoirs (194–203) preserves a series of poems that grew out of this crush; Norton tells us that the series of fifteen poems included in the essay "Clifton and a Lad's Love" (collected in *In the Key of Blue*, 1893) were also addressed to Brooke. As Symonds began exploring the meaning of his sexuality, he recalls in his memoirs (351), "I wrote many poems on Greek subjects…all feeding the fever of my heart, which was also kept alive by innumerable fair sights and passing episodes." The poems served as "the vehicle and safety-valve for my tormenting preoccupations. A cycle of poems gradually got written, illustrating the love of man for man in all periods of civilization…. The composition of the cycle lasted over the period between January 1866 and sometime after 1875" (367). He also mentions (311) writing "a great number of dithyrambic pieces in the style of Walt Whitman." Concerning the American, he said (467), "I find it difficult to speak about *Leaves of Grass* without exaggeration."

Several of the titles he lists now seem to be lost; most were privately printed and remain, bizarrely enough, still copyrighted (though no one seems to know who holds the copyright). Brian Reade in his anthology *Sexual Heretics* rescued two of the classical tales from oblivion. Taken from *Tales of Ancient Greece No. 1*, "Eudiades" recounts, in highly sensual language, Melanthias's love of the eponymous youth. He spots Eudiades first engaging in play with another boy. Like any traditional lovesick swain Melanthias woos Eudiades with flowers and songs and posts declarations of his love on a statue sacred to Eros. The story of Hylas helps the innocent Eudiades understand what is happening, and he accepts Melanthias's courtship. His "love began / To mould the calm boy to a passionate man," and he is ready to surrender his body. But Melanthias resists temptation, and they live virginal lives. The two become comrades in arms; defending Athens, they are killed on the battlefield together, leaving the poet—whose vision this is—to venerate them. Quite different, the strange "Midnight at Baiae," one of *Three Visions of Imperial Rome*, ends with a nude youth discovered in bed, his throat slit, the result apparently of a sadomasochistic encounter gone terribly wrong.

None has the power of a poem in three parts written in 1868 with a contemporary setting, fortunately preserved in the memoirs (347–51). The first part of *"Phallus Impudicus"* (347–51) records the poet's coming across a growth of stinkhorns, phallic-shaped mushrooms, in an Italian copse. It may well be a cruising ground since there "on the broken stone or roofless hut / Coarse shapes of shame and words of lust are cut." (*Shame* was apparently already becoming a code word for what would shortly be labeled homosexuality.) The poet is repulsed by the fungi. All the language he uses to describe them is negative:

> Poisonous and loathsome both to touch and smell,
> Rotten and rotting, wreaked the spawn of hell;
> Emblems of heat unhallowed, foul desire,
> Dry lust that revels in the fleshly mire.

But in the second part he awakens to "some hint of coming change." He has hired a "Sorrento lad" to accompany him on his journey. They take separate quarters for the night. When the poet arises the next morning, he passes into the youth's chamber and finds him lying naked, displaying to his gaze

> ......thighs and rosy nipples,
> Elastic belly, and soft sheltering velvet
> Short clustering down, luxuriantly wanton,
> Round the twin marble man-spheres shyly circling,

> Round the firm rondure of love's root of joy,
> The smooth rude muscle, calm and slow and tender,
> The alabaster shaft, the pale pink shrine,
> The crimson glory of the lustrous gland
> Lurking in dewy darkness, half-concealed,
> Like a rose-bud peeping from clasped silken sheath.

The sight is an epiphany: "from that day I nurse a deathless fire: / I am aflame with beauty." As for what the world may think, he decides he does not care. In the third part, the poet, now initiated into the phallic mysteries, observes Venetian men cruising each other, exposing themselves by pretending to urinate against a wall, and witnesses with new understanding a pickup.

At the end of 1868 he met Norman Moor, eighteen. By now Symonds was twenty-eight, married, and the father of two of his four daughters. He claims the relationship was chaste; from his description it could hardly have been pure. Two poems accompany the chapter about Moor in the memoirs (396–97, 403). In the mid-1870s Symonds met the nineteen-year-old Swiss hotelier Christian Buol. Yet again his memoirs serve to preserve a sensuous poem written about the youth asleep in bed beside him (503–04). He now published his first collection meant for the general public: *Many Moods*, 1878 (dedicated to his friend, the bisexual poet Roden Noel). It includes several narratives that skirt the edges of Victorian propriety. "The Lotus-Garland of Antinous," in heroic couplets, tells how Antinous sacrificed his life in order to save the life of his emperor, Hadrian. "The Meeting of David and Jonathan," again in heroic couplets, avoids phallic detail, but emotionally it could scarcely go further. "Callicrates" is a convoluted monologue in blank verse spoken by the title character's Spartan lover Aristodemus when they arrive in Hades after being slain in battle. "Love and Death"—the very title could unite all these narratives—tells in terza rima how two Athenian lovers, Cratinus and Aristodemus, the same name as above, sacrifice themselves to end a plague that is devastating the city state. Symonds returned to their story in "The Sacrifice: A Fragment" in his next collection, *New and Old*, 1880 (dedicated to another gay friend and eventually his literary executor, Horatio Brown), this time using blank verse. This volume also contains the pastoral "Hesperus and Hymenæus, or The Shepherd and the Star" in which an unnamed shepherd asks the evening star "To guide me to the shepherd whom I love." Hesperus instead entertains him with the story of how he seduced the inebriated Hymenæus and took him away to the heavens where all good lovers go.

A triad of poems published under the collective title "In Venice" foreshadow his relationship with the twenty-four-year-old gondolier Angelo Fusato, whom he would meet in 1881 when Symonds was over forty. In his memoirs he wrote (272): "How sharp this mixed fascination was at the moment when I first saw Angelo, and how durable it afterwards became through the moral struggles of our earlier intimacy, will be understood by anyone who reads the sonnets written about him in my published volumes." He proceeds to list the fifty-six in the order in which they should be read in *Animi Figura*, 1882, and *Vagabunduli Libellus*, 1884. The first two, emphasizing the impact of Fusato's eyes, are the most powerful. (It is a quality visible in photographs of the man.) The rest of the poems record a vacillating soul torn between "Shame and Desire" and social propriety, all in cloudy, abstract language with much talk of "madness," "Chimera," and "Maya." Not a one rises to the concrete simplicity of a sonnet about Fusato included in his memoirs (516). It ends:

......Our four hands, laughing, made
  Brief havoc of his belt, shirt, trousers, shoes:
  Till, mother-naked, white as lilies, laid
There on the counterpane, he bade me use
  Even as I willed his body. But Love forbade—
  Love cried, 'Less than Love's best thou shalt refuse!'

The memoirs go through 1891. One last series of significant gay poems was included in an 1893 essay, "In the Key of Blue." Musing upon the difficulties of describing tints of a color, Symonds set out to "try the resources of our language in a series of studies of what might be termed 'blues and blouses.' For this purpose I resolved to take a single figure—a *facchino* [Augusto Zanon, age twenty] with whom I have been long acquainted—and to pose him in a variety of lights with a variety of hues in combination." There follow prose passages interspersed with ten impressionistic poems that try to do with language what Whistler was doing with paint. Eight begin "A symphony of...," my ellipsis filled with two colors, one always blue. Written for the most part in rhyming couplets using iambic tetrameter, they celebrate the clothed male body in a variety of settings, but throughout you sense, "There throbbed a man's heart neath the shirt." And he ends the sequence by emphasizing the man

  Who warmed the cold hue, bright or dim.

Those grape-like curls, those brief replies;
These are thy themes—the man, the life—
Not tints in symphony at strife.

Symonds died in Rome of tuberculosis. Sean Brady has published *John Addington Symonds (1840–1893) and Homosexuality: A Critical Edition of Sources*, 2012. Regis's edition of the *Memoirs* is unabridged. Is it too much to hope for an edition of Symonds's gay poetry?

TEXTS: John Addington Symonds, *In the Key of Blue and Other Prose Essays* (Matthews & Lane, 1893); *Many Moods: A Volume of Verse* (Smith, Elder, 1878); *New and Old: A Volume of Verse* (Smith, Elder, 1880). SUPPLEMENT: *The Memoirs of John Addington Symonds: A Critical Edition*, ed. Amber K. Regis (Palgrave Macmillan, 2016). REFERENCE: Rictor Norton, *The Life and Writings of John Addington Symonds* (1840–1893) (online).

Paul Verlaine: *Hombres*; Love Poems / Arthur Rimbaud: Bawdy Poems (French)

Having committed myself to Jacques, I felt the need to better my understanding of French. During the week I was staying in an apartment in Metz just a few houses from where Verlaine was born. Since Jacques owned a copy of his bawdy poems, I decided to turn my hand at translating them. *A Lover's Cock* appeared in 1979; it was slightly revised in 1980. How I came into contact with Winston Leyland, the editor of *Gay Sunshine*, I no longer remember. On a trip to San Francisco, the three of us shared a meal. I remember Jacques's agreeing with Winston about the title, which I disliked. (In *My First Satyrnalia*, 1981, Michael Rumaker mentions picking up a copy at the Oscar Wilde Memorial Bookshop before returning it to the shelf, alas unbought.) Three decades later I returned to the poems and added others. The idea of bringing out an enlarged edition of *A Lover's Cock* fell through, and I turned to William Maltese to suggest we collaborate on a fictionalized biography of the two poets' relationship, incorporating the poems as part of the plot's progression. Though the resulting novel, *Ardennian Boy*, 2007, is pornography—quite well-written pornography, I like to think—it follows the facts closely. We do intersperse my translations of the latter poems from *Hombres* as if they were written earlier, and we invented the scenes on the ferry and in London to fill a gap in our knowledge of events at that time. But otherwise you can trust us, even at our most scatological.

Chafing from the restrictions of his life in the Ardennian backwaters, the adolescent Jean-Nicholas-Arthur Rimbaud (1854–1891) longed to escape to Paris. He made the first attempt at age fifteen during the Franco-Prussian War but was swiftly returned home. His third try was during the Commune, when he threw in his lot with some soldiers. Already the precocious genius had written over twenty poems that have been preserved. Now either something sexual happened or his vivid imagination conjured up a chain of fucks. If the former, it may have been consensual, but perhaps it was rape. The results, a triolet usually titled "The Stolen Heart" (Le Cœur volé), marks a new stage in his development as a poet. It was enclosed in a letter to a former teacher (a letter that, in the words of his biographer Graham Robb [81], has become "one of the sacred texts of modern literature," for it contained the celebrated statement *Je est un autre*: "*I* is someone else"). The poem nauseated the teacher. It begins simply: "My sad heart drools at the stern." The poet goes on to say, "With military erections / Their gibes have corrupted it." There remain behind "frescoes" and "nonsensical waves" as some sort of souvenir. These force the young poet to the question: "When they have shot their wads, / How to react, oh cheated heart?" One answer might be to write more poetry. Rimbaud at age sixteen turned out some of his greatest, including "The Drunken Boat."

It was also time to make one more attempt to get to Paris. He encountered a gay friend of the twenty-seven-year-old Paul-Marie Verlaine (1840–1896), who had already published two volumes of verse that Rimbaud much admired. Verlaine was married and newly a father, but his basic sexual orientation was toward men. Rimbaud wrote him, including samples of his poetry. Verlaine recognized immediately something important had arrived in French poetry. He may also have sensed something personal, for, as Robb (100) notes, "The five poems [Rimbaud] chose to send [Verlaine] are not simply representative samples of his work. They all have something in common: bottoms and acts of pederasty. The supposedly innocent young poet had put together a highly suggestive anthology for his potential patron." Rimbaud followed up "The Stolen Heart" with poems in which he speaks openly of taking a piss ("Evening Prayer"), enjoying a crap ("Squattings," and other poems), feeling an attraction to men ("Poets, Age Seven"), being groped by an official ("Customs Men"). The arrival of the uncouth teenager into the bourgeois household presided over by Verlaine's in-laws marked a decisive moment in both lives. The two actually lived together in Paris and London only some twenty months, with time-outs when Rimbaud returned home, before the fateful confrontation in Brussels in July 1873 in which Verlaine shot Rimbaud and was consequently imprisoned. But the chemistry between the two swept Rimbaud on through a series of astonishing poems, culminating in his two collection of prose poems, *A Season in Hell* and *Illuminations*, and turned Verlaine into a major poet beginning with the first volume after their rupture, *Romances without Words*, in which appears the lovely "Tears fall in my heart," with an epigraph by Rimbaud.

Probably egged on by Rimbaud, the two began playing with the possibilities of pornographic verse in contributions to *The Album Zutique*. This was a handwritten manuscript created by a group of bohemian poets who prided themselves on being literary outsiders (given to denouncing everything, *zut!*). Rimbaud and, by extension, Verlaine fit right in. Their poems were generally parodies of poets who they felt had sold out to the establishment. Twenty of the contributions have been attributed to Rimbaud, nine to Verlaine, with a joint "Sonnet to the Asshole." The last has often been reprinted in various translations. For the first time, so far as I know, the anus was elevated to the same stature as the penis. Verlaine wrote the octave. It describes the just-fucked "Dark, puckered hole," dripping with semen, farted out "To drip from the crack, which craves for it yet." Rimbaud picked up the sestet to describe an immediately following act of anilingus on the part of the fucker:

>My mouth too has often mated with that vent,
>My sobbing tongue tried to devour the rose
>Flowering in brown moisture....
>......the Promised Land
>Which with other milk and honey overflows!

Rimbaud then took the poem a step further, stripping it to its essence to create a twenty-eight-syllable sonnet. I could come up with only twenty-two in my translation and make it rhyme correctly: "Cap of / Silk, / Ivory / prick, / Clothes / Dark, / Paul eyes / Locker, // Sticks out / Tongue / On pear, / Sticks up / Prong / Shit fair!"

In addition to this naughty play, Rimbaud used the album to record his powerful "Memories of a Simple-Minded Old Man." In this poem he reminisces about his youthful awakening to sex. He describes how, at the country fair, he viewed the long penises of the donkeys with uncomprehending fascination. The scent of his mother's soiled petticoat and the sight of his little sister pissing both excited him. But above all he was tormented by strange yearnings for his father:

> Imagine: to be seated in his inviting lap, at hand
> The fly of his trousers which fingers wish to unbutton,
> To reach in and grab the thick, dark, hard cock
> Of the man whose hairy hand my cradle used to rock!

He bemoans that puberty arrived late for him. (Could this explain the striking difference between two photographs taken of him in October and December 1871?) Now he is impatient to "jack off." Verlaine was not quite keeping pace. *The Album Zutique* does include another intricate sonnet, "The Death of Pigs" (La mort des cochons). I tried to translate it, but was defeated by rhyme and its intricacy. When he was arrested after shooting Rimbaud, the police found him carrying a copy of "The Good Disciple," an inverted sonnet, a sort of literary jest illustrating Verlaine's desire to play the bottom to Rimbaud's top. It invites him, in the last line, to "Mount on my back and ride!" More important, Verlaine was writing some of his most beautiful love poems for the youth. "Green" (the title is in English) begins:

> I offer you boughs: leaves, flowers, and fruit;
> I offer you my heart, beating for you alone,
> Take, guard these humble gifts as your own,
> Only to your eyes will these presents seem sweet.

Meanwhile, Rimbaud was playing with four different versions of "O Seasons, O Châteaux." The earlier drafts permit the salacious reading:

> Who could possibly resist
> The magical study of Bliss?
> I am utterly in its thrall
> Each time his virile cock calls.

The final drafts are among his most anthologized. *A Season in Hell*, his only book that Rimbaud saw in print, has been taken as a reflection on their life together. In the section "Foolish Virgin," he seems to acknowledge his adverse influence on Verlaine. But recovered from his wound,

Rimbaud left the hospital and renounced poetry altogether. He was not yet nineteen years old.

The two men met one last time in 1876 before Rimbaud embarked on the wanderings that eventually led him to Africa and ultimately to his death in Marseille. Incidentally, at the time of Verlaine's arrest court-appointed physicians were ordered to examine him for evidence of "pederastic habits." As a result we know that he had a "short and not very voluminous" penis with an especially "small and tapering" glans and that his anus could "be dilated rather markedly...to the depth of about one inch" displaying "a widened infundibulum." The physicians concluded that "P. Verlaine bears on his person traces of habitual pederasty, both active and passive," of a fairly recent origin (Robb, 224). No similar information has come down to us about Rimbaud.

Verlaine had later affairs. On the rebound, in 1877 he fell in love with another teenager, his student Lucien Létinois. Upon the youth's death in 1883, Verlaine composed a suite of twenty-four poems in his honor. Verlaine's biographer Joanna Richardson (218) writes, "The comparison with Tennyson's 'In Memoriam' is inevitable; but Verlaine does not benefit from the comparative study." She judges them "an unsatisfactory whole. They remain a personal lament, a private elegy which is not dignified into a long and honest search for faith" (220). He later was enamored of the young Frédéric-Auguste Cazals, not realizing he was straight. Towards the end of his life he was involved with a series of female prostitutes. But Rimbaud continued to dominate his thoughts. As Richardson (229) says, "his love for Lucien Létinois and Cazals, his casual affairs with men and women had not lessened the intensity of his memories or his regrets." And it is literally because of him that Rimbaud became famous. In 1884 his appreciation of Rimbaud was collected in the volume *Les Poètes Maudits* (Accursed Poets). The same year he recalled with fondness, in his collection *Jadis et Naguère*, "Herculean nights" spent with the youth ("Poet and Muse"), although he also seems to have had second thoughts about their relationship as explored in another poem published in the same collection, "Crimen amoris."

In 1888 came an unfounded rumor of Rimbaud's death. The shock led him to review their life together in a hundred-line poem "Læti et Errabundi" (Latin, which can loosely be translated Footloose and Fancy Free). He celebrates their escape from "the pitiable female sex" and "vile prejudice":

> Fear of debauchery posed no restraint,
> Nothing could religious scruples now prohibit:
> For when one has surpassed every limit,
> Limits no longer offer a constraint.

Almost as if anticipating a post-Stonewall position, he goes on to assert:

> The romance of two living as one
> We write much better than 'normals'
> Can, for with us it is a case of equals
> United in strong and faithful passion.

He accuses straights of being jealous of their freedom, but feels indifferent "to all their gross scurrility." His vindictive attitude toward his wife momentarily derails the thrust of the poem. But he regains his footing as he moves into his final elegy in which he calls Rimbaud "my great and radiant sin." He finishes with a flourish: denying the possibility of Rimbaud's death, he announces, "No; no way! You live in me." In 1890 he published two sonnets to Rimbaud, again praising him. In 1895 he finally achieved his goal of publishing Rimbaud's *Poésies complètes*.

In this defiant mode he defended gay love in the abstract in an untitled poem:

> This passion which they alone now call love
> Is indeed love, tender and fierce;
> With, however, this striking difference;
> It is not, for sure, your ordinary, humdrum love.

He goes on to sneer at so-called normal love "Ah, the poor banal, animal love of straights, / Such limited tastes, such dull appetites, / All their inanities—not to mention pregnancies." He stresses the equality that lies between the partners in a same-sex relationship, so unlike the power differential played out between men and women. And finally he sees a gay relationship as nothing short of the need "To emancipate mankind from heavy nature." In another, unfinished poem from the period, one beginning "We don't belong to the herd," he traces the gay heritage through history. In "On a Statue of Ganymede in a Park in Aix-les-Bains," he calls Zeus's cup-bearer a "Beau petit ami," a term French *pédérastes* used to signal that someone was "one of us." It was also in this period that the series of fourteen pornographic poems collected as *Hombres* took form. Published posthumously, the volume opens with another celebration of our gay heritage. The second poem is a gay variant on Leporello's catalogue of Don Giovanni's conquests, "Mille e Tre," and the poet ends the volume by again describing his many lovers. Between these poems come verses describing individual sexual encounters. In some the emphasis is on the persons: a young rough (Poem 6), an adolescent (Poem 7), a restless sleeper (Poem 9), a couple taking delight in jacking off under the table of a café filled with straights (Poem 12). In others the focus is on the genitals in close-up. One describes the lover's penis (Poem 11); two address the glans of uncircumcised cocks (Poems 3, 4); Poem 8 begins forthrightly

> A bit of shit, a little cheese
>> Could never shock
>> My tongue or nose
> In rimming asses, sucking cocks.

Why is the volume called *Hombres* rather than *Hommes*? Presumably it is because the Spanish sounds more macho, both exotic and erotic.

Unlike with other writers of the period, the evidence for Verlaine's and Rimbaud's sexuality is so blatant, so ingrained in their biographies and their poetry, that it is difficult for critics and biographers to be coy about their sexuality. True, *Hombres* did not become part of the Pléiade edition of Verlaine's poetry until comparatively recently, but every scrap of Rimbaud's was printed early on. Richardson (354) sums up: "Verlaine's odyssey with Rimbaud holds the imagination. Never has there been a comparable liaison between two poets of recognised genius."

TEXTS: Arthur Rimbaud / Paul Verlaine, *A Lover's Cock and Other Gay Poems*, trans. Drewey Wayne Gunn & Jacques Murat, rev. ed. (Gay Sunshine, 1980). SUPPLEMENT: William Maltese & Drewey Wayne Gunn, *Ardennian Boy* (MLR, 2007). REFERENCES: Joanna Richardson, *Verlaine* (Viking, 1971). Graham Robb, *Rimbaud* (Norton, 2000).

A. E. Housman: *A Shropshire Lad* (English)

Peter Parker (1) in his "biography" of *A Shropshire Lad* notes that at the time of the collection's initial publication there were few indications "to suggest that *A Shropshire Lad* would become, and remain, one of the best-loved volumes of poetry in the language." A classical scholar, first at Oxford and then at Cambridge, Alfred Edward Housman (1859–1936) left behind a very slim body of poetry: forty-three poems in *A Shropshire Lad*, 1896 (*ASL*); forty-one in *Last Poems*, 1922 (*LP*); forty-eight in the posthumously published *More Poems*, 1936 (*MP*); and twenty-three (actually twenty-four) "Additional Poems" (*AP*) included in *The Collected Poems*, 1939. Gay themes of necessity are disguised in the two volumes published in his lifetime. Housman was still a teenager when the Criminal Law Amendment Act was promulgated. But clues enough present themselves to the reader. Take for example *ASL* 30:

More than I, if truth were told,
Have stood and sweated hot and cold,
And through their reins in ice and fire
Fear contended with desire.

In *ASL* 22 the poet picks up on a knowing glance he receives from a soldier; in *ASL* 51 he recognizes something of himself in a (presumably nude) Grecian statue in the British Museum; he alludes to Narcissus in *ASL* 15 and 20. Throughout he admires military men and identifies with criminals, often equating their lawlessness with love. E. M. Forster intuitively realized that *A Shropshire Lad* "concealed a personal experience…that the poet must have fallen in love with a man" (Parker, 128).

The slim volume appeared the year after Oscar Wilde was sentenced. Housman's gay brother Laurence knew Wilde, and Housman sent the playwright an autographed copy. His bitter reaction to Wilde's sentence, however, was not published until *The Collected Poems* (*AP* 18). In it a "young sinner" is being taken "to prison for…the nameless and abominable colour of his hair." The poem concludes with a sentiment echoed across many of Housman's poems: "He can curse the God that made him for the colour of his hair." Wilde's public disgrace was not the only incitement to Housman's outpouring of verse at the time. The same year he read an account of "a young naval cadet at Woolwich [who] realising that he was homosexual decided to shoot himself rather than give in to his 'evil' impulses" (Graves, 104). The poem about him was included in *A Shropshire Lad* (44). Here the poet seems to approve of the cadet's decision. One might question whether an older Housman would say the same. His sexuality fueled his rigid intellectualism to lead to his disdain of unjust laws and to his rejection of religion altogether. *LP* 12 forthrightly announces, "The laws of God, the laws of man, / He may keep that will and can; / Not I." "Hell Gate" (*LP* 31) depicts an open—and successful—revolt by two comrades against the idea of sin and punishment.

Last Poems was rushed into publication in order to get it to Housman's muse before his impending death. In 1879, while at Oxford, he fell in love with Moses Jackson. He must have guarded his feelings carefully. Even though the two shared rooms, first at Oxford and then in London, where Jackson's younger brother Adalbert joined them, Moses seems to have had no clue about Housman's intense feelings. Then in 1885 something happened that caused Housman to move out and Jackson to distance himself to such a point that the poet learned of Moses's 1887 marriage and departure for India only after the fact. A whole series of poems published posthumously attest to his sense of bewilderment and loss:

> Shake hands, we shall never be friends, all's over;
>   I only vex you the more I try.
> All's wrong that ever I've done or said,
> And nought to help it in this dull head:
>   Shake hands, here's luck, good-bye.
>
> But if you come to a road where danger
>   Or guilt or anguish or shame's to share,
> Be good to the lad that loves you true
> And the soul that was born to die for you,
>   And whistle and I'll be there. (MP 30)

With Moses away, he now grew closer to Adalbert. Laurence Housman felt certain that there grew to be a physical relationship between the two men, but in 1892 Adalbert died of typhoid. Housman recorded the vacancy his death left behind in another posthumously published poem headed "A.J.J." (*MP* 42). To the end of his life photographs of the two brothers hung prominently on a wall of his rooms.

Since Housman was such a private person, his sexual life is sealed from us. His biographer Richard Graves found evidence to suggest that he explored the greater freedom the Continent offered once he began his habit of taking yearly trips there beginning in 1897. Housman had some kind of a liaison with a Venetian gondolier, one Andrea, who is mentioned in *MP* 44 in conjunction with the intriguing lines "The tower that stood and fell / Is not rebuilt in me." Graves (155) found a document which seems to contain "references to a number of male prostitutes, including sailors and ballet dancers, together with a note of the price paid on various occasions for their services." Housman knew enough of the "Paris *Bains de va-*

peur" to call them "haunts of vice" (Graves, 159), and he later commented ambiguously on chauffeurs he hired for touring the French countryside (Graves, 250, 256). A later biographer waxed indignant about Graves's disclosures. Straights' vehement sexual hegemony never ceases to astonish me. As Housman himself says,

> The world goes none the lamer,
>   For ought that I can see,
> Because this cursed trouble
>   Has struck my days and me. (MP 21)

I hope Graves is right; I am much happier thinking that Housman achieved some degree of physical intimacy—"answered passions" (*MP* 12)—out of sight of judgmental eyes.

Though T. S. Eliot admired him, Housman's poetry was decidedly out of academic fashion by the time he published *Last Poems*. It was, after all, the year of Joyce's *Ulysses* and Eliot's *The Waste Land*, of the death of Proust (whom Housman read). He seems to have had no great influence on post-World War I poets. Musical composers have delighted in using his poems for settings. And Parker (4) stresses, "In the 120 years since [*A Shropshire Lad*'s] original publication it has never once been out of print."

TEXT: A. E. Housman, *The Collected Poems*, [ed. John Carter] (Cape, 1953). REFERENCES: Richard Perceval Graves, *A. E. Housman: The Scholar-Poet* (Scribner's, 1980). Peter Parker, *Housman Country: Into the Heart of England* (Farrar, Straus & Giroux, 2017).

C. P. Cavafy: "Days of..." (Greek)

Constantine Peter Cavafy (Konstantinos Petrou Kavafis, 1863–1933) pioneered both in using the Greek of the streets for poetic expression and in combining it with the officially recognized literary Greek. But the Alexandrian, as he became known in Greece because of his lifelong association with the Egyptian city, remained virtually unknown until after his death. In 1935, for the first time, a collected edition of 154 poems appeared. There remained 104 poems either uncollected or unpublished that had to wait until 1968 to join them. Even then there remained thirty unfinished poems. Cavafy is now recognized, of course, as one of the major European poets of the twentieth century. His poetry is very plain but, no matter the translation, memorable. (In fact, it seems impossible to do a bad translation.) His principal subjects are the passage of time ("Candles"), ancient history and myth ("Ithaca"; "Waiting for the Barbarians"), personal counsel ("Walls"; "The City"; "The God Abandons Antony"), the nature of art ("Sculptor from Tyana"; "Painted"; "I Brought to Art"), and erotic memories. A quarter of all the poems fall into this last category.

While on an extended visit with his relatives in Constantinople, 1882–85, he had his first gay experience with his cousin George Psilliary. He returned to Alexandria with his widowed mother, where he lived the rest of his life. He seems never to have formed a lasting bond. The manuscripts of three poems—"September of 1903," December of 1903," "January of 1904"—bear the initials "A.M.," whom Daniel Mendelsohn (521) identifies as Alexander Mavroudis, "a young man…whom Cavafy met during his 1903 visit to Athens, and who seems to have been the object of an intense but unconsummated crush." It has been suggested that Cavafy had an affair with Alexander Sengopoulos, who became his heir; but Mendelsohn (xxiv) points out that young Aleko may well have been an illegitimate nephew. He was very guarded about his sexual activities until he was almost fifty. The fact is not surprising, given the cultural atmosphere in which he found himself ("the society he lived in was extremely priggish," he writes in "Days of 1896") and his mother's dependence on him.

Beginning in 1911, "the year in which he published 'Dangerous,' the first of his poems that situated homoerotic content in an ancient setting" (Mendelsohn, xxxii), he began to write openly about his experiences. The erotic poems record the excitement of cruising bars, restaurants, tobacco shops, and streets wherever men congregate, the excitation of hookups in rented rooms. The memories are generally tied to a particular setting ("The room was threadbare and tawdry, / hidden above that suspect restaurant") and often summon up some particular aspect of the loved one's appearance (eyes that were "a deep blue, sapphirine"). If some of the poems indicate that he at first felt some degree of shame about his sexual cravings ("In Despair") and feared the possibility of "some devastating scandal" ("The 25th Year of His Life"), in his maturity he saw them as actually germane to his development as a poet, writing "In the dissolute life I led in my youth / my poetry's designs took shape; / the boundaries of my art were drawn" ("Comprehension"). After he and another man have risen from their bed of "illicit pleasure" and departed "separately, covertly, from the house," he muses, "Nonetheless, how the artist's life has gained. / Tomorrow, the day after, or through the years he'll write / powerful lines, that here was their beginning" ("Their Beginning"). Or again ("And I Got Down..."), after a visit to a brothel, he asserts,

The rooms I went to were the secret ones,
the ones they think it shameful even to name.
But for me there was no shame—for if there were
what kind of poet, what kind of craftsman would I be?

A series of five poems beginning "Days of..." (Days of 1896, etc.) have particularly caught the attention of later poets, who have imitated them or been inspired by them. Each focuses on the beauty of an impecunious youth who touched the poet emotionally, whose shabby setting could not disguise his natural grace. In these and other poems about twenty year olds, the man may momentarily worry about the nature of his desires as reflected through society's prejudices, but they generally transcend such narrowness and are "happy" when "they gave themselves to love" ("Two Young Men, 23 to 24 Years Old"). Instead of feeling debased, they are exalted by such "illicit pleasure."

Gregory Woods (*History*, 187) quotes Rex Warner's comparison of Cavafy and Eliot from his introduction to the first English translation. The two poets, despite their apparent differences, have much in common. But when it comes to sexuality, their differences become immense. Warner contrasted "Cavafy's eagerness to find value in ephemeral sexual encounters with T. S. Eliot's unproductive rejection and denigration of 'one-night cheap hotels.' ...Eliot's fastidious distaste for the sheer physicality of sex seems to have prevented his acknowledging its potential value even between silk sheets, let alone in the sordid settings which he was apparently unable to imagine being transcended by any kind of intercourse. For him the body was the object of fear and revulsion, perhaps especially when most intensely desired.... While Eliot tends to regard sex as an ineffable source of ugliness and degradation, Cavafy is more likely to treat it as both a source of immediate impressions of beauty and the inspiration for the eternal beauty of works of art." We have been fortunate in having a whole series of translators who have made Cavafy's poetry live; each volume has its own virtues.

TEXTS: C. P. Cavafy, *Collected Poems*, trans. Daniel Mendelsohn (Knopf, 2009). SUPPLEMENT: C. P. Cavafy, *The Unfinished Poems*, trans. Daniel Mendelsohn (Knopf, 2009).

Roger Casement: Love Poems (English)

Gay love poet—it is probably not a term one would immediately associate with Irish hero Roger David Casement (1864–1916). It was not until I read the *The Black Diaries* that I even knew he had written verse. Yet from his teenage years until he was hanged by the British for treason, he engaged in writing love, nature, and patriotic poems. He was particularly influenced by Keats and Shelley. His sister gathered sixteen of his poems for publication two years after his death. Herbert Mackey added thirty-five in an anthology he assembled in 1958. The love poems they included are implicitly addressed to men or are turned straight before the end in a cursory way. Both editors omitted the most important of the lot, "The Nameless One" (which, in fact, they may not have known). It was first published in 1959 in the Olympia Press edition of *The Black Diaries*. As part of his monumental study of Casement, Jeffrey Dudgeon reproduced the poem (568–69) from an autograph copy along with an extensive study of its history. In seven stanzas Casement examines what it means to be gay in an uncomprehending world. The meaning of the title has been debated, but it would seem to refer to Lord Alfred Douglas's poem "Two Loves." In the fourth stanza Casement raises the old question of Nature:

> Love took me by the heart at birth
> And wrought out from its common earth—
> With soul at his own skill aghast—
> A furnace my own breath should blast.
> Why this was done I cannot tell
> The mystery is inscrutable.
> I only know I pay the cost
> With heart and soul and honour lost.
> I only know 'tis death to give
> My love; yet loveless can I live?

I only know I cannot die
And leave this love God made, not I.

In a fragment of another poem published by Mackey, Casement contrasts Christ's love of and association with "Vile sinners." He accepts that God may "break my heart—but make it pitiful!" The same strain continues in an 1895 poem "Love's Awakening":

   O! God of love, how can it be accurst—
      This love that wakes, that thrills me thro' the night?
      This love that fills my being with delight—
   Of all the ills that stamp man's lot the worst?

This stanza is all that Dudgeon supplies. Mackey adds two more, the last turning it safely into a heterosexual poem. One obvious gay poem escaped his sister's censor: "The Streets of Catania," written in 1900 perhaps about an Italian lover named Casaldo. Setting his poem in the narrow streets where "shame" appears beneath the "throbbing" heart of Etna, Casement describes how

   Came like a highwayman, and went,
      One who was bold and gay,
   Left when his lightly loving mood was spent
      Thy heart to pay.

As a member of the British consular service, Casement became an important crusader in the fight against abuses of human rights. He documented extensive examples in the Congo and in Brazil. During this period he was also involved in two long-term liaisons and who knows how many brief sexual encounters. Extraordinarily handsome, charismatic, he was adept at picking up young men. These encounters he dutifully recorded in the so-called *Black Diaries*. Dudgeon's edition is a must read. It is a disarmingly frank record of one man's homosexual adventures at the turn of the twentieth century. Opening Dudgeon's edition at random, I find this typical entry (269):

   Sunday 5th March…Trams 1/-. 'How'? 3.6 [money spent] X [a mark
      Casement used to indicate a more than ordinary pick-up]   3.6
      Enormous 19 – about 7" and 4 thick. X   2.6
   …Supper at Jury's…Enormous Dublin under 19 Very fair thin leg
      knickers and coat white scarf. Blue eyes and huge huge stiff long
      and thick – a Limb.

When Casement was arrested by the British, the diaries were used to defame him, but ultimately the homosexual angle was minimized so as not to overshadow the charge of treason. As reported by Dudgeon (10), before his burial a medical officer at the prison examined the dead man's rectum and issued the report that he "found unmistakable evidence of the practices to which it was alleged the prisoner in question had been addicted. The anus was at a glance seen to be dilated and on making a digital examination (rubber gloves) I found that the lower part of the bowel was dilated as far as the fingers could reach." Thus he joined the ranks of Verlaine in having information preserved about him not ordinarily found in poets' files.

TEXT: Roger Casement, *The Crime against Europe*, ed. Herbert O. Mackey (Fallon, 1958), 159–214. SUPPLEMENT: Jeffrey Dudgeon, ed., *Roger Casement: The Black Diaries, with a Study of His Background, Sexuality, and Irish Political Life* (Belfast, 2002).

John Henry Mackay: *On the Margin of Life* (German)

Germany not only coined the word *homosexual* (in 1869) but also launched the earliest homosexual liberation movement. Though John Henry Mackay (1864–1933) was a supporter, Florence Tamage (284) notes that his "defense of homosexuality [was] part of a general anarchistic fight against any oppression of the individual" and "by refusing to offer any justification for homosexuality, he placed himself in an extremely marginalized position." She argues that, as a result, "his action did nothing to further the progress of homosexual liberation or education of the public." Even as she admires him, she strangely faults him for "his original presentation of homosexual relations, detached from any medical reference and any attempt at justification." Those omissions rather mark a step forward; Mackay felt no need to justify his feelings. He wrote six works in very different genres that he published, 1905–13, under the collective title *Books of the Nameless Love* using the pseudonym Sagitta to protect himself against the nefarious Paragraph 175. The fifth book, *On the Margin of Life* (*Am Rande des lebens*, 1909) consists of twenty-six poems in various forms about "those who thus meet, / On the margins of life." The book, however, might just as well have been called "Unrequited Love." The ofttimes mawkish verse is mostly addressed to teenagers ("Your trembling boyish body clings / so soft and warm against my own"), ending almost inevitably in the poet's being either stood up or left.

One of the more accomplished, "Whitsuntide" is typical. Consisting of 233 unrhymed lines, each having four stresses, it remembers an outing with a lad to the forest on the Havel River. The other pleasure-seekers gone, they kiss and pledge their love: "What is the world to me, its people, / If you only stay, your love and devotion!" But when they get back to Berlin, the youth loses himself "in the crowd's confusion," and the poet returns to his empty home: "In dreams of dead and deceptive days, / Alone as before and lonely as ever." The poem "Then into the Streets He Wandered" recounts the poet's encounter with a street hustler who promises him happiness—and does deliver, at least momentarily:

> For there on the next street corner
>
> [Happiness] waited—he saw it lean.
>
> And in a place safe and hidden
>
> He tasted it—all unseen.

"Defense" describes an appearance before a judge, the defendant presumably having been caught in a homosexual encounter: "I am a victim of the chance / Fate gave me over into your hand!" But the majority of the poems are laments. Mackay as a poet is not considered important enough to receive even passing mention in *The Princeton Encyclopedia of Poetry and Poetics*. Instead, it is his 1926 novel *The Hustler* that has secured his place in literature. He died of a heart attack ten days after the Nazi book-burning at Hirschfeld's Institut für Sexualwissenschaft, seven months before the death of the better known but deeply closeted cult figure Stefan George (1868–1933).

TEXT: John Henry Mackay, *Sagitta's Books of the Nameless Love*, trans. Hubert Kennedy (Peremptory, 2005), 221–330.

Lord Alfred Douglas: Early Poems (English)

One could almost wish that Lord Alfred Bruce Douglas (1870–1945) had never written "I am the Love that dare not speak its name." The last line of his poem "Two Loves," it has been quoted, referenced, and satirized from the time of Wilde's trials right up to the present, turning it into the gay cliché of all time. At the second trial, Wilde defended this love as "a great affection of an elder for a younger man as there was between David and Jonathan, such as Plato made the very basis of his philosophy, and such as you find in the sonnets of Michelangelo and Shakespeare. It is that deep, spiritual affection that is as pure as it is perfect" (Hyde, 201). "Two Loves," along with Douglas's sonnet "In Praise of Shame," appeared in the December 1894 issue of *The Chameleon*, a literary journal published in Oxford. Taking its title from Shakespeare's Sonnet 144, its form is that of a medieval dream vision. The dreamer is visited by a naked youth, Eros. He summons up two boys. The one "sang of pretty maids / And joyous love of comely girl and boy." The other "sighed with many sighs." Both claim the name of Love. But "the first did turn himself to me / And cried, 'He lieth, for his name his Shame'" and goes on to claim, "I am true Love." Thereupon, "Then sighing said the other, 'Have thy will, / I am the Love that dare not speak its name.'" *Shame* was a code word at the time denoting homosexuality. "In Praise of Shame," a sonnet, is another dream vision. In it "Our lady of strange dreams" reveals phantom shapes, one of whom "cried, 'I am Shame / That walks with Love.'" The dreamer is bid by the speaker to "see my loveliness, and praise my name." The dreamer concurs: "Of all sweet passions, Shame is the loveliest."

Douglas met Wilde (1854–1900) in the summer of 1891. The book version of *The Picture of Dorian Gray* had just appeared; Douglas's biographer Caspar Wintermans (27) reveals that "a signed copy was the first present [Douglas] received from Wilde." The attraction between the two men was immediate. Whether coincidental or not, the period following their meeting saw Wilde's great flowering as a dramatist and Douglas's debut as a serious poet. Douglas's gay poems, often surprising in their openness, include "Prince Charming," "De Profundis" (the title Robert Ross used when he published a portion of Wilde's accusatory letter to Douglas from prison), "In Sarum Close," "Hymn to Physical Beauty," "Sicilian Love Song," and "In an Ægean Port." One appeared in *The Artist* and three in *The Spirit Lamp*, magazines that were sympathetic to gay writings. After Wilde's imprisonment, brought about by the playwright's misguided lawsuit against Douglas's father, young Douglas wrote "Rejected," "St Martin's Summer," "Plainte Éternelle," "The Travelling Companion," and "Rondeau." The last records his feelings about Wilde. Douglas also wrote a gay closet drama in blank verse, *When the King Comes He Is Welcome: A Tragedy in One Act*.

These works along with other poems were collected in a small volume published in Paris in 1896 called simply *Poems*. All the gayest ones were subsequently suppressed by the author until 1933, when he issued two separate volumes, *Lyrics* and *Sonnets*. Even then, the sonnet "In an Ægean Port," despite being printed facing "In Praise of Shame," was slightly heterosexualized. *Poems* also included his vicious attack on his father, "A Ballad of Hate," likewise suppressed, and "In Memoriam," a sonnet dedicated to his brother Viscount Drumlanrig, who probably killed himself in order to cover up his sexual relationship with the married prime minister, the Earl of Rosebery. After Wilde's death Douglas paid tribute to him in his sonnet "The Dead Poet." As for Wilde's own poetry, it is certainly decadent, but it is hardly gay. Though his masterpiece, *The Ballad of Reading Gaol*, grew out of his imprisonment, it is based on a heterosexual murder. Still, the poem has been appropriated by gays. German filmmaker Rainer Werner Fassbinder, for example, interpolated sung stanzas from it into his film version of Jean Genet's *Querelle*.

The new century saw a different Lord Douglas. He married and fathered a son. Having rejected Christ for Apollo in his poem "Rejected," he now converted to Roman Catholicism. He repudiated his friendship with Wilde and viciously attacked Ross. He became embroiled in the outrageous 1918 trial involving Maud Allan, who was starring in Wilde's *Salome*. As he became more and more like his father, he too ended up being briefly imprisoned for libel. Almost certainly he would have approved the suit that Mary Whitehouse, the self-appointed moral guardian of the United Kingdom, brought against *Gay News* in 1976, under the Blasphemy Act of 1697, for printing James Kirkup's (1918–2009) "The Love That Dares to Speak Its Name." The poem describes a centurion making love to the dead Christ. It ends in quite a muddle with the speaker equating gay sex to mutual crucifixion and a means to arrive at both paradise and gay liberation. As a result of Whitehall's win, the poem cannot be reprinted in the U.K., though it is readily available online. Had she left well enough alone, the poem would have sunk under its own ineptitude; now it is required reading for anyone interested in gay history.

TEXTS: Lord Alfred Douglas, *Lyrics* (Rich & Cowan, 1935); *Sonnets* (Richards, 1943). REFERENCE: Hyde, H. Montgomery, *The Trials of Oscar Wilde* (Dover, 1973). Caspar Wintermans, *Alfred Douglas: A Poet's Life and His Finest Work* (Peter Owen, 2007). SUPPLEMENT: James Kirkup, "The Love That Dares to Speak Its Name" (online).

Mikhail Kuzmin: Poetry Cycles (Russian)

Part of the St. Petersburg Bohemian circle before the Revolution of 1917, Mikhail Alekseevich Kuzmin (1872–1936) was openly gay. He had a series of lovers, to whom he often dedicated his poems. His first great poetry cycle, "A Summer Affair" (1907), was dedicated to the army officer Pavel Maslow, who seems to have had the soul of a hustler. Comprised of twelve poems in various forms, it records, as his biographers John Malmstad and Nikolay Bogomolov (108) write: "an infatuation, the fleeting nature of which both parties sense from the outset; the torments of separation, which only intensify the poet's love; and his expectation of their new encounter as a Volga steamboat bears him back to his beloved." Only twelve years after the Wilde trial, the cycle celebrates in the second poem

> Hot embraces, heart's wild beating,
> Of snake-like arms the intertwinings
> Of limbs, the practiced palpitations,
> Of lips on flesh the practiced ardour,
> Buoyancy of a promised tryst
> And leavetaking across the threshold.

His biographers (28) remind us that the Russian press, both "Right and Left pilloried English society and the English system of justice, not Wilde." Still Kuzmin's openness was not admired by all and later got him as well as several of his lovers into trouble with the oppressive Stalin regime. The cycle opened Kuzmin's first collection, *Nets* (*Seti*, 1908). Its first three lines, which have nothing to do with the affair and everything to do with Kuzmin's search for a new style to take the place of outdated Russian symbolism, had an impact on other poets that seemed nothing short of revolutionary: "Where shall I find a style to catch a stroll, / Chablis on ice, a crisply toasted roll, / The agate succulence of cherries ripe?" Malmstad and Bogomolov (109) sum up, "The cycle is really the first of Kuzmin's major works fully to demonstrate the hallmark of his verse and prose at their best, in which the disparate moods of 'lightness' and 'gravity' find a rare balance."

Another cycle of ten poems included in *Nets*, "A Story Interrupted," describes Kuzmin's brief affair with the scene painter and set designer Sergey Sudeikin. It opens with a tribute to Sudeikin's portrait of the poet. He then recalls an evening together at a play. A meeting at a party seems to have been more intimate; at least the two men "manoeuvred behind the door together," and the poet sighed, "If only they happened more often, nights like this!" In the fourth poem he exclaims, "We're so lovey-dovey," and sums up, "We are faithful to the rules of a life that's gay and carefree." The story behind the fifth poem, "The Cardboard House," also provides the ending for a short story with the same title. The day after presenting Kuzmin with his gift, a Christmas decoration, Sudeikin left for Moscow to meet his fiancée. His departure marked the end of their sexual relations. The remaining five poems describe the poet's emotions as a result. He still maintains, "You are dearer to me with every moment, / You who have forgotten me, despise me, do not love me." And the three remained friends, even though the wife knew of their brief relationship, even sharing an apartment briefly 1912–13.

The "Alexandrian Songs" ("Aleksandriiskie pesni") span both these cycles. They were published in part in 1906 and complete in 1908, when they too appeared in *Nets*. The whole consists of twenty-six poems grouped in six sections. They were inspired by a trip he made to Egypt in 1895 with a cavalry officer whom he identified only as "Prince Georges." The latter died shortly after Kuzmin's return to Russia. They were actually written as songs set to music by the poet himself (he was an accomplished composer). His biographers (100) tell us, "It was as the author of the 'Alexandrian Songs' that Kuzmin made his first entrance into the cultural world of Petersburg after several were played at the November 28, 1905, concert of the 'Evenings of Contemporary Music.'" Here rather than speaking through his own voice or that of a scarcely disguised persona, Kuzmin adopts those of multiple speakers at different points in history. The section of seven songs entitled "Love" is downright giddy with the passion of one man for another: "my heart, my thoughts, my deepest meditations / are filled with voices endlessly repeating: / 'I love you, and my love shall have no ending!'" (2.2). A song from the section "Fragments" records a visit the speaker makes to a male brothel. Another from the same section not unexpectedly describes three sightings of Antinous, a figure who would show up in other Kuzmin poems. The entire cycle of songs appears in both collections translated by Michael Green.

Kuzmin died of pneumonia and a weak heart. By then the Soviet regime had reintroduced all the harsh measures against homosexuality that had been lifted after the Revolution, and many of Kuzmin's friends had been threatened or imprisoned (his last lover was executed after the poet's death). Almost forgotten, his impact on English letters began in earnest with Green's 1972 translation of the 1906 gay novel *Wings* (*Kryl'ya*), now recognized as a major work of modern gay fiction. His poetry has taken longer to find a readership. Kevin Moss assembled the gayest poems in his Gay Sunshine anthology *Out of the Blue*. "A Summer Affair" (retitled "This Summer's Love") also appears in Green and Stanislav Shvabrin's *Selected Writings*, but I find Green's earlier translations more poetic. However, you must go to this later volume for the 1919 four-poem cycle "Thrall" (also known as "Captivity"), "inspired by the arrest and imprisonment of Kuzmin's companion Yurii Ivanovich Yurkun in 1918" (Green & Shvabrin, 246); Kuzmin's last poetic masterpiece, the twelve-poem cycle *The Trout Breaks the Ice* (*Forel' razbivaet led*, 1929), a kind of retrospective of his life; and a miscellany of individual poems. Much of his poetry, as well as many of his works of fiction and plays and his very important diary, remains untranslated.

TEXT: Mikhail Kuzmin, *Selected Writings*, trans. Michael A. Green & Stanislav A. Shvabrin (Bucknell, 2005). SUPPLEMENTS: Mikhail Kuzmin, *Selected Prose & Poetry*, trans. Michael Green (Ardis, 1980), 139–63. Kevin Moss, ed., *Out of the Blue: Russia's Hidden Gay Literature* (Gay Sunshine, 1997), 89–114 (trans. Michael Green). REFERENCE: John E. Malmstad & Nikolay Bogomolov, *Mikhail Kuzmin : A Life in Art* (Harvard, 1999).

Aleister Crowley: Two Pornographic Collections (English)

Born Edward Alexander Crowley (1875–1947), the notorious occultist renamed himself to create a dactyl followed by a trochee, "the ideal measure for a famous name" according to a book he read while at Cambridge (Sutin, 48). Anyone so enamored of rhythm would naturally see himself as a poet. He published sixteen small volumes. The only ones still much read are his pornographic verses. The first collection in this vein was the salaciously titled *White Stains*. Published *sub rosa* in 1898 by Leonard Smithers, the publisher of *Teleny* and other prohibited works, its subtitle was *The Literary Remains of George Archibald Bishop, a Neuropath of the Second Empire*. The thirty-six poems, both homosexual and heterosexual in orientation, "run the gamut of the prominent perversions in the judgment of the late Victorian era: lesbianism, homosexuality, bisexuality, bestiality, sadism, masochism, priapic lust worshipped as the life force, necrophilia" (Sutin, 46). Most are designed to gross out the reader. The sonnet "Go into the Highways and Hedges, and Compel Them to Come In," for instance, celebrates urophagia and coprophagia in its opening quatrain:

> Let my fond lips but drink thy golden wine,
>   My bright-eyed Arab, only let me eat
>   The rich brown globes of sacramental meat
> Steaming and firm, hot from their home divine.

"Necrophilia" goes even further. More normal sounding, "A Ballad of Passive Paederasty" describes the poet's pleasure in playing bottom, while in the second of two "Rondels" he delights in playing the top. Almost lost among all the fetishes and role-playing are a few poems expressing the simple pleasures of love.

His next excursion into pornography was his assemblage of the materials that make up *Snowdrops from a Curate's Garden* in 1904. It was expressly designed to cater to the tastes of his wife, who was suffering from postpartum depression. Mostly heterosexual in nature, it collects "The Nameless Novel," three pieces of "Juvenilia," and "The Bromo Book." The latter is divided into poetic parodies and limericks, some of which involve same-sex male activities of a generally indecorous nature. Martin Starr (5) observes, "Throughout his life Crowley was bisexual in thought and less so in practice." The whole of *The Scented Garden of Abdullah the Satirist of Shiraz*, composed in 1905, is a sometimes comical, ofttimes tedious parody of the Persian Sufi poets and the writings of Sir Richard Burton. Supposedly *Translated from a Rare Indian Ms. by the Late Major Lutiy and Another*, it includes forty-two poems. Exactly half attempt to reproduce the form of the ghazal in English verse; the other half remain in prose, the supposed translator having been killed in battle during the Boer War. A vague storyline unites the whole. El Qahar, the poet, is in love with the fifteen-year-old boy Habib, or at least in love with his anus, his "podex." Somehow, he lost the youth to the enticements of a mightily-hung Nubian, whose giant member has so ruined the boy that his "podex has become like the twat of one sixty years an whore" ("The Blind Beggar"). Or again, where once Habib's anus resembled "the rose," now it resembles "nothing but…the podex of a peevish and filthy sodomite" ("The Comparisons"). Yet El Qahar remains so bewitched by the boy that he welcomes him back and promises him that his penis is still up to sodomizing him the entire night through just as once before "A thousand times that member rose and fell!" ("Zemzem"). So he summons him ("The Garden"):

> Come, O Habib, thy podex close
>   on El Qahar's enamoured tool!
> Though we mistake the world and God,
>   at least is no mistake in this.

The last two poems give the pretense of Persian poet, Anglo-Indian major, and Christian clergyman (who supposedly had completed Lutiy's work) away. The true inspiration for the work was his affair with a Cambridge student that began in 1897. Herbert Charles Pollitt, who preferred to be called Jerome, introduced "his younger friend to the Decadents in art and literature and generally made a poet out of the boy Crowley" (Starr, 7). The affair lasted little more than a year, but its importance is revealed in the penultimate poem, "The Riddle," which is an acrostic, the first letter of each line spelling out Pollitt's name. Here El Qahar and Habib alternate positions:

> To glut thy jasmine podex on
>   the member of thine El Qahar;
> To glut thine almond member in
>   the podex of thine El Qahar.

The last poem. "Bagh-i-Muattar," likewise is an acrostic. But this time it is Aleister Crowley's name that is spelled out—in reverse order (yelworC retsielA) as befitting his preferred passive role in same-sex couplings. Not published until 1910, *The Scented Garden* was his last poetry collection. From then on his voluminous writing would focus on sexual magick (his preferred spelling) and the creation of an alternate religion whose guiding principle would be, "Do what thou wilt shall be the whole of the law."

TEXTS: Aleister Crowley, *White Stains: The Literary Remains of George Archibald Bishop, a Neuropath of the Second Empire, 1898* (Birchgrove, 2011); *The Scented Garden of Abdullah the Satirist of Shiraz*, ed. Martin P. Starr (Teitan, 1991). REFERENCE: Lawrence Sutin, *Do What Thou Wilt: A Life of Aleister Crowley* (St. Martin's, 2000).

T. S. Eliot: *The Waste Land* (English)

In 1952 *Essays in Criticism* published John Peter's "A New Interpretation of *The Waste Land*." He reexamined the cubist poem—which until then had been viewed largely as an exposé of the social ills of the time—as an elegy for a dead male lover. In the process he essentially outed Thomas Stearns Eliot (1888–1965). The poet's reaction was disproportionate to the situation; he got in touch with lawyers to threaten legal action unless the essay was suppressed. As a result, in many libraries copies of that particular issue lack these pages. (The Jernigan Library's is intact). We can sympathize with the Nobel Prize winner, living as he was in an oppressive British milieu. Alan Turing's immeasurable service to his country had not been enough to save him from arrest. After the defection of Burgess and Maclean to the Soviet Union, with the winds of McCarthyism blowing across the Atlantic, the situation for gays in the United Kingdom became increasing perilous. In just a year's time Sir John Gielgud would be arrested for importuning in a public toilet.

After Eliot's death Peter's essay was reprinted (April 1969), with a postscript in which he identified the person being elegized as Jean Verdenal, a medical student living in the same Paris pension in which Eliot stayed in 1910–11 when he was twenty-two and Verdenal was twenty. Killed in the Dardanelles in 1915 during the early days of the Gallipoli campaign, his ghost flits across Eliot's oeuvre from the publication of *Prufrock and Other Observations*, 1917, which is dedicated to Verdenal's memory, to that of *Little Gidding*, 1942, in which he appears as a ghost. The dedication to *Prufrock* underwent a number of modifications before arriving at its present state, where it is coupled with a quotation from Dante's *Purgatorio*, Canto 21, in which Statius declares his love for Virgil, both emblems of gay Romans. The ghost seen in *Little Gidding* after a German air raid is also associated with, among other allusions, tags from the "sodomite cantos," *Inferno* 15 and *Purgatorio* 26. Between *The Waste Land* and *Four Quartets* Verdenal pops up unexpectedly in an April 1934 column in Eliot's *Criterion*, where the poet recalls "the memory of a friend coming across the Luxembourg Gardens in the late afternoon, waving a branch of lilac, a friend who was later (so far as I could find out) to be mixed with the mud of Gallipoli." In my first encounter with *The Waste Land*, I was titillated by the appearance of the homosexual Mr. Eugenides. Being imbued in the academic climate of the time, however, I assumed that prim Mr. Eliot was using him as an example of postwar corruption. I completely missed Eliot's avowal that the poem "was only the relief of a personal and wholly insignificant grouse against life" (Ricks & McCue, 577). I find it difficult to switch now to seeing it as an elegy akin to Tennyson's *In Memoriam*, but James Miller, who followed Peter's lead, has helped guide me in that direction.

The elegy opens with "The Burial of the Dead." The first lines—"April is the cruelest month, breeding / Lilacs out of the dead land"—remind us of Whitman's lament for Lincoln. Verdenal was killed on May 2, but Eliot may not have known the exact date. Peter coupled the lines with Eliot's aside in the *Criterion* to begin his rereading of the poem. Immediately there follows: "mixing / Memory and desire." What kind of *desire* one may ask. After briefly mentioning a visit to Germany (did Verdenal accompany Eliot on the trip he made there just before the outbreak of war?), the poem offers a profuseness of images of sterility and death, before breaking into a curious, even confusing image:

'You gave me hyacinths first a year ago;
'They called me the hyacinth girl.'
—Yet when we came back, late, from the hyacinth garden,
Your arms full, and your hair wet, I could not
Speak, and my eyes failed....

This girl is never directly referred to again, and no explanation is offered why a flower associated with the boy beloved by both Apollo and Zephyrus should be associated with a young woman.

The hyacinth garden does, however, recur indirectly in the notes Eliot appended to the poem. His note for Part 2, line 125 ("Those are pearls that were his eyes"), returns the reader to "Part I, 37, 48." Line 48 immediately makes sense ("Those are pearls that were his eyes. Look!"), but line 37 is the one with the hyacinth garden. The mysterious reference is cleared up when one discovers that the manuscript for Part 2 originally read, "I remember / The hyacinth garden. Those are pearls that were his eyes, yes!" Miller sums up, "What revision had put asunder was reconnected in the footnotes." He goes on to quote Wilson Knight: "the 'hyacinth girl' appears to be male." For the line about pearls must refer to Verdenal. The next extended scene in the published poem is the speaker's visit with a fortune teller. Using the Tarot, she identifies the major characters—the drowned Phoenician Sailor (whose eyes were pearls), the stand-in for Verdenal; Belladonna, the wife, inescapably Vivienne Eliot; and the protagonist himself—and then introduces a seemingly minor character—a "one-eyed merchant," the homosexual Mr. Eugenides. The last scene in the section is an encounter with a fighter who saw combat in the same area where Verdenal was killed.

Part 2 consists of two extended scenes. The first is between the speaker and presumably his wife. She suffers from neurasthenia brought on by a loveless marriage. The speaker's emotions instead are invested in the Phoenician sailor. Was Eliot remembering an earlier part of Verdenal's service when the speaker muses, "I think we are in rats' alley / Where the dead men lost their bones"? The editors for Eliot's complete poems identify Rats Alley as the name of one of the trenches in the Somme battlefield. (Miller notes that the poet Louis Simpson equated "bones" to "boners." Similarly, in the library copy of Miller's book I am using, someone has penciled in the margin beside "one-eyed merchant," "one-eyed snake?") If indeed Eliot was in love with Verdenal, he married Vivienne on the rebound, just a month after receiving word of Verdenal's death. He would separate from her in 1932 and thereafter have nothing to do with her, but already the great rift between husband and wife is clear, and the drowned sailor is somehow involved.

Sexuality of all types, along with reminders of death, permeates Part 3. Here the speaker is in as bad shape as the wife in Part 2. Not only does he think about Verdenal's death ("my brother's wreck," a line not in Shakespeare's *The Tempest*, which he is quoting) but also his own father's in 1919. Battleground imagery perhaps lies behind "White bodies naked on the low damp ground," along with another reference to rats and bones. Here appears Mr. Eugenides, who invites the speaker to a weekend in a Brighton hotel known for its discretion about its guests' indiscretions (this last information courtesy of Ricks and McCue's annotations). And like that, the speaker turns into Tiresias, the man who became a woman who became a man. Part 3 ends with a reference to St. Augustine. Here come together an acknowledgment of the intensity of love, Augustine's confession of his love for a male friend, and a reminder of Augustine's association with the Phoenician city of Carthage in preparation for Part 4, the death of Phlebas the Phoenician. When the drowned sailor appears, he is linked through verbal echoes with Mr. Eugenides: there "merchant," here "profit and loss"; there "currants," here "current." The reference to bones returns. "Whirlpool" echoes "the Wheel" that the fortune teller refers to. One thing neither Peter nor Miller addresses is the reason for an association between Verdenal and Phoenicia (or the reason Mr. Eugenides comes from Smyrna, Turkey, the country in which Verdenal was killed).

Seemingly the most straightforward of the five sections, Part 5 tantalizes in a number of places. For the passage that begins "Who is the third who walks always beside you?" Miller suggests that the speaker might be Vivienne Eliot and the third, whom she cannot discern whether "a man or a woman," is again the French friend. I assume the "black cock" that appears is a weathervane and nothing more (but after reading some of Eliot's previously unpublished poetry, I am not sure). With the sermon of the thunder the most interesting aspects are the changes made between the original draft and the published poem. In response to the first thunder clap, the speaker responds thus in the manuscript:

......we brother, what have we given?
My friend, my blood friend, beating in my heart,
The awful daring of a moment's surrender
Which an age of prudence cannot retract—
By this, and this only, we have existed,
Which is not to be found in our obituaries.

"My friend" recurs in his response to the second clap. There is also a reference to a figure who intrigued Eliot: Shakespeare's Coriolanus. In an oblique way could he be thinking about the homoerotic friendship between Coriolanus and Aufidius and the literal death the latter brings the former? Most intriguingly, in the response to the third thunder clap, the original action was in the past tense, not the conditional in the published version:

......your heart responded
Gaily, when invited, beating responsive

> To controlling hands. I left without you
> Clasping empty hands I sit upon the shore
> Fishing, with the desolate sunset behind me

For Miller (135) the sermon of the thunder has "brought about the direct confrontation with the truth of the poet's past, and the commands and his responses must remain in his consciousness as the way to the cure for his impotence...and as the means for restoring his voice as a poet. Only by such confrontation and salvaging of the self can the poet-protagonist come to fruitful terms with his malaise."

It was long thought that the original drafts of the poem had been lost. It was announced in 1968 that they had been discovered as a part of the New York Public Library collections. The file also contained drafts of poems Eliot associated with *The Waste Land* either thematically or as a source for lines. One is the masturbatory fantasy "The Death of Saint Narcissus." In it the youth goes through a series of metamorphoses: a tree with entangled roots and branches, a fish "With slippery white belly held tight in his own fingers," and a young girl whose rape somehow introduces Narcissus to "the taste of his own whiteness." Satiated, he is left "green, dry and stained / With the shadow in his mouth." There are still other poems that show Eliot's fascination with homosexuality: "The Love Song of St. Sebastian," lines from "Petit Epître," some curious allusions in "Ode," and "Improper Rhymes," which reveal Eliot's obsession with body functions and buggery. "The Love Song of J. Alfred Prufrock" particularly comes alive when a gay reading is applied to it. The original manuscript had as an epigraph lines from *Purgatorio* 26, Eliot's favorite passage about homosexuals preparing for heaven. Concerning the "you and I" of the opening line, Ricks and McCue (376) quote part of a letter from Eliot: "I am prepared to assert that the 'you' in *The Love Song* is merely some friend or companion, presumably of the male sex." This pair at nightfall wander through streets bordered by "one-night cheap hotels" (the kind used for short-term sexual encounters?). Along the way Prufrock, though something of a dandy, identifies with "lonely men in shirt-sleeves." Their destination is a fashionable party where the women will be "Talking of Michelangelo." Prufrock does not feel at ease with these women and accepts that they will largely ignore him. In the end, both he and his male friend, in anticipation of Phlebas, will "drown."

Was Eliot gay? Many of his contemporaries assumed he was. They commented on his secretive night life and his penchant for wearing make-up. A large coterie of his friends before World War II were gay. Vivienne Eliot's biographer, Carole Seymour-Jones (*Painted Shadows*, 2001), not only accepts his homosexuality as a fact, but names partners and asserts that he introduced some of them into his home, where he and his wife had separate bedrooms. It is almost as if Eliot was deliberately strewing clues about his sexuality in his poems, just begging to be outed, only to panic when in essence he was.

TEXTS: T. S. Eliot, *The Waste Land: A Facsimile and Transcript of the Original Drafts including the Annotations of Ezra Pound*, ed. by Valerie Eliot (Harcourt Brace Jovanovich, 1971). SUPPLEMENT: Christopher Ricks & Jim McCue, eds., *The Poems of T. S. Eliot*, 2 vols. (Johns Hopkins, 2015). REFERENCE: James E. Miller Jr., *T. S. Eliot's Personal Waste Land: Exorcism of the Demons* (Pennsylvania State, 1977).

Fernando Pessoa: *Antinoüs* / António Botto: *Songs* (Portuguese, English)

Every gay encyclopedia I have seen with an entry on Fernando António Nogueira Pessoa (1888–1935), generally considered Portugal's greatest modern poet, has almost identical disclaimers. Robert Howes is representative: "Although there is no conclusive proof that Pessoa was homosexual, the fact that he never married, the extreme reserve he maintained about his private life, and his friendship with the openly gay poet António Botto point in this direction" (Dynes, 978). Certainly his long poem "Antinoüs," published in 1918, is indisputably a gay poem. Written in English (Pessoa grew up in South Africa and was perfectly bilingual) in loosely structured rhymed verse, the poem registers Emperor Hadrian's anguish at the death of his beloved Antinous. Early on, as he views the youth's naked body, he recalls their sensual lovemaking quite explicitly:

O fingers skilled in things not to be told!
O tongue which, counter-tongued, made the blood bold!
O complete regency of lust throned on
Raged consciousness's spilled suspension!

Hadrian goes on to remember how Antinous was wont "thy dangling sense to cloy, / And uncloy with more cloying, and annoy / With newer uncloying till thy senses bled." He says the youth's "hand and mouth knew games to reinstall / Desire." He speaks of "sucked lust," "every body-entrance to his lust," and, at length, how they spent long periods "playing with lust." Sensuality is prologue to Antinous's deification, which takes up the major portion of the 359-line poem, mentioning in passing the glorification of Ganymede. The gods make a mysterious appearance at the end.

Like much of Pessoa's Portuguese poetry, his English love sonnets, also published in 1918, are gender-neutral. Richard Zenith found an unpublished and incomplete Portuguese poem in the Pessoa archives dated 1919 which he provisionally entitles "A Fragmentary Gay Poem." Written in the first person, the poem goes beyond "Antinoüs" in its expression of desire, though modified that the sexual object may be man or woman. All the explicit examples offered, however, are male. Pessoa is unusual in creating a series of male poetic voices, which he called heteronyms, each with his individual personality. One of these, Álvaro de Campos, is identified as having homosexual tendencies. Perhaps for that reason he is attracted to Whitman, who heavily influences both his poetics and his thought. In his 218-line "Salutation to Walt Whitman" Campos acknowledges the American as the "Great pederast brushing up against the diversity of things, / Sexualized by rocks, by trees, by people, by their trades, / Itch for the swiftly passing, for casual encounters, for what's merely observed." Howes finds "overtones of sadomasochistic fantasy in both Campos's 240-line "Triumphal Ode" (not included in *Poems*) and the 904-line "Maritime Ode." In the latter we find such lines as these:

> Oh, my heroes, hairy, coarse, adventurous and criminal!
> My seafaring beasts, you husbands of my imagination!
> Fortuitous lovers of my oblique sensations!
> I'd like to be your One-and-Only lover awaiting you in every port,
> You, the abhorrent, loved with the pirate blood of her dreams!

Her refers back to the poet's expressed wish "To let my passive body be the grand sum-total-woman of all women" to be violated at sea. But such lines are almost lost in the turmoil of images and emotions that propel the poem along. What interests Campos, as avatar of Whitman, above all is "All the ways of expressing all emotions."

Pessoa championed the work of António Tomás Botto (1897–1959). He came to his defense when the younger man was attacked for his "praise of Greek love," and he translated Botto's poems into English in 1933. The collection, however, was not published until 1948, presumably because of its content. Howes writes that the poet "was highly sociable and was well known for his Bohemian life-style, his taste for sailors and his wicked tongue, which made him many enemies." He also notes that, "despite his open homosexuality, he married and his wife...stood by him to the end" (Aldrich & Wotherspoon, [vol. 1], 64–65). *The Songs* (*Canções*) includes eighty-nine poems, of which only three or four are heterosexual. They are tainted with more than a whiff of misogyny. Kissing is his preferred sexual outlet. (Or is this a euphemism for genital activity?) Settings tend to be enclosed spaces at night, often the bed chamber. Poems with exterior settings praise such manly types as athletes, Angolan dancers, and a bullfighter. The poet is very appreciative of the beauty of male flesh. But, as Howes points out, "the majority [of the poems] form part of an ongoing dialogue with an anonymous lover or lovers, in which only the voice of the poet is heard." In Botto's lyrics *eros* and *thanatos* are often linked, though he may be alluding to "the little death" of sexual fulfillment. Postcoital goodbyes and unfulfilled rendezvouses are almost as prevalent as actual love-making. The poet is keenly aware of the capriciousness and falsehoods that can accompany declarations of love.

Pessoa's translations are limpid, a pleasure to read. Here is a representative poem entire (Boy 6):

> Who is it that clasps me to him
> In the half-light of my bed?
> Who is it that kisses me
> And bites my breast till it bled?
> Who is it that speaks of death
> In my ear, so slow, so sweet?
> It is you, lord of my eyes,
> Who have my dreams at your feet.

At age fifty Botto and his wife emigrated to Brazil. He died there as the result of being struck by a car. The last edition of *The Songs* published during his lifetime appeared in 1956.

·∥·

TEXTS: António Botto, *The Songs*, trans. Fernando Pessoa, ed. Josiah Blackmore (Minnesota, 2010). Fernando Pessoa, *Poems*, trans. Edwin

Honig & Susan M. Brown (City Lights, 1998); *Selected English Poems*, ed. Tony Frazer (Shearsman, 2007).

Wilfred Owen: Erotic Poems (English)

His war poetry, especially after Benjamin Britten's use of it in the 1962 *War Requiem*, so dominates our image of Second Lieutenant Wilfred Edward Salter Owen, M.C. (1893–1918), that it was not until I listed the poems in which gay images appear that the impact of Owen's contribution to gay literature hit me. His biographer Dominic Hibberd (xix) provides evidence that the poet "recognized and accepted [his sexuality] without much difficulty." In a 1912–14 poem "O World of many worlds" Owen says that he feels like "a meteor, fast, eccentric, lone, / Lawless" in contrast to those who "hold course unalterably fixed." He acquired an important circle of gay friends, beginning with the French poet Laurent Tailhade, who met him in France in 1914 and "quite slobbered" over him (Hibberd, 135). Tailhade introduced Owen to the newly fashionable French cult of decadence. When Owen returned to England to enlist, he encountered poet and bookstore owner Harold Monro. Sent to the Craiglockhart War Hospital in 1917 for treatment for shell shock, he met, and fell in love with, Siegfried Sassoon (1886–1967). The latter encouraged Owen in his development as a poet (and would edit the first, posthumous collection of his poems). A few months later Owen met Robert Graves, and then Robert Ross, Wilde's faithful friend. At Graves's wedding (his rite of renunciation of his earlier homosexuality), Owen met Charles Scott Moncrieff (1889–1930), the future translator of Proust. Scott Moncrieff fell in love with Owen, and the two may even have been momentarily intimate. He in turn introduced Owen to his lover, the risqué poet Philip Bainbrigge (1890–1918). Osbert Sitwell (1892–1969), whom he met through Ross, rounded out the homosexual coterie he now found himself a part of.

A few of his poems hint that Owen was also given to cruising the streets and the waterfront. One wonders whether he composed more openly gay poems than the ones that have come down to us. We know that his brother Howard destroyed and mutilated letters and a diary to expunge from the record any traits he deemed damaging to his brother's reputation. For that matter, Owen himself burnt much material before being sent back to battle the last time. Still, of the 103 poems plus fragments that have come down to us, a goodly number reflect same-sex relationships. "Impromptu" praises a lover's hand and eyes. In "Storm" the poet imagines himself as a tree inviting the "brilliant danger" of lightning from a "face... charged with beauty." "To—" compares a moment two lovers share to the innocence of children at play, despite their awareness that war and time threaten to cut their happiness short. In "With an Identity Disc" he invites a "sweet friend" to wear his identity disc after his death so that "thy heart-beat kiss it night and day." "The Promisers" records his disappointment when a cherished friend does not show up. "Music" exults the way "Love's body" has opened him to the fullness of "Life's symphony." "The One Remains" expresses his longing to find "All beauty, once for ever, in one face." "Autumnal" describes the end of "a love that had been dear." "The Peril of Love" describes his tendency to become "a prey of impulse" and give over to "fierce infatuation." Then there is the enigmatic "How Do I Love Thee?," which, though seemingly addressed to a woman, contains the statement, "I do love thee even as Shakespeare loved." Several poems describe the power of a very male Eros: the aforementioned "To—," "To Eros," "Purple," and "The Time Was Aeon." In the latter St. Paul leads a mob of "railers, hot with hate" in battle against "the naked likeness of a boy." There are also such poems as the witty "Maundy Thursday," in which the poet kisses not the silver cross but "the warm live hand" of the acolyte holding it, and the medieval-like whimsy "Page Eglantine,"in which the speaker looks to his page to serve this night as "my quire" and "my wine."

Then there are those poems that move towards an even more explicit homosexuality. After taking secret "antidotes," the poet in "A Palinode" turns away from Nature to embrace the City with "passion." An encounter with a sailor on the train in "It Was a Navy Boy" goes nowhere. "Six O'Clock in Princes Street" finds the poet semi-cruising the Edinburgh thoroughfare. "The City Lights" finds him "along the waterside," where he "sinned." "The Rime of the Youthful Mariner" is an exercise in sadomasochism ending in some sort of erotic coupling. "Who Is the God of Canongate?" is a fairly explicit dialogue with, first, an Edinburgh and, then, a London rent boy with whom men "lift their lusts and let them spill." Just as explicit is "I Am the Ghost of Shadwell Stairs." The poet—a "ghost," a "shadow"—is cruising the London docks. Lit by a "purple" streetlight, he feels "a strange tide turns," and in the end, "I with another ghost am lain." Inexplicably, Owen's editor omits "Reunion," the most direct of all the

sexual poems, not even including it among the fragments. Two drafts are reproduced online as part of the Oxford University's digital archives. The title may stem from the theory of love put forth in Plato's *Symposium*. The first draft begins:
> I saw you, I sought you.
> I sought you, I caught you,
> And we were two,
> Were two against the world's taboo.

As a result, even when the majority try to come between them, they fail. The first draft ends, "And Pan shall make all worlds our dancing halls." The second draft (which also has a revealing line, "I needed, you ceded") ends with a vision of the embracing solidarity of comradeship: "We shall be many / Against the enemy." One can only imagine what Owen's untimely death (he was killed seven days before the armistice) deprived us of.

TEXT: Wilfred Owen, *The Poems*, ed. Jon Stallworthy (Norton, 1986). REFERENCE: Dominic Hibberd, *Wilfred Owen: A New Biography* (Ivan R. Dee, 2003).

Federico García Lorca: *Ode to Walt Whitman*; *Sonnets of Dark Love* (Spanish)

Picture the moment: in the fall 1929 the young Puerto Rican scholar and bilingual editor of the *Alhambra* magazine, Ángel Flores, takes an older Columbia University student, Federico del Sagrado Corazón de Jesús García Lorca (1898–1936), only a few months after his arrival to the States, to an apartment building in Columbia Heights, Brooklyn. The circumstances of the visit are unclear, and a variant account makes the setting a bar (though that hardly accords with the scene presented). A party is in progress. The host, the American poet Hart Crane, is surrounded by sailors. Lorca, who supposedly is learning English, has made little progress in the language; Crane, despite his love of exotic words, is basically monolingual. Flores gives up trying to act as an intermediary between the two and lets them converse in broken French. When he realizes that they both share a common sexual interest in the sailors, he discreetly withdraws. What ensues the rest of the evening remains unknown. At the time, Crane was in the throes of finishing *The Bridge*, in which the span across the East River becomes symbolic of the American spirit. It includes a long tribute to Whitman and is shot through with quasi-concealed gay imagery. Lorca was beginning to map out his *Poet in New York* (*Poeta en Nueva York*), an expressionistic look at those marginalized by society. It includes "Sleepless City (Brooklyn Bridge Nocturne)" and "Ode to Walt Whitman," and it allows the poet to explore his own sexuality. There are even linguistic similarities between the two works, and it might be instructive to compare Lorca's *lógica poética* with Crane's logic of metaphor.

The trip to New York was Lorca's first excursion outside Spain. He was in part fleeing the tensions between him and the painter Salvador Dali (Lorca's ode to him, 1926, reflects happier times). There were various causes for the rift, but they were magnified by filmmaker Luis Buñuel's jealousy (Lorca perceived the surrealistic film *Un chien andalou*, 1929, as a direct attack on him). But the immediate catalyst seems to have been the ending of an unhappy love affair with the sculptor Emilio Aladrén Perojo. In New York, despite his limited English, he immersed himself in theater, the life of Harlem, and the general bustle of a large city so unlike Madrid. Little hints from the poems leave you wondering whether he also took advantage of the sexual outlets that the city offered. The outline of the work that would become *Poet in New York* began to take shape in his mind, though its contents were to be provided by whatever actually happened to him. Individual parts were published separately. Most notably, the ode to Whitman appeared in a limited edition as a chapbook, 1933. *Poet in New York* first appeared posthumously in 1940, in incomplete form as a bilingual edition translated into English by Rolfe Humphries. A desire for love is a major motif throughout the book. There is a sense of betrayal in the "Fable of Three Friends to Be Sung in Rounds." Lorca's friend Rafael Martínez Nadal, who did much to pull Lorca's posthumous reputation out of his family's imposed closet, says it is a remembrance of Lorca's affair with Aladrén and added "that he could identify the other two 'friends' without difficulty" (Maurer, 272). The poem builds to an assertion that the three have "murdered me." In an early draft the "I" is explicitly named Federico. The gay sonnet "Adam," though written in New York, was not included, perhaps because much of its language anticipated the poem to Whitman.

The ode provides the culmination of the poet's ambivalent experiences in the city: "Not for a moment, Walt Whitman, lovely old man, / have I failed to see your beard full of butterflies." Clearly, Lorca reveres the American poet, dead only six years before he was born. But equally clear, he is uneasy about the company in which he thus finds himself, one with "the faggots"

> gathered at bars,
> emerging in bunches from the sewers,
> trembling between the legs of chauffeurs,
> or spinning on the platforms of absinthe.

Paul Binding (140–41) asserts that, from Lorca's viewpoint, Whitman can be "censured for his failure to do justice to the pain and evil in life," for not having acknowledged, as Lorca writes, "the darkest swamp." Following Binding's lead, one can read the final stanzas as Lorca's awareness that "the failure of homosexual life to live up the Whitmanesque image of it is inextricable from the failure of American society to live up to Whitman's social pastorals for it." But Lorca himself barely confronts the reality of the struggle for economic survival that has begun in economically depressed America: the understandable reasons behind the existence of "urban faggots," hustlers, "who drink prostitution's water with revulsion." His list of the pejorative terms used for homosexuals in the U.S., Cuba, and Mexico and across the Iberian peninsula comes across to a present-day reader like a slap against the face. Binding also raises the question whether Lorca instinctively felt that Whitman had a tendency to see people *en masse* and perhaps too exclusively from a homosexual standpoint. Lorca accepts "the little boy who writes / the name of a girl on his pillow" alongside "the boy who dresses as a bride." Still the poem ends on an up beat, after a final salute to "lovely Walt Whitman." It is a deeply personal poem that we have been permitted to overhear, not a call for liberation.

From New York the poet sailed to Havana, the experience providing a coda for *Poet in New York*. Back in Spain he threw himself into theater. He did not progress with his unfinished gay play *El público* (*The Audience*). But his sympathy for the marginalized, the silenced ones, led him to create his great trilogy about frustrated women (*Blood Wedding, Yerma, The House of Bernarda Alba*). He prepared *The Tamarit Divan* for publication. Based on Arab verse forms, which he saw as part of his Andalusian heritage (Emilio García Gómez had published his anthology in 1930), Lorca responded to their homoeroticism. In 1935 he published his elegy on the death of the bisexual bullfighter Ignacio Sánchez Mejías, whom he had personally known. And he composed the eleven Petrarchan sonnets now known as *Sonnets of Dark Love* (*Sonetos del amor oscuro*). Their existence was long the subject of rumor, but their publication was blocked by Lorca's protective family. After they were finally published in a pirated edition in 1983, the family relented and an approved version came out the next year. Could one have anticipated that one day they would be co-translated by Lorca's niece? The subject of the sonnets is disputed. Traditionally he has been identified as Rafael Rodríguez Rapún, an apparently straight engineering student who had become associated with theater (and who was also assassinated by the fascists). But recently documents have come to light indicating that the person addressed was the gay teenager Juan Ramírez de Lucas, with whom Lorca wanted to escape the increasingly dangerous political climate of Spain to emigrate to Mexico. Ramírez's parents opposed the plan. The private nature of the poems leads to an emotional and sexual intensity that outstrips Lorca's earlier homoerotic verse even as it resorts to symbolic obscurity/revelation that, decoded, would not be out of place in Whitman's *Leaves*.

The sonnets begin with a sense of urgency, the couple seemingly engaged in sex. He urges his lover ("Sonnet of the Garland of Roses") to "Delight in the fresh landscape of my wound, / break reeds and delicate streams, / drink blood poured on a thigh of honey." Openings, phallic shapes, and liquid spilled on the upper leg offer "delight." Binding (210) reminds us that well into the twentieth century a folk belief held that "semen was blood that had been changed in the testicles." In "Sonnet of the Sweet Complaint" Lorca thinks about the feel of "your breath / …on my cheek at night." Alone, he wishes for "the flower, pulp or clay / for the worm of my suffering." He acknowledges the difference in their age and the power differential in their love. It is not all sex. The poet exults in a telephone call. He begs his lover to write to him. The sequence builds to "The Beloved Sleeps on the Poet's Breast." It opens: "You will never understand how I love you." In the previous, untitled poem Lorca has asserted how his love is natural. Now he calls it a *norma*, a law that rules "both flesh and morning star." He is all too aware, however, of enemies waiting for them in ambush. The final poem, "Night of Sleepless Love," provides the sequence's climax, in two senses of the word. The poem is built on a series of oppositions, which get lost in the translations. In the first quatrain, night up, the poet cries, the lover laughs. Does this indicate a sadomasochist dynamic? Or simply the different sensations felt in anal intercourse? In the second quatrain, night down, the lover cries. He is now a "Cristal de pena," probably a play on the similarity between *pena* (pain) and *pene* (penis). Penis, pain, and lover all interchangeable, he/it cries "for deep distances" while the poet suffers over the lover's "weak heart of sand." The first tercet moves to dawn. The couple is engaged in mutual oral sex, sixty-nining. Literally their mouths press "to the icy jet / of endless blood that spills." "Icy" translates *helado*, a common word, Binding (210) reminds us, for ice cream, "which male issue rather resembles." Though too free, a richer, more connotative rendering of the lines might be: "our mouths suck the creamy jet / of life-giving liquid that spurts." Binding thinks the "closed balcony" referred to in the final tercet stands for the anus; I would see it as Lorca's whole being, now open to the sun, the power of love reviving his "shrouded heart." The gay poet Rafael Campo, who has also translated the entire sequence using slant rhyme to preserve the formal aspects of the sonnets, seems to agree with me.

With Wilde, Lorca has become an iconic gay martyr. He was assassinated by the Spanish *Guardia Civil* both for his political activities and his sexuality. Binding has studied the corpus from a gay perspective. Despite its title, Ángel Sahuquillo's work tells us more about the academic response to the poet than it does about his poetry and plays and their relationship to a gay tradition. By the way, García Lorca's name can confuse. His family name is García, and he is correctly alphabetized with the *G*'s in indices. In typical Spanish fashion his mother's name, Lorca, is added on, and it has become traditional in English to refer to him by it only.

TEXTS: Federico García Lorca, *Poet in New York*, trans. Greg Simon & Steven F. White, ed. Christopher Maurer, 3rd ed. (Farrar, Straus & Giroux, 2013); *Sonnets of Dark Love / The Tamarit Divan*, trans. Jane Duran & Gloria García Lorca (Enitharmon, 2017). SUPPLEMENT: Rafael Campo, trans., "Sonnets of Dark Love," *Diva* (Duke, 1999), 84–94. REFERENCES: Paul Binding, *Lorca: The Gay Imagination* (GMP, 1985). Ian Gibson, *Federico García Lorca: A Life* (Pantheon, 1989). Ángel Sahuquillo, *Federico García Lorca and the Culture of Male Homosexuality*, trans. Erica Frouman-Smith (McFarland, 2007).

Hart Crane: *White Buildings* (English)

Almost everyone seems to agree that Crane's gayness informs much of his poetry even as he had to conceal the fact because of the prejudices of the era in which he was writing. For most straight critics that suppression allows his poems to be universal despite his sexual orientation, while for gay critics they are universal just because of his sexuality. Everyone seems to agree that the poetry is often obscure, sometimes to the point where meaning is lost. In an attempt to relieve that obscurity some of the criticism becomes more opaque than the poetry itself. Thomas Yingling, who has written a full-length study, often caused my eyes to glaze over. Sometimes a reading seems so idiomatic that it probably satisfies the critic alone. Is the moon really "phallic," as Gregory Woods (*Articulate Flesh*, 152) insists, just because the tidal sea's "vast belly moonward bends" (Voyages 2)? Much of Crane, I know, escapes me. Tennessee Williams instantly felt a shock of recognition upon reading him.

Harold Hart Crane (1899–1933) early acknowledged his sexuality. His first published poem, which appeared when he was only seventeen, was titled "C 33," Wilde's cell number (actually C.3.3.) used as a pseudonym for the publication of *The Ballad of Reading Gaol*. There followed a number of other similarly coded poems, published but uncollected. They all seem surprising for a teenager at the time of the First World War even as they foreshadow his later strategies. Take "Annunciations." On the surface it describes the appearance of a plant growing out of the earth, hints at the virgin birth ("a dove's flight"), and ends with apparently a childbirth. But the plant's sap is "anxious milk-blood" (semen?) which, "aroused," causes "a quickening quiver." The human act involves "moans of travail of one dearest beside me" followed by "high cries" hushed during the early hours "before dawn." Are we actually present at some sexual act involving two males? Does the idea of such a reading exist only because one knows Crane was gay? But then, could the poem's lexicon have come into existence had Crane not been gay? "Modern Craft" is pretty up front: "My modern love were [sic] / Charred at a stake in younger times than ours." These apprentice works climax in the most accessible homoerotic poem from the period (not published until after his death). "Episode of Hands" recalls an incident in which a factory owner's son bandages the wound of a worker whose fingers have been injured by the machinery. His task finished, "The two men smiled into each other's eyes."

Crane's first collection, *White Buildings*, appeared in 1926. In one case he cut a line that he probably considered too obvious. "Possessions," his poem about "this fixed stone of lust," describes a casual pickup in Greenwich Village. The poet having taken the other man back to his apartment, the poem included the italicized line below in its printing in *The Little Review* (Woods, 146; Fisher, 191; italics mine):

I know the screen, the distant flying taps
And stabbing medley that sways—
Rounding behind to press and grind,
And the mercy feminine that stays.

There follow other poems in the collection, in particular "Recitative," that reward a gay reading.

It closes with a series of six poems published under the collective title "Voyages." Woods (150) quotes an earlier (and straight) critic R. W. B. Lewis for praising "Voyages" as "that rarity in American literature—genuine and personal love poetry," going on to extravagantly call it "the only truly moving and beautiful poetry of male homosexual love in English," arguing that "Crane has succeeded in making the passionate love of male for male representative of every kind of human passion." Crane's biographer Clive Fisher (230) is only slightly more reserved in describing it as "one of the most beautiful love lyrics in modern poetry." Crane met Emil Opffer, a Danish sailor in the merchant marine, in New York in 1923. Opffer was by necessity often at sea, but in 1924 he persuaded Crane to move into the same apartment complex where he lived, located at 110 Columbia Heights in Brooklyn. Crane discovered that his new bedroom was the same John Roebling, the engineer who designed Brooklyn Bridge, had used to oversee construction of the span after he was crippled. Their affair led Crane to return to a short poem he had written earlier about the playful innocence of children on the beach. He now saw the sea theme, so obviously connected to Opffer's profession, as a vehicle to explore "the wrapt infections of our love." You can find in "the dark confessions" all sorts of sexual allusions, but the overarching theme is the intertwining of the eternity of the sea, the finality of death, and the brevity of love and sexual passion. The final wrapping is language itself. One other poem, never completed, was begun for Opffer after their relationship had frayed: "The Visible the Untrue."

Even before the two men met, Crane had been mulling ideas that would lead to his epic *The Bridge*. It was published in 1930. Gay critics find a rich subtext that straight readers probably miss. Woods (140) takes delight in the fact that it took nearly half a century before Robert Martin (in an article, not in his book) would "explicate satisfactorily Hart Crane's observation, in 'The Tunnel,' that love has become 'A burnt match skating in a urinal.'" In many ways the poem is comparable to Eliot's *The Waste Land* in its mingling of the idiosyncratic and the larger cultural context. But despite its autobiographical elements and its ties to Whitman ("Cape Hatteras"), it seems to me far less personal than Eliot's grouse. Meanwhile, Crane continued to publish lyrics. His second projected collection, "Key West," produced his last poem, "The Broken Tower." It is one of his greatest. Such a stanza as the following is universal:

> And so it was I entered the broken world
> To trace the visionary company of love, its voice
> An instant in the wind (I know not whether hurled)
> But not for long to hold each desperate choice.

Could anyone other than a gay man have captured the intricate implications created by Crane's particular choice of words? His dive from the ship returning him from Mexico cut short whatever might have been and set forever his image as a *poète maudit*. In retrospect, his suicide was foreshadowed by his destruction of his portrait painted by the Mexican artist David Siqueiros. Soon after his death gay American poet and artist Marsden Harley (1877–1943) wrote "Un Recuerdo – Hermano – Hart Crane R.I.P." and painted the haunting *Eight Bells Folly: Memorial for Hart Crane*.

TEXT: Hart Crane, *Complete Poems and Selected Letters*, ed. Langdon Hammer (Library of America, 2006). REFERENCES: Clive Fisher, *Hart Crane: A Life* (Yale, 2002). Thomas E. Yingling, *Hart Crane and the Homosexual Text: New Thresholds, New Anatomies* (Chicago, 1990).

Luis Cernuda: *Reality and Desire* (Spanish)

Cernuda and Lorca met in Madrid in 1927, but their friendship, according to Lorca's biographer Ian Gibson, dates from Lorca's return from New York. Gibson writes, "Cernuda was to write some of the frankest—and finest—poetry ever produced in Spain on the theme of homosexual love and its frustrations, and while we know disappointingly little about the nature of his friendship with Lorca, it is probably safe to assume that, in the 1930s, their shared homosexuality was the source of mutual confidences and appreciation" (200). Luis Cernuda Bidou (1902–1963) had earlier discovered André Gide's writings; they gave him permission to accept himself as he was. Upon Gide's death in 1951 he wrote an elegy expressing his sense of debt, "In Memoriam A. G." Similarly, he wrote an ode "To a Dead Poet (F.G.L.)" upon Lorca's assassination in 1936—incidentally outing Lorca for readers who had not before been aware of the older poet's sexuality ("Look at the glowing boys / You loved so much in life"), and followed it up near the end of his life with a meditation on the meaning of Lorca's growing reputation, "Once More, with Feeling." Though Gibson stresses how introverted Cernuda was, he fell in love with Serafín Fernández Ferro, to whom Lorca had introduced him, and published *Forbidden Pleasures* (*Los placeres prohibidos*, 1931), a volume described by Juan Godoy as "unprecedented in Spanish literature because of its openness about the poet's homosexuality." Cernuda was crushed when the affair ended. Godoy goes on to contrast Lorca and Cernuda: "Lorca defends freedom to love in all its manifestations. Cernuda speaks of gay love as if heterosexual love were something lower, or not even acceptable. His openness brought critical neglect during his lifetime, but ironically has now resulted in his recognition as one of the most important poets of twentieth-century Spain" (Haggerty, 179–80).

Even during his surrealistic period of *A River, a Love* (*Un río, un amor*, 1929), Cernuda's poetry is more readily accessible than Lorca's. In the same decade the latter was crafting his ode to Whitman and his dark sonnets, Cernuda was writing straightforwardly in "Blackbird, Seagull": "The sailor's golden muscles, / His cool salty lips, / Hold me captive in a world of illusions." "The Poet's Glory" rejects a society that would "try to limit love" ("Forcing an overcoat on the little boy in chains under the divine sun") and promises

> My love is yours;
> Ah for just one long night
> Let your warm dark body slip
> Light as a whip
> Underneath mine......
> And let the bottomless spring of your kisses
> Pour into me the fever of a passion gone dead between us,
> Because I'm sick of the vain labor of words.

Even as his life in Spain became untenable, he defiantly wrote in "Love from the Shadows," a rare rhyming poem (unrhymed in all translations): "You return among shadows, shadowy force / Of a different love. The lowly world hurls insults. / But life belongs to you: rise up and love." By then he had begun his Whitman-like practice of incorporating each new volume of poems into his masterwork *Reality and Desire* (*La realidad y el deseo*), first appearing in 1936 and reaching its fourth edition in 1964. In addition to love, his recurrent themes include beauty, nature, celebrations of the body, the Spanish people and their spirit, language and poetry, his larger cultural heritage, including gay heroes, the passage of time, and the entanglement of *eros* and *thanatos*.

He went into exile as a result of the Civil War, going from France to Britain, where he remained until 1947 (and where he fell in love with a Glasgow student). That year he emigrated to the U.S. Going by the evidence of the poems, the period spent in the U.K. and the U.S. was not sexually or emotionally fulfilling. In 1949 he visited Mexico for the first time. Two years later he met Salvador Alighieri, almost thirty years younger than he, married and with a child. As a result, he chose to permanently relocate to Mexico, where he lived until his death from a heart attack. There, once again surrounded by his native language and deeply in love, he wrote some of his most beautiful poems. They are also his gayest since *Forbidden Pleasures*. They are tinged with sadness. Whereas death seems merely a trope in his earlier work, in his last two volumes it takes on a reality of its own, as if Cernuda somehow foresaw that his life would be cut short. *With Time Running Out* (*Con las horas contadas*, 1956) includes his sixteen meditations on the power and significance of his love for Alighieri. "Poems for a Body" he called them collectively, but they are more about the spirit and the way love transfigures it.

Salvador's given name in Spanish signifies "savior," and that is the role he assumes in the suite. There is no narrative progression, though one can piece out that the affair was largely one-sided and brief. It begins with an address to Salvador himself (a point Stephen Kessler loses by translating his name). In Poem 3 the poet himself appears by name: "I, this unknown / Luis Cernuda, who lasts // For just a flash / Of hopeful love." He takes comfort in his writing. He begs Salvador to return to him (Poem 5). He chastises himself for not being able to keep quiet about his feelings (Poem 6). He feels awe that such powerful emotions can come to him at his age (Poems 7–8) and marvels how "pure encounter brought you to life" (Poem 9). In Poem 10 he echoes the biblical Ruth in asserting that "My land is you," that "You are my people. // Exile and death / For me are where / You are not." He tells Salvador he is his "hell and paradise" (Poem 11). But the younger man has freed him, even if Salvador does not care (Poem 12). He praises his lover's "beautiful body" (Poem 14) which "Puts flesh on a myth" (Poem 16). The sequence is one of the greatest series of love poems written in the twentieth century. Salvador, a body builder whose dark skin gained him the nickname El Chocolate, also appears in some of the prose poems called *Variations on a Mexican Theme*.

In *Desolation of the Chimera* (*Desolación de la Quimera*, 1962) Cernuda pays tribute to artists of all kinds who came before him, some straight, but most gay. His homage to Verlaine and Rimbaud, "Birds in the Night" (its title in English), has a directness and a depth of personal emotion that challenge the reader who wants poetry to be pretty. Looking, in his imagination, at the plaque placed on the home the two Frenchmen shared in London, Cernuda calls them

> Prisoners of their fate: the impossible friendship, the bitterness
> Of separation, and then the scandal; and for this one
> The trial, and two years in jail, thanks to his habits
> Condemned by society and law, at least up to now; for that one on his
>   own
> To wander from one corner of the earth to the other,
> Escaping to our world and its celebrated progress.

For a poem about King Ludwig II, "Louis of Bavaria Listens to *Lohengrin*," Kessler (210) notes that "Cernuda uses the Spanish equivalent Luis, no doubt as an echo of his own name." In the poem the king has suffered from "Deep eyes, sun-browned skin, / The grace of a young body," perhaps much as Cernuda suffered under Salvador's spell. But Wagner's fierce music comforts him: "The melody enables him to know himself, / To fall in love with who he truly is. And in the music he lives forever."

Cernuda has attracted few English translators. Reginald Gibbons's *Selected Poems*, 1977, offers forty-five poems and ignores many of the gayest ones. Rick Lipinski includes seventy-eight poems in *The Young Sailor and Other Poems*, 1986, but commits some real bloopers such as confusing *hiel* (bile) and *hielo* (ice). Kessler offers 109 poems in two volumes, plus the complete prose poems in a third. He occasionally leaves me shaking my head, as in "Best Loved Word," where he builds to the revelation of Cernuda's favorite word and then leaves it in Spanish. (*Andaluz* is simply *Andalusian*—why make it a mystery?). But all said, his is the most trustworthy and, in the case of Cernuda's final poems, the most powerful translation.

TEXT: Luis Cernuda, *Desolation of the Chimera*, trans. Stephen Kessler (White Pine, 2009); *Forbidden Pleasures: New Selected Poems (1924–1949)*, trans. Stephen Kessler (Black Widow, 2015).

Xavier Villaurrutia: Nocturnes (Spanish)

I was enamored of the idea of Mexico long before I visited the country. My first summer there in 1965 simply confirmed my feelings. My dissertation at the University of North Carolina was expanded as *American and British Writers in Mexico, 1556–1973* for the University of Texas Press. To my delight, a Spanish translation occasioned a mention by Octavio Paz in one of his essays. By that time, however, I had fallen in love and begun my French adventure. But through 1971 I spent as much time as possible in Mexico, having deliberately accepted a job at Texas A&I / Texas A&M University–Kingsville because it was only two hours from the border. Not until I was cleaning out books from my parents' home did it occur to me that my passion for the country may well have been kindled by an aunt's birthday present of *The Bobbsey Twins in Mexico*. I then remembered the paper cutout I had of a Mexican hacienda. During my Mexican years I read a great deal of Mexican fiction and nonfiction in translation. (My Spanish was never up to tackling a long work.) I remember no poets other than Paz. Certainly I have no memory of hearing about a group of rebellious writers of the 1920s and 1930s who had loosely banded together in Mexico City as *Los Contemporáneos*. A number of them were as open about their homosexuality as it was possible to be at the time: notably Carlos Pellicer, Elías Nandino, Jorge Cuesta, Xavier Villaurrutia, and Salvador Novo.

Xavier Villaurrutia y González (1903–1950) is the only one to be fully translated: his major work was translated by Eliot Weinberger in 1993 and his complete poetry by D. M. Stroud in 2004. Villaurrutia's output is relatively slight: his reputation rests largely on one work, *Nostalgia for Death* (*Nostalgia de la Muerte*, 1938, 1946). Altogether, his corpus numbers a little over a hundred poems, a figure one arrives at only by counting individual titles that make up suites of poems. But it yields much pleasure, not least when it is read with a gay eye. *Nostalgia for Death* consists of nineteen Nocturnes and six Nostalgias. "Statue Nocturne" is dedicated to his lover of the 1920s, the painter Agustín Lazo, who allegedly gave up art upon hearing of Villaurrutia's premature death. The poem may describe one of Lazo's paintings. (His portrait of the poet appears on the cover of *Homesick for Death*.)

"Love Nocturne" is addressed to Villaurrutia's later lover Manuel Rodriguez Lozano, another painter. "Sea Nocturne," dedicated to Novo, muses upon the relationship between the ocean and blood. It becomes unclear whether "your secret rumor" belongs to blood or to Novo; whichever, the poet promises to "keep our secret." The "Bedroom Nocturne," in which he celebrates "the sweat moistening our thighs / that embrace and struggle and, finally, give in," is delivered to no particular lover. In the Nostalgia section the deeply closeted Langston Hughes unexpectedly shows up as the dedicatee of "North Carolina Blues." In 1934–35 Hughes was in Mexico, where he had spent much of his childhood. On this occasion, Villaurrutia wrote an article about him for one of the national newspapers. But why North Carolina? So far as I know, Hughes had not been there since 1931, and Villaurrutia never. The poem, or perhaps it is better described as a suite of eight oriental-like verses, is quite sexual: it "reeks of human flesh."

Paz has rightfully called Villaurrutia's "Los Angeles Nocturne" his most erotic poem. Dedicated to the gay Mexican movie producer Agustín Fink, with whom Villaurrutia visited L.A. in 1936, it is a fairly explicit description of an evening spent cruising the city streets. The movement of the men is likened to a river's flow as

they stroll, they stop, they walk on by.

> They trade glances, they risk smiles,
> they pair off improbably.

Following age-old rituals, matches are struck, doors are opened, "the heart [is] caught between two orgasms." Then, mysteriously the men are transformed into angels of desire (the poem's title could also be translated as "Angels Nocturne") who visit the aptly-named city "to chant the songs, the pledges and the swearwords / in which men concentrate the ancient mystery / of flesh, blood, and desire." Using simple aliases (Dick, John), these heavenly creatures,

> They stroll, they stop, they walk on by.
> They trade glances, they risk smiles.
> They pair off improbably.

In the rented rooms, when they strip, they reveal "celestial" tattoos before they "fall back into bed," where they dream of men, "not of angels."

This poem is followed immediately by "Rose Nocturne," written for José Gorostiza, another *contemporáneo* and probable lover. Villaurrutia compares various parts of his body to the pink flower. He begins by describing what the rose is not. It is not "like baby's skin," nor is it "the resurrection rose." It is not "the pink flash of fire," nor is it "the sailor's compass rose." It is not the flower itself, the pink rose. Then he begins to list what his "rose" is. It is a "digital rose," although what the finger is exploring goes unmentioned. It is "the pink shell" of the ear listening. It is the "rose incarnate of the mouth." And it is—well, at this point I am unsure what it is. There is no stanza break, so one is led to think the poet is still describing the mouth. All the translations I have seen agree that the stanza builds to the statement that "it is the labial rose, / the wounded rose." But some of the terms Villaurrutia uses to get there lead me to wonder if he is not in fact describing a man's anus, its lips yielding and expanding. In the next stanza the poet calls it "the rose of eyeless wakefulness." The final stanza evokes the image of smoke and ash and carbon that makes a pinpoint of light in the dark without taking up space, apparently a shared cigarette after sex.

After *Nostalgia* Villaurrutia's poetic production slowed down even further. But the poems often become more explicit. In the first of his two sets of *décimas* (or "tenners," as Stroud labels them), we find this (Death Decima 7):

> In the rubbing, in the contact,
> of ineffable delight,

of caress supremely light
leading out into the act,
we accept mysterious pact
in a long, delirious spasm
where hallucinating chasm
and infernal agony
forge together what is me
and what is you in one orgasm.

Save for a set of satiric "Boston Epigrams" with which the volume ends, his final volume, *Canto to Spring* (*Canto a la primavera*, 1948), could just as well be called *Canto to Love*. Twelve poems celebrate its power, "more than for sex and power."

Carlos Monsiváis in his introduction to Novo's memoir *Pillar of Salt* (32) quotes an epigram that Novo wrote about Villaurrutia:

This little actress, so fine and small
our very favorite Lilliput
whose ass accommodates one and all,
do we exaggerate to call him slut?

The memoir itself speaks of Novo's early encounters with Villaurrutia, resulting in the two of them and their two lovers renting a studio in Mexico City together. It gives unexpected insights into Mexico City of the time.

TEXT: Xavier Villaurrutia, *Homesick for Death / Dead Nocturnes: The Complete Poems*, trans. D. M. Stroud (Saru, 2004). SUPPLEMENT: Salvador Novo, *Pillar of Salt: An Autobiography with 19 Erotic Sonnets*, intro. Carlos Monsiváis, trans. Marguerite Feitlowitz (Texas, 2008).

Richard Bruce Nugent: "Smoke, Lilies, and Jade" (English)

It struck me upon rereading "Smoke, Lilies, and Jade" how much Richard Bruce Nugent (1906–1987) and other writers (and painters) associated with the Harlem Renaissance of the 1920s and 1930s anticipated the New York School of poets (and painters). Nugent was the only one out of the closet, but other important poets were also gay: notably Claude Mc-

Kay, Langston Hughes, and Countee Cullen. They were city poets. They formed a coterie of friends who supported each other and competed with each other. (The relationship between Wallace Thurman's novel *Infants of the Spring* and Nugent's novel *Gentleman Jigger* shows how complicated their friendships could be.) They were multi-talented, also writing novels and plays. Nugent was a painter, a dancer, and an actor (part of the cast of the original *Porgy and Bess*). How much like Frank O'Hara he sounds in a line from his prose poem like the following: "Harold was there...and Constance and Langston and Bruce and John...there was Mr. Robeson." He quotes part of "one of Hughes's poems" ("Boy," not published until 1928). Thurman similarly used real names and transparent pseudonyms in his novel *Infants of the Spring*, 1932. Their Harlem readers would, of course, have recognized the references instantly. Nugent was the only writer who was also a serious painter. Other gay artists include Beauford Delaney and James Richard Barthé, along with the honorary Harlemite, photographer Carl Van Vechten.

Nugent's poem was published in the one issue of *Fire!!* in fall 1926. Its explicit bisexuality created a minor furor—though "Not quite enough criticism," Thomas Wirth (15) tells us, "to get the publication banned in Boston (which might have generated enough publicity to rescue the fledgling quarterly from the financial difficulties that ended its run with the first issue)." The piece sketches out a bare narrative: nineteen-year-old Alex (generally seen as a self-portrait) is picked up by a Spanish-speaking youth (based on Juan José Viana, a kitchen employee in the hotel where Nugent was working as a bellhop) using a classic line, but in Spanish to Alex's delight ("perdone me señor tiene usted fósforo"). They proceed to Alex's room and bed. Alex nicknames the youth Beauty; Beauty in turn calls Alex "Dulce." However, Alex is also pulled toward Melva. He concludes, "one *can* love two at the same time," but clearly Beauty has the stronger attraction. The poem is filled with lush imagery, unexpected uses of color, and varied levels of sensory appeal ("a field of blue smoke and black poppies and red calla lilies"). It takes the form of long paragraph–stanzas composed of short clauses and phrases separated by ellipses. One such unit ends:

> Alex opened his eyes...into Beauty's...parted his lips...Dulce...Beauty's breath was hot and short...Alex ran his hand through Beauty's hair...Beauty's lips pressed hard against his teeth...Alex trembled...could feel

Beauty's body...close against his...hot...tense...white...and soft...soft...soft....

An excerpt was used in Isaac Julien's 1989 film *Looking for Langston*. Spoken aloud, one hears even more clearly its inventive poetic qualities.

Nugent had used the same form for "Sahdji," another prose poem, included the year before in an anthology edited by Alain Locke, the gay "dean" of the Harlem school of writers. Set in Africa, Sahdji's story is narrated by an unidentified artist. She is "the favorite wife" of the chieftain Konombju and deeply in love with him. Mrabo, a son by another wife, is in love with her. A fourth enters the narrative: "Numbo idolized Mrabo...Numbo was a young buck...would do anything to make Mrabo happy." One day on a hunt, when all eyes are focused on the prey, Konombju is killed by an arrow. His funeral pyre is prepared: Sahdji "looked at Mrabo and smiled...slowly triumphantly" and joins her husband in death: "Mrabo stood unflinching...but Numbo, silly Numbo had made an old man of Mrabo." Dr. Locke would have understood the two men's relationship. Both poems are reprinted in Wirth's introduction to the multi-talented Nugent, which includes reproductions of his art along with his creative work and historical reminiscences.

Wirth also includes more conventional poems. In "You Think to Shame Me," the loved one tries to put down the speaker for his "promiscuity." He admits:

> True—many is the body I have explored
> Feverishly with my lips and tongue
> And many are the lips I've kissed.
> Many the boy who, fever-fired, searched
> With blind weapon to pierce me through.
> And did—with my assistance.

But he defends himself: "such happenings are a search for a real thing, / And each is the real thing until done and proved not." He remembers too how they met: in a men's room, the other disgusted by the graffiti written on the wall above the urinals. Questioned how men could so expose themselves, the speaker proposes some answers, but the poem closes with his own rather ambiguous question to the other.

Wirth ends the volume with an interview he had with Nugent towards the end of his life. Nugent talked about another 1925 poem, "Shadow," included in the volume, which he said had been misread as being about race when actually it was about society's stigmatization of the homosexual.

The poem includes the lines, "A shadow am I / Growing in the light, / Not understood as is the day." In the interview he asserted, "I have never been in what they call 'the closet.' It has *never* occurred to me that it was anything to be ashamed of, and it never occurred to me that it was anybody's business but mine." Nugent did complicate his life by falling in love with a woman, marrying her, but never satisfying her sexually. Outlasting all his peers, he became the final historical voice of the vibrant movement. He is the central figure in Rodney Evans's 2004 film *Brother to Brother*.

TEXT: Richard Bruce Nugent, *Gay Rebel of the Harlem Renaissance: Selections from the Work*, ed. Thomas H. Wirth (Duke, 2002). REFERENCE: A. B. Christa Schwarz, *Gay Voices of the Harlem Renaissance* (Indiana, 2003).

Sandro Penna: Boy-Love Poems (Italian)

Unlike the Uranians with all their cloying sentimentality, their pretense about the purity of their motives, Sandro Penna (1906–1971) has the virtue of admitting forthrightly that he was turned on by underage Italian lads found on the streets, in movie theaters, out in the country. He wrote (from *This Strange Joy*),

> Always boys in my poems!
> But I can't talk about anything else.
> Everything else bores me.
> I can't sing you Salvation Army songs.

Jack Shreve cites an interview in which Penna insisted that he was a pederast, not a homosexual (Malinowski, 297). When he gives an age for a boy in his poems it is always between twelve and fifteen. Adolescents are not the only theme of his poetry. He describes the countryside, alludes to small events, mentions journeys, muses over the past, and expresses a sense of loss and isolation. Death is ever present. But contacts with boys, sudden glimpses of them, are the major theme. Penna is always discreet about sex, however, and leaves his reader to imagine naked couplings; his language, though colloquial, is never vulgar.

His first collection, because of the fascist government, did not appear until 1938. It was followed by others after the war until he had published over 400 poems. They are all short, chiseled works, ranging from two to twenty lines. Much admired in his lifetime, his work was championed early on by the bisexual (but closeted) poet Umberto Saba. After the war he met Pier Paolo Pasolini as a result of the latter's favorable review of his second collection, and the two became friends. According to Gregory Woods, for many years the two men competed "to see who could make love with the greater number of boys along the overgrown banks of the Tiber and in the scattered urinals of Rome's ugly urban landscape" (Summers, 542). Woods records also that in 1956 Penna met a fourteen-year-old boy, Raffaele Cedrino, "with whom he formed a relationship that lasted until 1970" (Haggerty, 675). According to translator George Scrivani (10), Penna died of "an accidental overdose of sleeping medicine."

There is no comprehensive edition of his poetry in English. Four volumes of selected poems have been published, each titled after one of his poems. W. S. Di Piero's *This Strange Joy*, 1982, with 121 poems, provides the only bilingual text. Scrivani's selection of sixty-four poems, *Confused Dreams*, 1988, is published in a tiny edition just right for sticking in your shirt pocket before taking a hike or going on a plane ride. Blake Robinson includes 135 poems, along with twenty-three prose pieces, in *Remember Me, God of Love*, 1993. Though he does not give us the Italian, he does identify the source of each poem. More recently Peter Valente chose 161 poems for *A Boy Asleep under the Sun*, 2014. He notes that they are not literal translations; what he has done is to take the original poem, rethink it in English, and then record its essence. There is much overlapping, enough to make me aware that translating Penna is not as easy as it would seem.

As for which volume to recommend, I go back and forth between Di Piero's and Scrivani's. The latter offers the most naked boys, including several gems about cruising that all the others omit. With Scrivani we are permitted to accompany the poet "into the cool / of a railway urinal," where he is "Ready now to abandon / body and soul / amid radiant white porcelain" (misspelled *procellan*). He remembers how on one such occasion "The kid left the urinal / with his sex / still hanging out." He calls it "adorable negligence." Yet another poem records a moment probably just before or during the war in which

The rose in all its glory
wasn't half so beautiful
as when he made love

to the sleepless sentry
in that crowded
urinal at dawn.

The poet delights in catching boys unaware in the streets or fields while they are pissing. And once he catches a boy as

He left the field abruptly,
still half naked,
and immediately disappeared.
In the warmth of that moment,
a warm odor remained,…
a few flies—
among them, me.

As he says,

The sexual problem
has occupied my whole life.
Whether it will turn out
good or bad,
I ask every chance I get.

If his volume just did not have so many typos.

There are plenty of boys in Di Piero's choices. But the final two words in one of his translations—"A sudden wind blew up. And my sweet rough / summer friend got up from the grass, /but already hot, completely dressed"—seems emblematic of his taste. True, the poem ends with a hint of nakedness, but very discreetly so:

We made a warm bed our playground.
But in sleep we fell in love with caves again.
Later, white in the wind, a lonely handkerchief
flashed in the night.

Such handkerchiefs show up periodically in Penna's poems, emblematic of desire fulfilled.

The last two lines of a quatrain that Di Piero translates are worthy of being engraved on a monument to the poet:

I'm always standing by a window,
always so much in love with life.
Joining words to men was the brief
adequate gift the gods gave me.

TEXTS: Sandro Penna, *Confused Dream*, trans. George Scrivani (Hanuman, 1988); *This Strange Joy: Selected Poems*, trans. W. S. Di Piero (Ohio State, 1982).

W. H. Auden: *The Platonic Blow*; Love Poems (English)

I must have known fairly early on that Wystan Hugh Auden (1907–1973) was gay; I'm pretty sure I knew about Chester Kallman by the time I was in graduate school. By then I must also have read *The Platonic Blow* (now more often known as "A Day for a Lay") since it was published in 1965. So why did I not realize how much gay love poetry Auden had written? In part, it is because his poetry is gender-neutral, and in the 1960s we were innocents. I must have been in my late thirties before it sank in that the "sleeping head" in "Lullaby" is male ("Lay your sleeping head, my love, / Human on my faithless arm"). As late as 1994 it took the movie *Four Weddings and a Funeral*, in which John Hannah reads "Stop All the Clocks" ("He was my North, my South, my East and West"), to cause me to pay attention to that poem. In part also it was because I knew mostly the anthology pieces, and other than "Lullaby" they were seldom Auden's love poems. Of course, had I read Humphrey Carpenter's biography when it appeared in 1981, it would not have taken me so long.

As early as age fifteen Auden was sexually attracted to school mates. At Oxford he was the center of a gay circle including the novelist Christopher Isherwood, the poet Stephen Spender, and the journalist Tom Driberg (who introduced him to Eliot's poetry, a major influence on his own). He was sexually active, freely seeking anonymous pickups when the occasion arose, but almost from the beginning he was seeking love. His crushes yielded his first gay love poems, some of which Carpenter reproduces. Many found their way into subsequent publication, often with a different or no title. Since Auden tended to either discard or extensively revise earlier poems as he compiled successive editions, no one volume meets the needs of a gay reader. We are stuck for the moment with Edward Mendelson's 1976 edition of *The Collected Poems*. If you want to be complete, for the earliest poems you have to turn to his edition of *The English Auden* also. Working from Carpenter and consulting John Fuller's

Commentary, I come up with the following candidates to consider for a volume of Auden's erotic poetry.

The earliest love poems that he chose to conserve are "The Letter" and "The Secret Agent." So guarded as to be emotionally and linguistically obscure, they were written for either of two youths who did not respond to his sexual overtures, so it is not surprising that a sense of frustration hangs over both poems. Upon leaving Oxford, he spent a time in Berlin, which he described as "the buggers [sic] daydream" (Carpenter, 90). There he had a series of affairs with various boys. One Kurt Groote apparently made a special impression. He is mentioned by name in the first part of "1929" (as is Gerhart Meyer, another of his lovers) and is the subject of "Too Dear, Too Vague." Mendelson inserted a "short" written during this time into the *Collected Poems*. It reads in full:

> I'm beginning to lose patience
> With my personal relations;
> They are not deep,
> And they are not cheap.

Auden also wrote "This Loved One," which mocked Isherwood's affair with a Berlin boy.

Upon returning to England, Auden took up the role of schoolteacher in Helensburgh, Scotland. "What's in your mind" would seem to date from this time. The poem urges an unidentified "D.W." (the initials are penciled on Auden's personal copy of the poem) to use his "great big serpent" to strike at the poet's "heart." Carpenter (131) maintains that Auden "had no affairs with pupils, but only with [a] young man who was in his late teens and lived near the school," whom he referred to as "a chum." Poems which grew out of this affair include "That night when joy began" and "For what as easy." The first returns to the battleground imagery of "The Secret Agent," as do many of Auden's poems at the time. Fuller (173) reads it thus: "Night is associated with sexual tumescence ('narrowest veins'), morning with the end of the one-night stand. The lovers expect to be challenged by the morning as by a sentry, but, unbelievably, peace has been made: now they can see no end to their love."

In the fall of 1932 Auden changed posts and began teaching in Colwall, England. Initially, no love interest was in sight, and he sought sex on trips out of town. Then, according to Carpenter (157), in 1933 he fell in love, again with someone much younger. From this crush came a series of sonnets that he published but did not collect. Fuller says the poem "Through the Looking-Glass" also grew out of the infatuation. The poet gazes upon a portrait of the boy painted by the school's art teacher and, narcissistically, sees his younger self in the image. Freudian theory comes into play as the poem turns into self-analysis, but hope is held out that "the birth of natural order and true love" may yet be celebrated. The sonnet "Meiosis" comes from the same period, but here the poet addresses the sperm released in the moment of orgasm, leaving the reader free to imagine pretty much anything he wishes about the pair involved.

Other writing projects took Auden's attention. Not until 1936–37 did he bring forth further love poems. But four he collected from this period—"Dear, though the night is gone," a dream poem; "Fish in the unruffled lakes"; "Stop all the clocks," though in its initial appearance in a play it was recited by a woman), and "Lullaby"—are some of his most powerful verse. He also addressed a poem to the sexually timid composer Benjamin Britten ("Underneath an abject willow"), urging him to "Strike and you shall conquer." In the context of these serious examinations of the mysteries of the heart, the satirical "Uncle Henry" seems out of place at first. It portrays a lisping caricature of an old auntie who, "Weady for some fun," regularly leaves his wife to take off for Mediterranean cities

    Where I'll find a fwend,

don't you know, a charmin' cweature,

    like a Gweek God and devoted:

        How delicious!

It ends with a toast "to women for they bear such / lovely kiddies!" Auden delivers a different kind of putdown to the American novelist Frederick Prokosch, who had printed some of his poems in limited editions. Prokosch, proud of his genital endowment, sent Auden a number of nude photographs, clearly hoping to entice the poet into a sexual encounter. Instead, in *Letter to Lord Byron*, Auden makes fun of him (though not by name) for dropping into the mail his "photo in the rude." The presence of these poems serve to remind us how camp permeates much of Auden's work from early on.

In 1939 Auden and Isherwood emigrated to the U.S. (Auden was naturalized in 1946.) Here he began a new chapter in his love life. In April the two were part of a program for the League of American Writers. Harold Norse showed up with his boyfriend, the eighteen-year-old Chester Kallman. The youths sat on the front row and blatantly flirted with the Englishmen. According to Carpenter (257), "A short time later, Kallman told

Norse: 'Wystan is in love with me.'" Their affair lasted, after its fashion, till the end of Auden's life. Carpenter (259) tells us that "Chester was sexually 'well hung' which always appealed to Auden," whose favorite sexual activity was sucking off his partner. Unfortunately for their sexual compatibility, Kallman's "preference in bed" was "anal passive" (Carpenter, 261). A flood of love poems now came flowing from Auden's desk: "The Prophets," "Like a Vocation," "The Riddle," "Heavy Date," "Law like Love," "The Hidden Law," "Warm are the still and lucky miles," "If I Could Tell You," "Leap Before You Look." The poet cannot believe his good luck; he harbors doubts of all kinds about the affair, including whether it will last; but he convinces himself "we / Our life-day long shall part no more." And then, not two years into the relationship, Auden discovered that Kallman was going to bed with another man. His idealism was shaken. For him their relationship was nothing less than a marriage. "In Sickness and in Health" he had pledged "That this round O of faithfulness [i.e., their wedding rings] we swear / May never wither to an empty nought." Kallman, callously or realistically, decreed that the two men could remain friends, but they would never have sex again, that he, Kallman, would search for sexual satisfaction elsewhere and Auden could do the same. Though unhappy about the situation, Auden accepted Kallman's conditions. Having started teaching again, he availed himself of students and, when they were not available, male prostitutes. Poems from this period include "Though determined Nature can," "My second thoughts condemn," "Alone," "Canzone," and "The Lesson." By the time of the postwar poem "In Praise of Limestone," he seems to have made peace with the situation. Much later, in "The More Loving One," he writes: "If equal affection cannot be, / Let the more loving one be me."

In 1948 Auden wrote *The Platonic Blow*, i.e., the ideal or nonpareil blowjob. Perhaps because the title can so easily be misunderstood, it has come to be called, almost universally, "A Day for a Lay" (from the opening line). Auden never publicly claimed it. Nor did he disclaim it, and copies circulated among his friends. One of these was published in 1965. It is a pity that Mendelson did not include it at least as an appendix (especially since he claims the text is defective), but it is readily available in a number of anthologies. Carpenter (359), in an uncharacteristic prissy tone, judges: "As poetry, 'The Platonic Blow' is negligible; as pornography, it has been much admired by readers with similar sexual preferences to Auden's." The poem is vintage Auden in its form (even if copied from Charles Williams), its ingenious internal and end rhymes, and its imagery. Its thirty-four quatrains, written in various pentameter measures, rhyme *abab*. The poem opens with a pickup in the street: Bud, a twenty-four-year-old mechanic from Illinois. The poet invites him to his home. After a beer, he makes his move: "I found what I hoped. I groped. It was large"—indeed, "Nearly nine inches long and three inches thick." Both naked,

> We aligned mouths. We entwined. All act was clutch,
> All fact, contact, the attack and the interlock
> Of tongues, the charms of arms. I shook at the touch
> Of his fresh flesh. I rocked at the shock of his cock.

The poem proceeds to detail the poet's homage to Bud's genitals, taint, and hole, until finally "His ring convulsed round my finger. Into me, rich and thick, / His hot spunk spouted in gouts, spurted in jet after jet." In 1974, using voice-over to recite the entire poem, Peter de Rome's movie *Adam & Yves* visually and explicitly enacts the actions being described.

Mendelson was not unwilling to insert several other poems into his posthumous edition that prove Auden's interest in sex continued to be strong. "Three Posthumous Poems," 1964–67, describe different kinds of hustlers he sought as release. In "Aubade," "happy / after a night of love," he accepts himself as "an ecto-endomorph / cock-sucker." Writing to Kallman about his loneliness in New York ("Minnelied"), he says, "steps can be taken, even / a call-boy can help." "Glad" recounts his troubled but rewarding experience with a married Viennese youth named Hugerl K—. Carpenter (396–97) describes the complicated relationship in his biography and records (451) that Hugerl and his wife attended Auden's funeral. Using the haiku form, Auden wrote during this same period: "Loneliness waited / For Reality / To come through the glory hole." In "Talking to Myself" (which he dedicated to Dr. Oliver Sacks), Auden examines his naked body. Looking at his penis, he feels, "*His architecture / should have been much more imposing: I've been let down!*" But he has "gotten used to Your proportions," and he concludes that, "all things considered, I might have fared far worse." He goes on,

> Seldom have You been a bother. For many years
> You were, I admit, a martyr to horn-colic [an involuntary erection]
> (It did no good to tell You—*But I'm not in love!*):
> how stoutly, though, You've repelled all germ invasions,
> but never chastised my tantrums with a megrim.

TEXTS: W. H. Auden, *Collected Poems*, ed. Edward Mendelson (Random House, 1976). Gavin Geoffrey Dillard, ed., *A Day for a Lay: A Century of Gay Poetry* (Barricade, 1999), 40–44. REFERENCES: Humphrey Carpenter, *W. H. Auden: A Biography* (Houghton Mifflin, 1981). John Fuller, *W. H. Auden: A Commentary* (Princeton, 1998).

Jean Genet: Poems to Criminals (French)

In 1948 Jean Genet (1910–1986) collected his six poems in a volume called simply *Poèmes*. They form three pairs, each inspired by a different French youth whom Genet found sexually and emotionally attractive, but they are meditative rather than narrative. The first pair was inspired by Maurice Pilorge, whom Genet probably knew only by hearsay. In 1939 at age twenty-five (Genet thought he was twenty) he was sentenced to the guillotine for a murder he had committed, its motive disputed. "The Man Condemned to Die" was written, and published as an unbound booklet, in 1942 while Genet was in the Fresnes prison for theft. The poet summons up his memory of Pilorge and proceeds to create a number of vignettes that mingle sex and violence:

> This apparition comes forth from the awesome sky
> Of love's crimes. Child of the depths
> Astonishing splendors will be born from your body,
> Perfumed cum from your charming cock.

Biographer Edmund White (180–81) sums up its importance: "The poem is the prototype for Genet's later fictional explorations of prison. Already in this first composition Genet touches on several familiar themes. He invokes Devil's Island as a tropical haven for loves between convicts. He equates the solitary masturbator in prison with the inspired writer. He dreams of a powerful, pitiless, sadistic man and his pretty blond Ganymede. He elevates homosexual love in general and fellatio in particular with poetic figures derived from Villon, Ronsard, Baudelaire and Rimbaud. He explores androgyny, or more precisely in rapid alternation he assigns masculine and feminine qualities to the same youth." He blasphemes by demanding his penis be venerated the same way the Virgin is (White points out that "most of the words for the male sex organ happen to be feminine"). And the poet prays not to the Christian god but to Hermes, who among other attributes was the "patron of thieves." The fifty-two quatrains (rhyming *abab*) and four cinquains (rhyming *abbab*) mix "traditional eloquence" and raw sexual slang. It is an audacious beginning for an unconventional literary career.

In 1944 Genet arranged to have the poem printed properly, along with a new one, "Funeral March," as *Secret Songs*. The new poem is a series of thirteen love poems to Pilorge, cast in various verse forms. As such, they are much more accessible on a first reading. Their purpose as a whole may be summed up by a quatrain in Section 7:

> To keep you pleased O gamin of a deep beauty
> I will remain dressed to the very day I die.
> Your soul leaving your decapitated body
> Will find in my strong body a white [or blank] resting site.

In 1943, while serving time in the Santé prison, Genet met twenty-three-year-old Lucien-Guy Noppé. According to White (226), "The encounter with Guy inspired Genet to begin writing *Miracle of the Rose*" for which he served as the model for Bulkaen. (He also appears as Guy in *The Thief's Journal*.) Thus his presence to some extent must lie behind Genet's third poem, "The Gallery," though "most of the poem is a homage to a murderer called Harcamone, …the name of the hero of *Miracle of the Rose*" (White, 222). The poem, however, was dedicated to Nikos (Nico) Papatakis, the manager of a Saint-Germain-des-Prés nightclub whom Genet met in 1944. Sartre cites Genet as saying: "I wrote two poems that had no relationship one to another. I mixed them, hoping to give more obscurity, more density to my verses" (White, 282–83). Perhaps for this reason the scene keeps shifting from the boat rowed by prison slaves to woods where "a golden doe shakes with fear" to some indefinite space. Sexuality pulses through the poem. I don't think I have ever read another in which flatulence plays such a part.

> Harcamone with green arms prestigious queen flying
> Above your scent by night and the woods woken up
> By horror of his name this mourning convict sings
> On my ship and his song leaves me broken-hearted.

White (222) further complicates the poem by revealing that "golden doe" is prison slang for "a runaway boy…who has been sodomized for the first time." For him the major theme is transformation. Genet's fourth poem,

"The Parade," addresses Guy directly. In one long passage the image of the rose dominates. But I confess: just as I think I am following Genet's rapid changes of thought, he slips away from me. The poem ends: "But to roam my body take off your shoes." I don't seem to have the gift of Genetic barefootedness.

The last pair of poems were inspired by the eighteen-year-old bisexual Lucien Sénémaud, whom Genet met in 1945—either through the actor Jean Marais, in prison, or on the Cannes beach. He also appears in *The Thief's Journal*. The first poem for him (though printed last in the collection) was "The Fisherman of Suquet." (Suquet is the old quarter of Cannes, originally inhabited mostly by fishermen.) Language upwells from the poet, deeply in love: "I gush out and become swamp wanting edge / When the will-o'-the-wisps turn blue at night / Tongue of fire watching over my passage." At times the human situation is very concrete, very specific, usually sexual; at other times the figures succumb to a surge of romantic images to be felt rather than analyzed. Prose and poetry alternate; a miniature surrealistic drama plays out between "the thief" and "the tree," "the night," and "the gunner." White (284) judges, "If 'The Fisherman of Suquet' is, despite frequent lapses, Genet's best poem, it succeeds because it is fully dramatized and generally abandons rhyme and metre, which Genet now manipulates with perfect naturalness." The other poem dedicated to Sénémaud is "A Song of Love." Again we have a flood of images, symbols, taken from Genet's private mythology. In the opening quatrain he evokes a celestial shepherd in wintertime, a penis coated with frost from the poet's breath, and daybreak. Before the godlike creature before him the poet is ready to prostrate himself. He accepts his abuse. Such also provides the poet his strength. The poem, by the way, has no relationship to the movie *A Song of Love* (*Un chant d'amour*) which Genet filmed in 1950. But the short film was shot in Papatakis's nightclub, and Sénémaud is one of the prisoners.

Two different translations of the complete poems appeared in 1981. I was in at the beginning of Steven Finch's *Treasures of the Night*—but then I also later knew Paul Mariah, whose last issue of *ManRoot* had multiple translators. As a special feature, it has two different versions of "A Song of Love," one by Frank O'Hara and one by Paul. Jeremy Reed and George Messo published their translation of *The Complete Poems* in 2001, but it appears to be unavailable in the U.S. (I have not seen it.) Winston Tong and Bruce Geduldig's rhyming translation of "The One Condemned to Death" appears in Gavin Dillard's *A Day for A Lay*.

TEXT: Jean Genet, *Treasures of the Night: The Collected Poems*, trans. Steven Finch (Gay Sunshine, 1981). REFERENCE: Edmund White, *Genet: A Biography* (Knopf, 1993).

Paul Goodman: *Hawkweed* (English)

I found Paul Goodman's (1911–1972) *Hawkweed* in a now defunct bookstore in downtown San Antonio in 1968, the year after it was published. I probably pulled the modest green-covered paperback off the shelf because of the impact of the author's counterculture treatise *Growing Up Absurd*. I vaguely knew also that he was one of the founders of gestalt psychology. My eyes dilated as I read conventional-looking poems filled with the kind of language I had previously encountered only with Ginsberg. Scott McLemee explains, "traditional verse forms (such as sonnets and haiku) and elevated diction are...mixed with colloquial dialect, street scenes, ...descriptions of 'cruising' and casual sexual encounters" (Summers, 334). For example, Sonnet 44 begins:

Transfigured both the fucked and the fucker's face
no longer beautiful, terrible, austere,
more alike than people otherwise appear,
every breath draws nearer the animal race.

I lugged the paperback around with me for years and gave it up only after I verified that all its poems had made it into the thematically arranged *Collected Poems*. I confess that upon now rereading them for the first time in a long time, I am not as enthralled as I originally was.

Goodman's fiction is autobiographical, but no comprehensive biography of the writer exists. Kingsley Widmer provides a chronology in his largely unsympathetic study of the work, but it is light on names and relationships. Goodman was bisexual; it is probably fair to say, however, that he loved males and used females. Rejecting the institution of marriage on principle, he was in two common-law relationships for thirty-five years and fathered three children. But he was always in search of male partners, ceaselessly cruising to the point of being a nuisance. He was fired from three teaching jobs, including one at Black Mountain College, for his sexual relationships with students. In 1949 while at Berkeley he took Robert Duncan's boyfriend Jerry Ackerman (resulting in Duncan's "The Venice Poem"). Lots of first names are dropped in his poems, but from the evidence of Jonathan Lee's documentary film *Paul Goodman Changed My Life*, 2011, there never was a community of lovers; rather lots of casual encounters. Wives and children are interviewed for the film, but no male lover comes forth to talk about their relationship. In 1969 Goodman published an essay "The Politics of Being Queer" in *Nature* magazine. His comparison of gays to African Americans using the N-word must have jarred sensibilities even then. Some of the poems are likewise unsettling for the same reason—often more so, as some of them also pander to sexual myths about size.

Gay poems weave in and out of *Hawkweed*; gay lines pop up unexpectedly in verse not otherwise about sexuality. As various interviewees in the film stress, sexual relations were fundamental to his understanding of himself as an anarchist. So, in his discussion of music, "Saint Cecilia's Day, 1941," he casually mentions how "Central Park, it once was wild and gay / with bushes for the privacy of love / before another Moses [Robert Moses] gave it laws." Even in the meditations he writes about his deceased son, "Sentences for Matthew Ready," he casually mentions sexual encounters with guys he has picked up. One's sexual life, in Goodman's view, is not something apart, hidden, from the rest of life; rather it is an important aspect of it. For Goodman there seems to have been no difference between *loving* and *making love*. Three sections of the *Collected Poems* are titled "Making Love." One page (277) captures perfectly Goodman's sense that one cannot separate emotions from sex. Of the two poems on the page, the first opens "His cock is big and red when I am there / and his persistent lips are like port wine." The second one begins, "We have a crazy love affair, / it is wanting each other to be happy."

Goodman seems to be almost forgotten these days. Joe LeSueur in his memoir of life with Frank O'Hara (121) commented, "Memoirs by his colleagues barely mention him. (Was he really so disliked, even hated, by his peers? It would appear so.)" Gregory Woods and Richard Howard are among the few to take his poetry seriously. Quite a bit of it is also read in the documentary film. The "Little Prayers" section of the *Collected Poems* concludes:

My genius, God, as an author
has been to bring it all together
   and show that even this
   unlikely combination can exist,
and now this mess of poems too.
Maybe—but I cannot know—
   the whole adds up to more
   than the parts of my disorder.
Maybe. Maybe not.

TEXT: Paul Goodman, *Collected Poems*, ed. Taylor Stoehr (Random House, 1973). REFERENCE: Kingsley Widmer, *Paul Goodman* (Twayne, 1980).

Tennessee Williams: Erotic & Autobiographical Poems (English)

How did this very naïve, rural Southern boy know so early that Tennessee Williams held an important key to my understanding of myself? At age sixteen I snuck out of a Beta Club convention in Asheville to see the film *The Rose Tattoo*. At age twenty, still closeted, I was explaining to my even more naïve friends at Wake Forest what *Suddenly Last Summer* was all about. I am clueless how I even came to my knowledge; sex was still a major mystery and would remain so for two more years. At age twenty-two I was supposed to be working on a thesis at the University of North Carolina on Faulkner, but I found myself reading Williams. Finally, I gave up and asked to change topics. UNC was fairly progressive, but the drama teacher assured me that Williams would not endure, that I would be better off writing about someone like Arthur Miller. The more courageous George Harper, a Yeats specialist, took me on but refused to let me explore *Streetcar* alone, as I wanted to. The results were *A Study of the Southern Neurotic Women in Three Plays by Tennessee Williams*: the writing is beautiful, if I may say so; the contents, not worth looking at. It was during this period that I found *In the Winter of Cities* with its distinctive cover in the same bookshop where Coleman Barks first encountered Rumi.

The young Thomas Lanier Williams (1911–1983) as poet was greatly influenced by Sara Teasdale and Edna St. Vincent Millay. He was twenty-five when a friend, another aspiring writer, introduced him to the poetry of Rimbaud, Crane, and Rilke. The first two had such an impact on him that they later became characters in plays of his: Crane in *Steps Must Be Gentle*; Rimbaud in *Will Mr. Merriwether Return from Memphis?* Rimbaud's sister is mentioned in the poem "Those Who Ignore the Appropriate Time of Their Going." Crane's encounter with a sailor appears in "Androgyne, Mon Amour," Crane and Rilke are coupled in "Evening," and Crane is invoked again in a poem first published in *The Collected Poems*. Williams stole Crane's own collected poems from the Washington University library in St. Louis and lugged it around for decades as an amulet before it eventually disappeared. By then, as the editors of his collected poems point out, he had learned how to subvert Teasdale and Millay to his own purposes. "The Siege" looks conventional in its use of quatrains rhyming *abcb*. But then the reader realizes that its subject is cruising and that its language is far from genteel as may first appear ("tottering pillar of blood" in the first line turns out to be an erection). By the end even the pretty rhyme scheme has disappeared. Coming to Williams after reading Rimbaud and Crane (as well as Auden's love ballads) leaves one fiercely aware how underrated his poetry is. It was originally gathered in three volumes: as part of *Five Young American Poets*, Third Series, 1944; *In the Winter of Cities*, 1956, expanded 1964; and *Androgyne, Mon Amour*, 1977. The same themes are found in his poetry as in his plays and fiction: time, mortality, problems of communication, loneliness, desire, intangible fears. Many of the poems are about his family and the people he's met. But the greatest part are highly personal, though more elliptical than his *Memoirs*.

Not surprising, the poems in *Five Young American Poets* that allude to sexual encounters are discreet. In "The Summer Belvedere," "Mornings on Bourbon Street," "Pulse," "The Dangerous Painters," "the fierce encounter at / the broken gate" is barely glimpsed. He became bolder in *In the Winter of Cities*. It contains two of his poems most anthologized in gay collections, about different kinds of sexual partners. "Life Story" describes the aftermath of sex between two men in tragic-comic terms. Each is eager to tell his story to the other; neither is interested in listening. It ends on the macabre note: "Well, one of you falls asleep / and the other one does likewise with a lighted cigarette in his mouth, / and that's how people burn to death in hotel rooms." Though it could be set in any city, "The Interior of the Pocket" describes one of the hustlers Williams saw in Italy. The type shows up again in his novel *The Roman Spring of Mrs. Stone* and in his next to last published poem.

Though it did not appear until 1982, "The Blond Mediterraneans: A Litany" seems to recall Williams's 1948 trip to Italy. His biographer Donald Spoto (147) writes that "he had taken a young Italian lover named Salvatore (who was called Raffaello in Williams's *Memoirs* and in letters)." By then Williams had had numerous boyfriends and had been in two longer relationships, one of which had ended just before the trip. After discussing the nature of Italian hustlers, Williams ends his poem on a cynical note: "you know, Salvatore, a smile, an embrace / is not much in the way of a contract, is it?" Williams had met Frank Merlo in 1947, but it was not until his return from this trip that they began sharing a house. He dedicated his play *The Rose Tattoo* to Merlo, whose presence can be felt everywhere in it. Williams's pet name for him was Little Horse, the title of a deceptively simple 1956 poem. Throughout their years together, Merlo remained faithful. Williams, however, rejected the idea of monogamy, and the relationship became increasingly rocky. Perhaps already these tensions show behind the plaintive last lines of this poem: "My name for him is Little Horse. / I wish he had a name for me." They established a sort of base in Key West. "The Island Is Memorable to Us," reflects their initial enchantment. "A Separate Poem" marks the troubled end: "Oh, yes, we've lost our island. / Time took it from us." Williams reviews their life together, allowing glimpses of what Merlo meant to him and of what he has lost, until at the end "When we speak to each other / we speak of things that mean nothing of what we meant to each other." In 1963 Merlo was diagnosed with terminal lung cancer and quickly died as Williams's own life spiraled out of control.

He may well have been thinking of Merlo as he wrote "Shadow Wood," with its damning last stanza:

> For tenderness I would lay down
> the weapon that holds death away,
> but little words of tenderness
> are hard for shadow man to say.

Merlo's ghost visits him in "His Manner of Returning." Williams shows him his Key West gazebo with a "brass plate" engraved with names of people "whom I've loved," including Merlo's own "between the rose vines that are beginning to climb"—to have the ghost retort, "Loved? You?" "Androgyne, Mon Amour" reviews his life; certain lines in particular seem to recall Merlo. There is also his poem about his 1962 trip to Tangier without Merlo to visit Paul and Jane Bowles: "Tangier: The Speechless Summer." His companion was the poet Frederick Nicklaus. Williams records his increasing boredom with the youth, but we get no hint of what Merlo's absence means to him.

Williams's libido clearly drove him until the end. He directly confronts sexual desire in "The Comforter and the Betrayer." The penis is an animal living in "the kingdom of dark," enveloped in "shadow," fearful of "the uncontested mystery of the gods" that is light. Williams contends, though, that one must "Trust / this betrayer. He is your only comfort." As he became more dependent on drugs and started hiring sexual companions, his gayness slipped more and more openly into his poems: "Young Men Waking at Daybreak," "You and I," "Wolf's Hour," "The Rented Room."

Across his life Williams was fascinated by religion and mythology. "The Christus of Guadalajara," clearly influenced by Crane, depicts a "womanish" figure who "whispers love and love" but seems incapable of action. "San Sebastiano de Sodoma" celebrates the martyr, not the painting, not forgetting to cite the legend that Sebastian was the lover of the Emperor Diocletian. "Orpheus Descending" focuses on the "broken" poet who learns "the passion there is for declivity in this world" before being "dismembered by Furies." Williams makes no mention of Orpheus's celebration of male-male love, perhaps not surprising given the fact that the poem was published in 1952. Williams returns to these figures, sometimes in disguise, repeatedly in his plays.

He left uncollected a poem that, nevertheless, became something of an anthem for him. Dating from 1941, it was published, without a title, by his first biographer in 1961. The opening stanza sounds a frantic note of optimism:

> I think the strange, the crazed, the queer
> will have their holiday this year,
> I think for just a little while
> there will be pity for the wild.

He speaks of "places known as gay," "secret clubs and private bars." The four quatrains build on this affirmation "before, with such a tender smile, / the earth destroys her crooked child." With the change of one line (to make it more affirmative) he incorporated the poem into a short play he worked on in the late 1950s, *And Tell Sad Stories of the Deaths of Queens*. But it had already formed the basis of an eighteen-stanza song sung between scenes in his short play *The Mutilated*. Unfortunately the editors of *The Collected Poems* chose not to reprint the entire work. The song is not quite yet a call for gay liberation, but it is the closest Williams gets in his poetry and is a far advance beyond the somewhat similar "Carrousel Tune": "Each of us here thinks the other is queer / and no one's mistaken since all of us are!"

TEXT: Tennessee Williams, *The Collected Poems*, ed. David Roessel & Nicholas Moschovakis (New Directions, 2002). REFERENCE: Donald Spoto, *The Kindness of Strangers: The Life of Tennessee Williams* (Little, Brown, 1985).

James Broughton: "Wondrous the Merge" (English)

James Richard Broughton (1913–1999) described himself as "a pansexual androgyne." (He was one of San Francisco's Sisters of Perpetual Indulgence: Sister Sermoneta.) He had his first gay experience before he was fifteen; he had his first straight experience when he was seventeen. He was lovers with Harry Hay, pioneering gay activist; Emil Opffer, Hart Crane's former lover; and Kermit Sheets, an actor and playwright; as well as Pauline Kael, later a renowned film critic, with whom he had a daughter. He married Suzanna Hart and fathered two more children. (The three-day marriage ceremony was filmed by Stan Brakhage.) Then in 1974, twenty-five-year-old Joel Singer entered his life. They were married by a minister in Canada in 1976 and remained partners until Broughton's death. Broughton was a member of the San Francisco literary renaissance, publishing his first collection of poetry in 1947, and was a founding member of the Art in Cinema movement, directing his first independent film in 1948. His 1968 film *The Bed* was one of the first to introduce full frontal nudity. (Since Byron–Verlaine–Casement led me into asides about penis size, I should report that with Broughton you can judge for yourself. There exist a whole series of nude photographs and films to choose from.) His gossipy autobiography *Coming Unbuttoned* covers his life until his meeting with Singer. A 2013 documentary film, *Big Joy: The Adventures of James Broughton*, offers insight into his life from the ending of World War II until his death.

Depending on which reference or anthology you consult, Broughton as a poet is not worth mentioning (Fone, Woods), is of minor importance (Dynes, Summers), or is a central figure in twentieth-century gay culture (Nelson *et al.*). Present consensus seems to be that his films are his most important contribution, though he insisted his films are poetry. (Seventeen are available on three DVDs.) Of his written word, Charles Krinsky writes: "Broughton's poems combine simple language with formal experimentation to express emotions ranging from optimism to defiant anger. They celebrate the human spirit as a force of nature but also depict the social and psychological constraints that impede personal liberation" (Haggerty, 145). *Packing Up for Paradise* was, with the help of Jim Cory, the last selection of his poetry that he made before his death. In Jeffery Beam's eyes, it ensures "Broughton's place among the great poetic mystics such as Rumi, Whitman, and Blake" (Nelson, *Contemporary*, 48). A section called "From the Gospel According to Big Joy" reveals its indebtedness to Rumi by its dedication to Coleman Barks.

Gay poems are scattered throughout the volume, but I wish to focus on the twenty poems, 1970–96, in the Ecstasies section, which reflects his life with Singer. (The section takes its name from a 1983 volume.) It opens with a statement of Broughton's outlook on life: "Sing Out for Eros." In it he extols the mind, the emotions, the body, sex, and their link to the spiritual: "Listen to your angels / ripening your secrets." It is followed by a pre-Singer poem, "Anthem of St. Priapus," that indicates his preparation to meet a male lover. The middle stanza implores another:

> Let me drink deep of thy sacred fountain
> its bitter-sweet honey-hot milk of love.
> Let me lie drunken at thy throbbing spring.
> This is the mouth and the taste of God.

The fourth poem recounts Broughton's meeting with Singer. In answer to Whitman's 1855 question, "Who need be afraid of the merge?" Broughton exclaims, "Wondrous the Merge." He says of Singer,

> Then on a cold seminar Monday
> in walked an unannounced redeemer
> disguised as a taciturn student
> Brisk and resolute in scruffy mufti

he set down his backpack shook his hair
and offered me unequivocal devotion.

The poem evokes Joseph Campbell's directive, "Follow your bliss." (Broughton also transcribed the statement as "Follow your own weird.") The description of their first days together from anyone else would sound like the scrawls of a lovesick teenager, but the mixture of concrete events and spiritual correspondents are in keeping with the poet's rhapsodic, and playful, vision. There follow a series of poems that further demonstrate Broughton's refusal to compartmentalize experience. His playfulness shows up most exuberantly in "Kingdom Come," its title a *double entendre*. The opening stanza reads: "While I bask in your radiating arms / my sore coccyx and my cool buns / warm their shivers against your loins." He compares Singer to a St. Christopher who provides him with "a new flight plan" that lifts them into planetary orbit. He renounces the need "to crave any further crown / when I reign supreme in a radiant kingdom— / the omnipotent warmth of your arms." The second half of the section of poems begins with "Once Upon" and "Two Adams in a Sonoma Wood." More poems celebrate "a habit of mutual excess" and the joys of "brisk dueting." The section concludes with mementoes of the couple's pilgrimage to Asia. In "Leaving the Taj Mahal" Broughton addresses the fact that "doubtless I shall have to die / before you [space] my young Beloved." He playfully begs Singer to construct "a transilluminated bed like this" when he does. In a sense, he received his wish: Singer has faithfully promoted Broughton's legacy. As the last poem in the section, a kind of coda written just three years before his death, says, they were, and are, "Twin flames ever in blissful blaze."

All poetry is performance pieces, none more so than Broughton's. He celebrates "Nipples and Cocks" with the gusto of Ginsberg. There is a "Song of the Phallus," in which the penis speaks: "I am the very fountainhead / of rapture and remorse." What first sounds like a children's rhyme, "This Little Duck"—which raises the questions, "When will my little duck grow up big" and "When will my duckling stand up straight"—becomes something altogether different when you change the vowel in *duck* and say the lines again. One of Broughton's last poems, "Memento of an Amorist" itemizes basic tenets: "I've never met a cock I didn't like"; "Say that I give compassionate attention / to mankind's need for a taste of bliss"; "I never look for a lover. I am one." Auden renounced his poem "September 1, 1939," in which he had written, "We must love one another or die." Broughton rebukes his dead contemporary by restoring the line at the end of his own "Shaman Psalm," verses (reprinted in *All*) recited across a short film of the same name made with Singer: "Love one another / or die."

TEXT: James Broughton, *Packing Up for Paradise: Selected Poems 1946–1996*, ed. Jim Cory (Black Sparrow, 1997). SUPPLEMENTS: James Broughton, *All: A James Broughton Reader*, ed. Jack Foley (White Crane, 2006); *Coming Unbuttoned* (Query, 2016).

Robert Friend: Narrative Poems (English)

Before I read *Dancing with a Tiger*, Robert Friend (1913–1998) was not even a name for me. The selection offers a sampling of six volumes of his published poems plus uncollected verse. Gabriel Levin's informative introduction provides an overview of his life as he moved from New York to Puerto Rico, later Europe, and finally Israel, where he taught at the Hebrew University of Jerusalem and had Palestinian lovers. Editor Edward Field's preface serves Friend less well. It could be entitled "I and Robert." Field offers little insight into the poet and provides no clue to his editorial principles. None of the three poems that Jim Elledge includes in his anthology *Masquerade* appears in Field's selection. Field's subheadings hint at some thematic principle at work, but it results in poems from Friend's first, 1941, volume jostling against poems not published until his final, 1995, one. We are told which original volume each poem comes from, but there is no explanation how the "uncollected poems" fit into Friend's opus. Thus, it is difficult to discern whether there was any progression in Friend's thought or technique. Field offers no explanation for omitting poems from the last chapbooks. (Levin, 16, tells us that *After Catullus* "vexed some of his friends and delighted others.") The ninety-three poems we are given, however, demonstrate clearly why Friend is worthy of our attention.

Let's start with the two most atypical ones. "The Teacher and the Indian" is a narrative of an uneasy relationship told in ten vignettes. A New York City freshman English professor takes interest in his only Native American student. After an afternoon in a bar together, "That night / they found themselves in a single bed." During their affair, the student takes his teacher to the Museum of Anthropology, where he proudly shows off artifacts from his people. He writes a series of remarkable mini-autobiographies. The professor learns that the student's first lover was ironically a cowboy. The student confesses to also having sex with a train engineer, "a rough character / who picked him up in a bar." Unlike the essays, conversation is only "empty talk," and the teacher grows bored. They have a few last fucks, including a brutal one in which the student for the first time takes his teacher anally. But the affair is over. Five years later, the student now an Army sergeant, they meet up again. They grope each other under the table at a public bar—"Happy hour! / Amiable, awkward, strangely innocent! / Their last together." Altogether different is the abstract "Thomas Triangle and Seymour Square," which humorously describes two very different types of lovers: "Triangles suffer pangs of pure fire. / Squares burn smokily / with desire, desire, desire." After cataloguing the various ways they differ, both personally (Seymour types his letters; Thomas writes his) and sexually (Thomas loves; Seymour goes to the hammam), the poet asks whether the two can ever form a relationship: "is there no circle of love / to enclose them both?"

A sort of autobiography emerges. "Ars Poetica" looks back to his first teaching experience in Puerto Rico. William Carlos Williams visits. Friend is set "to argue the cause of the sonnet," but the older poet "soon diagnosed the case" more accurately and points him in the direction of the male bathers enjoying the San Juan beach. The poet acknowledges in "The Perfect Fool": "my lower self, you are a perfect fool, / queer as they come, without a blush or shutter, / You itch, I scratch." But sex proves to be only sex ("The Bridge"), and love remains illusive ("At the Top"). In "The Punishment," the speaker recalls a straight man he was in love with. One day the straight guy, in revenge for some "great wrong," fucks the poet:

> It was not the punishment that I deserved.
> The real punishment came later
> when I realized that you would never
> punish me again.

He often muses upon the fact that no sooner does he find himself with someone than he wishes he were by himself again: in "Sleeping Alone" he wryly observes, "I dreamed of two / in a big wide bed," but having found someone,

> I dream of a single
> narrow bed
> cool and white
> where I can lie alone
> all night.

He seems to accept his inability to give himself to another ("The Irrational Source") and admits that he is trapped in a kind of narcissism ("The Truth"). One sees a progression in the tiger poems. In "In the Valley," 1941, the beast seems symbolic of the id let loose to threaten orderly life. In "The Tiger," 1964, it becomes more directly symbolic of sexuality itself, with all "the strategies of desire." In "Dancing with a Tiger," 1995, the beast deserts the poet, leaving him "strangely relieved / to find myself alone."

Friend pays tribute to his gay predecessors. Standing "At the Tomb of Oscar Wilde," he bemoans that gay life still has not moved beyond campy burlesque and fugitive meetings in urinoirs. "Two Moons over Taxco" would appear to empathize with Hart Crane's plight in Mexico. "Rereading Cavafy" reminds the poet of an experience he himself had with "a handsome young Greek" with whom he exchanged shirts ("Shirts"). "Alfred Chester" is an elegy to his friend who also emigrated to Israel. I particularly like "Housman's Venetian Visits." Obviously indebted to Richard Graves's biography, it opens, "I would like to imagine another love for Housman / that provided solace for his stubborn heart." Friend takes comfort, like I do, in the idea that, post-Jackson, Housman did not live a miserable life of chastity. Then there is Friend's witty three-liner "For Gabriel" (presumably Levin): "You show me yours and I'll show you mine. / Don't get me wrong. I mean our poems. / They, too, are a nakedness we must explore."

TEXT: Robert Friend, *Dancing with a Tiger: Poems 1941–1998*, ed. Edward Field (Menard, 2003).

Harold Norse: Poems about Various Subjects (English)

Norse's autobiography reveals his hurt at not being recognized as a major figure in cultural histories, of always being relegated to the fringes. He tries to establish his importance by reminding us of his role in bringing Kallman and Auden together; his friendships with Williams, Ginsberg, Baldwin; his introduction of Ian Sommerville to William Burroughs; his part in refining Brion Gysin's cut-up method of composition. He leaves the impression that he bumped into everyone who was someone (or going to be someone) in Greenwich Village, Rome, Paris, Tangier, Palma, and elsewhere. Repeatedly, he remembers famous writers and composers praising him for this or that achievement. Yet few memoirs mention the "feisty little Brooklynite sexpot" (Ned Rorem, *Knowing When to Stop*, 348), and he appears, if at all, in biographies only as a walk-on. Joe LeSueur in his book on Frank O'Hara (56) calls Norse "one of the great blowhards of American poetry." Born Harold Rosen (1916–2009), the illegitimate Norse created his last name as an anagram. His collected poems, *In the Hub of the Fiery Force*, 2003, make a dauntingly thick volume of 615 pages whose organization does not serve him well. The same is true of his two selected volumes: *Carnivorous Saint*, 1977, which, to quote Douglas Field, "established Norse as a leading gay liberation poet" (Hawley, 820), and *The Love Poems*, 1986. Norse badly needs an editor. And I'm not sure that he found the one called for in Todd Swindell, though his selection, *I Am Going to Fly through Glass*, chosen from across the entire collected volume, attempts to create a kind of autobiography.

A handful of Norse's poems stand up well. These include tributes to other writers: "Remembering Paul Goodman," "We Bumped Off Your Friend the Poet," about Lorca, "Dream of Frank O'Hara," and an excerpt from "Homo" about Byron, along with an attack on various oppressors of gays. I am bemused how he paid Jacques and me the ultimate homage by lifting and rearranging a great deal of our translation of Verlaine's "Dans ce café" as his own. His portraits of anonymous men linger in the mind: the shy attendant in "Gas Station," a fourteen-year-old boy in the supermarket in "Indian Summer Afternoon," a bullied boy who committed suicide in "Requiem for St. Ronnie Kirkland." Travel poems ("Now France," "Greek Islands") and pseudo-shamanistic poems ("I Am in the Hub of the Fiery Force") seem to me the weakest.

In his introduction to *Carnivorous Saint* Norse denounces a gay reviewer who criticized Winston Leyland's anthology *Angels of the Lyre* for categorizing the poets and stereotyping homosexuality. You can almost hear Norse snort as the writes, "while nobody complains about a straight volume or anthology of poems about sex and love, including all the gory details...somehow if a homosexual poet does the same, it's sordid and sleazy." The titles of some of the poems are indicative: "Mysteries of the Orgy," "Naked Men in Green Heated Water," "Let Go and Feel Your Nakedness," "The Gluteus Maximus Poems" and the saucy "Prick Poem." The latter is simply a rhyming list of names we give our favorite organ, but it is a delight:

> Well, call it the cock, dick, prick or peepee
> crank, dork, joint, pisser, sweetpea,
> tootsie roll, lollipop, weenie, piece of meat,
> sausage, salami, banana, somethin' to eat,

and so forth for five more couplets. Then there is the satiric "I'm Not a Man." It includes such lines as, "I'm not a man. I do not feel superior to women," "I'm not a man. I write poetry," and "I'm not a man. I don't want to destroy you." Apparently each time Norse read it aloud, he felt the need to stress that it was not autobiographical, presumable because of the line, "I have acne and a small peter." Indeed, a nude photograph of him, seemingly no longer available on the internet, proves the second half of the line is inaccurate. When I first read Norse in the late 1970s, he seemed like a major find. This time I understand why he is so largely ignored. In particular, Norse never really found a distinctive voice or a truly burning subject.

TEXT: Harold Norse, *In the Hub of the Fiery Force: Collected Poems of Harold Norse, 1934–2003* (Thunder's Mouth, 2003). SUPPLEMENT: Harold Norse, *Memoirs of a Bastard Angel: A Fifty-Year Literary and Erotic Odyssey* (Thunder's Mouth, 1989).

Robert Duncan: "The Torso" (English)

Grove Press's gay editor Donald Allen's groundbreaking anthology *The New American Poetry*, 1960, gave prominence to a set of affiliations that he had already begun defining in the press's *Evergreen Review*. He grouped postwar poets into the Black Mountain poets, the San Francisco Renaissance, the Beat Generation, and the New York poets. Though the groups were mixed in terms of gender and sexuality, gays were prominent in all four. Allen tied Robert Edward Duncan (born Edward Howard Duncan Jr., 1919–1988; adopted as Robert Edward Symmes) into the Black Mountain group but pointed out that he was also a member of the San Francisco group. Geographically, he belongs to the latter. In the late 1940s Duncan and two younger poets, Jack Spicer and Robin Blaser, launched the so-called Berkeley Renaissance. The excitement they created spread to other poets. Duncan provided links to Black Mountain students Jonathan Williams, the founder of Jargon Press, to Michael Rumaker, who wrote *Robert Duncan in San Francisco*, and to John Wieners. While living in Boston, Spicer and Blaser also became close to the mentally disturbed Wieners and to Steve Jonas. Michael Duncan and Christopher Wagstaff assembled a visual treat of the writers and painters associated with Duncan, 2013. Once Allen Ginsberg blazed into town, his larger-than-life personality dominated much of the subsequent San Francisco scene, but Duncan always remained a force. And he must always be credited as the first important writer to voluntarily out himself nationally, in his essay "The Homosexual in Society," *Politics*, March 1944. Illustrative of the consequences of such a bold act at the time, in October John Crowe Ransom, editor of the *Kenyon Review*, rejected Duncan's poem "An African Elegy," after having already accepted it for publication, writing, "We are not in the market for literature of this type." (Being the drama queen I can be, when I learned this fact, I marched over to my bookshelves, seized Ransom's *Selected Poems*, and dumped it into the trash can. I have never read Ransom since.)

Duncan was cross-eyed; everyone who encountered him commented on his double vision. (How he was drafted at the beginning of the war remains a mystery to me; he received a dishonorable discharge when he announced he was a homosexual.) His life itself seemed wracked by strange cross-purposes. After a series of romances (including one with actor Robert De Niro's father), he was embraced by painter Burgess Collins, who went by the single name Jess. In 1950 they entered what they considered a marriage, which lasted until Duncan's death. But whereas Jess wanted monogamy, Duncan had a series of flings behind his back all his life, finding Jess's preference for "mutual masturbation and occasional oral sex" (Jarnot, 334) less than fully satisfying. These included brief liaisons with the poets George Stanley, Tom Savage, Aaron Shurin, and the Australian Chris Edwards, as well as other painters and various students. He even tried to seduce their straight roomer Stan Brakhage under Jess's nose, causing Jess to evict the future underground filmmaker. Something of an exhibitionist, Duncan stripped for a poetry reading in 1955 (Ginsberg later imitated him) and was fond of displaying his hairy back. At least one photograph exists on the internet of Duncan reading in the nude. After one particularly egregious infidelity on Duncan's part, Jess took revenge by seducing Blaser. That led to a growing rift between the two poets. Spicer and Duncan began to quarrel when Spicer felt Duncan was selling out. They ultimately became bitter antagonists. And poor James Broughton had to put up with Duncan's periodical outbursts of displeasure because of perceived affronts. The biographers of both Duncan and Spicer make similar comments. Lisa Jarnot (169) says simply, "Bay Area camaraderie went hand-in-hand with strife." Lewis Ellingham and Kevin Killian (366) record that, whereas "Competition and cooperation characterized the early poetic relations within the Berkeley Renaissance structure," "internecine struggle" prevailed among the San Francisco group to the point that, when Spicer died, "it was but a small turn for the remaining participants to focus angers upon each other."

Within Duncan's poetry, Terrence Johnson argues, "The theme of love so interacts with his other themes that any attempt to separate gay and nongay poems is meaningless" (Summers, 210). Also, because of the nature of Duncan's poetry, it is easy to miss gay references, they are so coded or indefinite. Jarnot describes the impact individual lovers had on individual poems. But she also remarks (343) on the fact that poems often resort to "ambiguity of subject…partly to shelter Jess from yet another infidelity." Unfortunately, there is no ideal collection to recommend for gay readers. The two-volume collected poems, 2012–14, is expensive. Robert Berthoff's selection leaves out a great many poems that are pertinent, but it is the most readily available. Perhaps its most regretful omissions are "The Venice Poem" (which grew out of his relationship with Jerry Ackerman, Spicer's boyfriend whom Duncan stole, only to lose him to Paul Goodman), "Sonnet 1" (an eighteen-line unrhymed poem about Dante's vision of "men / who lust after men"), and "These Past Years" (a review of his "sweet marriage" to Jess). Karl Stenger observes that Duncan's poems "leave the reader little room for compromise; one either loves them or hates them. While some critics have criticized Duncan for being mannered, tedious, pedantic, disorganized, or superficial, others have called him not only the most talented but also the most intelligent of modern poets" (Nelson, *Contemporary*, 137). My problem is that I find none of his work memorable. By constructing the poem as a field, he provides me no landmarks to order my pursuit of his thought. It bothers me that his series of poems called "Structure of Rime" have neither formal structure nor rhyme.

"The Torso," presumably written about Jess and published in *Bending the Bow*, 1968, seems to be his most anthologized gay poem. It is fairly representative of his work. Words cascade down the page, appearance substituting for form. It opens,"Most beautiful," and names three trees indigenous to California. After a space, we have "Is he…" (the ellipsis part of the line). Next comes three lines, italicized, from Gaveston's opening speech in Marlowe's Edward II. Another space precedes a series of lines about "Truth," "illusion," "chambers of my male body," and "an idea in Man's image," before an italicized question introduced by another ellipsis—"*…homosexual?*"—completes the line above: "Is he homosexual?" There follow references to "the treasure of his mouth," the "commingling" of their souls, "Paradise," and "a fire in me, [space] a trembling / hieroglyph." Then begins an inventory of the man's body. Duncan offers rhapsodic commentary about his lover's clavicle, nipples, navel, and pubic hair. The most we get about the penis is the flowery (pun intended) description of "the stamen of flesh in which his seed rises." Duncan acknowledges "a wave of need and desire." He then says, "This was long ago." Falling in love "has brought me into heights and depths my heart / would fear [space] without him." His lover's voice breaks in to assert his importance to Duncan's life. The poem concludes with Duncan's simple statement, "For my Other is not a woman but a man," followed by another line, again italicized, from Gaveston's speech about his happiness to return to his king. And that's pretty typical of the rest of Duncan's poems.

TEXT: Robert Duncan, *Selected Poems*, ed. Robert J. Bertholf, rev. ed. (New Directions, 1997). REFERENCES: Michael Duncan & Christopher Wagstaff, *An Opening of the Field: Jess, Robert Duncan, and Their Circle* (Pomegranate, 2013). Lewis Ellingham & Kevin Killian, *Poet Be like God: Jack Spicer and the San Francisco Renaissance* (Wesleyan, 1998). Lisa Jarnot, *Robert Duncan: The Ambassador from Venus* (California, 2012).

Rod McKuen: *Alone...* (English)

In the late 1960s, early 1970s, Rodney Marvin McKuen (1923–2015) achieved the unheard of for poetry: his collections became American best-sellers. The flower children reveled in his musings about sex and love. Meanwhile, the critics, including my colleagues in English, sneered at him. Accepting their assessment, I never bothered to check out any of his volumes. Then one day, years later, I was in a used-book store and came across copies of the paperback selections that he published 1974–83, illustrated with photographs of the hunky-looking author. I pulled one down to have a look. I was lucky, I now realize, that the volume I chose was *Alone...*, 1975. It took me only a few pages to realize: this guy is gay. Yet McKuen is conspicuous for his absence from gay literary history. What gives? Well, to be honest, I wouldn't be asking the question had I chosen another volume. Although there is not a one without some poems that yield greater pleasure when read from a gay perspective, McKuen does have a narrow range, and after a while his love poems all begin to sound alike. His penchant for concealing the gender of his partner can annoy, even if you accept McKuen's insistence that sexual labels narrow the person and limit his experiences. He steadfastly refused to identify himself as gay, straight, or bi. But he was active in the San Francisco Mattachine movement as early as 1953. The cover of his Crisco/Disco album *Slide – Easy In*, 1977, blows his cover, so to speak, and he took a public stance against Anita Bryant with his song "Don't Drink the Orange Juice." Later he was involved in AIDS fundraisers. And then there is the mystery of what part Edward McKuen Habib played in McKuen's life (he appears in a few late interviews and is named in the obituary). I think it is time for us to look at McKuen as a gay poet, even if we ultimately decide he is only a minor one.

Alone... (the ellipsis is part of the title) has the longest and most personal (if still guarded) introduction of the seven volumes. It opens with the prose poem "Solitaire," which mentions "the meatrack" so casually that you could miss the reference. Throughout the volume we find casual references that easily lend themselves to a gay reading: such phrases as "inch by inch the night" ("Thursday Evening"), "the shadows / that I've had to learn / to love" ("Shadows and Safety"), "moving in on strangers" and "the newfound friend" ("Video Tape"), "chased my nakedness / down a lonely beach" ("Kearny Street"), "spoken in a code" ("What Common Language"), "another blind man's breath" ("Eighteen"), and the statement "I need the sureness / of the shadow world again. / To make me whole" ("Where the Big Boys Play"). The poem "Holidays," about "Rented rooms"

 and people
 who forget your name
 before you finish
 going down the stairs,

makes sense only as a sexual encounter between two men. The same is true for "Advance / Retreat," which opens: "No woman held a man / the way that you / hold onto me just now." In "I Roll Better with the Night" he recalls

 Firm friendly hands
  slipping slowly
 into my back pockets,
 pressing hard and holding me.

The invitation in "Fiore / 1812"—"Come into me / as I've lately come / inside of you"—could be read spiritually, I suppose, but it is more easily read sexually. In "Thursday Evening" he exults,

 It's somehow
  miracle enough
 that Amstel beer in
  Amsterdam
 made us drunk enough
 to meet at all.

In "Night Song" he wryly says that if one fails to pick up someone on a Saturday night, at least he has the consolation of the Sunday paper. A poem such as "Oakland Bus Depot, 1951" leaves ambiguous the "you" who "never arrived." Is it a friend he was supposed to pick up? Or is it a pickup that never occurs?

 Two poems that grew out of his experiences during the Korean war are pretty explicit. In "Soldier, One / Tagu, Korea – 1955" the poet passes another soldier, who "stands apart a little / from the rest." He raises the question: "Passing past each other / our eyes meet in challenge, / or is it recognition?" He hopes it was "recognition." "Private Spencer" describes a soldier whose "eyes are lonelier / than most." The poet watches him being cruised by a woman unaware that she is not "what he wanted / at all."

Even more explicit is the short poem "Closet," which is filled with word play. It bemoans those who

> …spend their lives
> in gyms around the world
> afraid to face the fact
> that what they really want
> is one, two,
>   maybe three
> trips around the world
> with Joe or Jack or Jim.

He is equally straightforward in "July 14." He remembers how he started to advise "Paul" that

> *it's ok to drop your pants*
> *to old men sometimes*
> *but I wouldn't recommend it*
>   *as a way of life.*

But then he reflects: "but who's to say which way is better / till they've been there / and come back safe."

What effect, if any, did his poetry have on youths searching for a sexual identity at the time? Is there any anecdotal evidence to show? Unlike Ginsberg's, it would have been safe to read and discuss in public. And it was readily available. A few articles published at the time of McKuen's death support the idea that he has had more influence on gay identity than we presently realize.

TEXT: Rod McKuen, *Alone…* (Pocket Books, 1975).

Allen Ginsberg: *Howl* (English)

Irwin Allen Ginsberg (1926–1997) would have been a poetic force no matter what, but the San Francisco Police Department unintentionally jump-started his national and international reputation. The poet read *Howl* before an audience at the Six Gallery in San Francisco on October 7, 1955, to great acclaim. Lawrence Ferlinghetti, owner of the City Lights Bookshop, sent him a note that, by implication, heralded him as the new

Whitman. Ferlinghetti published *Howl and Other Poems* in the spring of 1956. In June he was arrested for willfully and lewdly printing, publishing, and selling obscene and indecent writings. The case was tried without a jury in October 1957. The judge ruled the defendant as not guilty of the charges, one of the important cases from the period that began protecting gay free speech. Both *Time* and *Life* magazines followed the case. Even in rarified Wake Forest I knew about Ginsberg and Ferlinghetti. For years the forty-page collection was one of the books most often stolen from the A&I library, indicative of student interest in the poet's work. The poem that so shocked the poor police detective is now routinely included in college anthologies.

Howl is a quasi-mystic and righteously indignant incantation bewailing the state of post-war America. It is divided into four parts. The first, written in the past tense, describes America's destroyed children: "I saw the best minds of my generation destroyed by madness, starving hysterical naked." The second section, written in the present tense, seeks the source of their destruction. Moloch—"the Canaanite fire god, whose worship was marked by parents burning their children as propitiatory sacrifice" (Ginsberg's footnote)—becomes a metaphor of the forces ranged against the saintly counter-culture that Ginsberg is leading. In the third section (still in the present tense), addressed to Carl Solomon, an inmate in a New York psychiatric hospital, the poet identifies with the insane, the natural man in this fallen world. The poem concludes with a verse footnote, declaring that we must return to a kind of Edenic purity: "The world is holy! The soul is holy! The skin is holy! The nose is holy! The tongue and cock and hand and asshole holy!" Typical of the very personal nature of Ginsberg's poetry, the footnote addresses "Holy Peter holy Allen holy Solomon holy Lucien holy Kerouac holy Huncke holy Burroughs holy Cassady holy the unknown buggered and suffering beggars holy the hideous human angels!" Barry Miles's edition of *Howl* offers copious footnotes identifying the various personages.

The poem simply accepts both the drug-culture and homosexuality as normal. Lines such as the following were recited in the trial, to the real or feigned consternation of the district attorney:

> who howled on their knees in the subway and were dragged off the roof
>   waving genitals and manuscripts,
> who let themselves be fucked in the ass by saintly motorcyclists, and
>   screamed with joy,

who blew and were blown by those human seraphim, the sailors,
  caresses Atlantic and Caribbean love,
who balled in the morning in the evenings in rosegardens and the
  grass of public parks and cemeteries scattering their semen freely to
  whomever come who may,
who hiccuped endlessly trying to giggle but wound up with a sob
  behind a partition in a Turkish Bath when the blond & naked angel
  came to pierce them with a sword.

The film *Howl* appeared in 2010 with James Franco playing Ginsberg. It consists of three interwoven parts: Ginsberg's discovery of himself as a poet, a dramatization of the trial, and Eric Drooker's animated creation of the poem, read in its entirety by the star. It is just one of some twenty movies in which Ginsberg appears as a character (being played by Daniel Radcliffe in a recent one). Ginsberg himself appears as an actor in some fifteen. He also became an avid photographer, taking snapshots of everyone in his circle. Several compilations of his photographic work have been published. He himself, often in the nude, was the subject of many famous photographers' camera work. As a result the basic outline of his life and that of his fellow Beats is more intimately known than that of most writers.

Of the other gay poems in *Howl and Other Poems*, the wittiest is "A Supermarket in California." The poet pursues the aisles of a modern supermarket in search of Whitman and Lorca. He finds the latter up to something among the watermelons. Whitman shows up "poking among the meats in the refrigerator and eyeing the grocery boys." The poet asks, "Where are you going, Walt Whitman? The doors close in a hour. Which way does your beard point tonight?" Ginsberg's depressed vision of present-day "America" returns to the themes in *Howl*. After denouncing the wrong turns our country has taken, the poet considers, "It occurs to me that I am America." The poem concludes with a warning: "America I'm putting my queer shoulder to the wheel." "Many Loves" was not part of the original collection, but Ginsberg includes it with the section in his *Selected Poems*. Carrying an epigraph from Whitman, it recreates in explicit detail his first sexual encounter with Cassady.

It takes 1216 pages to contain Ginsberg's *Collected Poems*. His selected poems provides a handier introduction. He himself introduces it by saying, "This volume summarizes what I deem most honest, most penetrant of my writing." It contains a useful Index of Proper Names. After Cassady,

Kerouac, and Orlovsky, Christ, Blake, and Whitman occur most often. Ginsberg was never hesitant about pushing his correspondence to Whitman, not only on the poetic but also the personal level. He recounted how Whitman slept with Edward Carpenter, who slept with Gavin Arthur, the twenty-first president's grandson, who slept with Cassady, who slept with Ginsberg. I have to feel at least a tinge of regret that I did not try to enter the seminal succession when I met Ginsberg alone at the MLA Convention in Houston in 1980.

TEXT: Allen Ginsberg, *Selected Poems 1947–1995* (HarperCollins, 1996). SUPPLEMENTS: Allen Ginsberg, *Howl: A Graphic Novel*, with Eric Drooker (Harper Perennial, 2010). Barry Mills, ed., *Howl: Original Draft Facsimile, Transcript & Variant Versions...* (HarperPerennial, 1995). REFERENCES: Mike Evans, *The Beats from Kerouac to Kesey: An Illustrated Journey through the Beat Generation* (Running, 2007). Bill Morgan, *I Celebrate Myself: The Somewhat Private Life of Allen Ginsberg* (Viking, 2006).

James Merrill: *The Changing Light at Sandover* (English)

In deference to his mother, James Ingram Merrill (1926–1995) remained poetically and, with straight friends, socially closeted throughout the 1950s and 1960s. The divorced wife of one of the founders of Merrill, Lynch may have been personally homophobic, but her real concern seems to have been how *she* would be regarded by the social register should it come out that her son was a queer. Even when Merrill and David Jackson, his partner for life, started living together, they maintained the pretense of Jackson's marriage—though Merrill's campy mannerisms probably gave the game away to most. There were moments when the closet door swung ajar, sometimes startlingly so as in "A Renewal" (*The Country of a Thousand Years of Peace*, 1959). It depicts lovers on the edge of a breakup who reconcile when "Love buries itself in me, up to the hilt." Other times it's just a hint of a gay sensibility informing the poem. "Charles on Fire" (*Nights and Days*, 1966), my favorite poem of his, describes an evening with friends, seemingly all males. Someone shows off, lighting a match to a glass filled with brandy. It cracks, the flame sliding over "Charles's glistening hand" before being extinguished, leaving him "flesh again," a fact he checks with an "unconscious glance / Into the mirror." The images are quintessential Merrill. The gay presence is reinforced by allusions to Proust, Cavafy, even when the poet resorts to the genderless neutral to describe lovers.

Merrill was apolitical, a bystander to gay liberation. But he becomes a bit braver in his first post-Stonewall collection, *Braving the Elements*, 1972. "The Emerald" is his imaginary declaration to his mother: *"there will be no wife; / The little feet that patter here are metrical."* Langdon Hammer, his biographer (515–16), defends his timidity, holding that from the beginning "his poems had been, from one angle, the story of a gay writer repeatedly affirming his desire and his way of life against the pressure of a censuring culture. He had kept coming out, and coming out farther, in his work." *Divine Comedies*, 1976, contains "The Book of Ephraim," the first part of Merrill's "postmodern apocalyptic epic" (whatever that means). Hammer (545) notes that "Merrill was writing for the first time with utter frankness about his relationship with Jackson." I might question "utter frankness," but the poem is the result of the couple's attempt to refashion their lives after two decades of seeking love and sex in the beds of others. Theirs was an open relationship from the beginning; each knew the other's partners (though Merrill's partners generally did not know about the further partners he took behind their backs). Merrill and Jackson (JM and DJ) begin playing with the Ouija board, contacting dead friends (Auden), Merrill's mentors (Yeats, Stevens), imaginary characters, and spirits (Ephraim). The results are twenty-six sections, each beginning, in sequence, with a letter of the alphabet. The sections are written in a variety of poetic forms. Given that the Ouija board has only capital letters, the various respondents to the movement of the willow-ware cup that the couple use in lieu of a planchette scream at us from the page.

Merrill had no plan in mind when he published "Ephraim." But the idea grew to return to the Ouija board for a full-fledged trilogy, Dante's *Comedy* floating in the back of his mind. The initial result was *Mirabell's Books of Number*, 1978. It is divided into ten sections, one for each Ouija number 0–9. Part 3.3 raises the question of the couple's homosexuality. DJ says,

> What part, I'd like to ask Them, does sex play
> In this whole set-up? Why did They choose us?
> Are we more usable than Yeats or Hugo,

Doters on women, who then went ahead
To doctor everything their voices said?
We haven't done that. JM: No indeed.
Erection of theories, dissemination
Of thought—the intellectual's machismo.
We're more the docile takers-in of seed.
No matter what tall tale our friends emit,
Lately—you've noticed?—we just swallow it.

This leads to Mirabell's answer:

LOVE OF ONE MAN FOR ANOTHER OR LOVE BETWEEN WOMEN
IS A NEW DEVELOPMENT OF THE PAST 4000 YEARS
ENCOURAGING SUCH MIND VALUES AS PRODUCE THE BLOSSOMS
OF POETRY & MUSIC, THOSE 2 PRINCIPAL LIGHTS OF
GOD BIOLOGY. LESS ARTS NEEDED NO EXEGETES.

Then came *Scripts for the Pageant*, 1980. This section turns to the last resources of the Ouija board: YES, &, and NO. Angels, historical figures, friends, and literary people have their voice as DJ and JM continue as mediums. Auden and Kallman play prominent roles. Reviewer Charles Molesworth gushed that Merrill's "work asks comparison with that of Yeats and Blake, if not Milton and Dante," before going on to claim, "But the clearest analogue may be that of Byron, who, desiring a scale both intimate and grand, yet wanting a hero, decided to fill the role himself" (Polito, 177). The three sections were united as *The Changing Light at Sandover*, in 1992, with a new Coda whose final word is the opening word of "The Book of Ephraim." I read the entire 560 pages while I was in my second stay at M. D. Anderson. The thought of rereading it gives me a headache. My sketchy notes at the end of the volume read: *text = self-referential; poet = self-indulgent, self-centered; quest, the meaning of life in a Ouija board!; personal, scientific, religious; science-fiction, mythology, literature (limited), music (limited); godlike.* Merrill may have felt deeply, but he was no profound thinker. Both a stage and a film version, *Voices from Sandover*, directed by his last lover, Peter Hooten, were failures.

His *Collected Poems* (which does not include the mock-epic) takes up 885 pages. When he won the Bollingen Prize for *Braving the Elements*, a *New York Times* editorial complained "of the tendency of Yale's library 'to reward poetry that is literary, private, and traditional'" (Hammer, 529). One either loves Merrill or is indifferent. He was never part of a movement, but his coterie of friends included like-manner gay poets: Witter

Bynner, his mentor and first lover Kimon Friar, Richard Howard, Daryl Hine, Alfred Corn, and his literary executor J. D. McClatchy. Merrill died of an AIDS-related heart attack. His mother died in 2001, a year before Jackson. Merrill and Jackson are buried side by side.

TEXT: James Merrill, *The Changing Light at Sandover* (Knopf, 1995). SUPPLEMENT: James Merrill, *Selected Poems*, ed. J. D. McClatchy & Stephen Yenser (Knopf, 2008). REFERENCES: Langdon Hammer, *James Merrill: Life and Art* (Knopf, 2015). Robert Polito, ed., *A Reader's Guide to James Merrill's* The Changing Light at Sandover (Michigan, 1994).

Frank O'Hara: "I do this I do that" (English)

> New poet, Frank O'Hara. Piece of cake. A comer.
> And Ashbery, his chum. Too opaque. A bummer.
> —Kenward Elmslie, "Touche's Salon"

In the early 1960s five New York poets were singled out as the New York School of poets by analogy with the New York School of painters. And in fact there were friendships and influences between the poets and painters, facilitated by Frank O'Hara's early liaison with Larry Rivers and his employment with the Museum of Modern Art. The poets were Barbara Guest, James Schuyler, Kenneth Koch, O'Hara, and John Ashbery. Three—Schuyler, O'Hara, and Ashbery—were gay, and Koch, according to O'Hara's lover Joe LeSueur (127), "could easily have passed for gay." There have been several books about the movement, including an entire encyclopedia by Terence Diggory, 2009, and an illustrated survey of painters and poets assembled by Jenni Quilter, 2014. Though most people hearing the term New York School would probably think first of the painters, Christopher Schmidt gives three reasons why the label is fitting for the poets:

- their "shared tropism toward the visual artists."
- their mixture of "references to high and low culture."
- their "ability to capture the discordant rhythms, combustive energy and occasional loneliness of New York City" (Hawley, 815).

Besides their approach to verse, they shared other commonalities. LeRoi Jones (Amiri Baraka) and later Frank Lima were on the fringes for many years, but the five central poets were all white and basically uninterested in African-American or Spanish-Harlem cultures. Instead O'Hara wrote "Ode: Salute to the French Negro Poets." Other than Guest, they were all male. Schuyler, Koch, and O'Hara served in World War II. The three gay men were comparatively open about their sexuality in the McCarthy era, though Ashbery escaped to France during this period and remained the most closeted in his poetry. He, O'Hara, and Koch were Harvard graduates, and, unlike the Beats, there always seems to be a whiff of elitism about them even when they slum. Like the Beats, however, their allusions are often personal. I found LeSueur's memoir about his ten years with O'Hara an enormously helpful introduction to how to read not only O'Hara's poetry but also Schuyler's.

Ashbery may presently have the highest reputation of the five, but the dean of the New York School of poets was unmistakably Francis Russell O'Hara (1926–1966), his influence continuing even after his death in a Fire Island beach accident. If the New York School of poets has not entered the culture so intimately as have the Beats, O'Hara's death, his striking good looks, and the nude paintings of him by Rivers and by Wynn Chamberlain have entered the gay mythos. His "out" poems offer an altogether different kind of democratic celebration than the kinds Ginsberg offers. O'Hara is a name-dropper, sometimes the full name, often only the first. His poems often seem a private joke to be shared by the in-group. That coupled with what appears to be almost impenetrable chunks of language I found off-putting when I first tried to read him. For years the only poem of his that I liked was his witty "Why I Am Not a Painter." LeSueur's memoir, an act of unabashed hero worship, changed all that. Despite the names dropped and the confessional nature of some of the scenes he describes, O'Hara's poems can be as personally accessible as Ginsberg's.

Take O'Hara's "At the Old Place." This is a poem that describes eight gay men's evening out, spent first drinking and then dancing. It opens:

Joe is restless and so am I, so restless.
Button's buddy lips frame "L G T TH O P?"
Across the bar. "Yes!" I cry, for dancing's
my soul delight. (Feet! feet!) "Come on!"
Through the streets we skip like swallows.
Howard malingers. (Come on, Howard.) Ashes

malingers. (Come on, J.A.) Dick malingers.
(Come on, Dick.) Alvin darts ahead. (Wait up,
Alvin.) Jack, Earl and Someone don't come.

The childlike description (run, Frank, run) of grown men is amusing in itself. But the poem becomes more interesting when we realize, via LeSueur, that it is a transcript of an actual evening that occurred a month or so after he and O'Hara began sharing an apartment. Anticipating texting, the mouthed letters stand for "Let's go to the Old Place," a gay dance bar in Greenwich Village. The participants are LeSueur, Ashbery (Ashes, J.A.), the artist John Button, the pianist Alvin Novak (Button's lover), Howard Griffin (Auden's one-time secretary), the musician Richard Stryker (Harold Norse's lover, to LeSueur's dismay), Earl McGrath (the composer Menotti's secretary, later a music-industry executive, apparently bisexual), and the San Francisco poet Jack Spicer, who had a crush on O'Hara. Knowing who is who makes the later lines describing O'Hara's pleasure as "Wrapped in Ashes' arms I glide" move to a new register. Likewise "Joe's two-steps, too, are incredible." McGrath's and Spicer's reluctance to join them at first before they finally "drift / guiltily in" can be understood in different ways.

Many of O'Hara's poems, the greater part of which were published posthumously, evoke such scenes with his friends and lovers, sometimes in gossip-sheet detail: "Johnny and Alvin are going home, are sleeping now / are fanning the air with breaths from the same bed ("Poem"); "I remember JA / staggering over to me in the San Remo [bar] and murmuring / 'I've met someone MARVELLOUS!'" ("John Button's Birthday"). He may be best known for what he himself labeled his "'I do this I do that' poems." That is, he simply details what he did, often during his lunch break. His first widely distributed collection was in fact titled *Lunch Poems*, 1964.

O'Hara's *Collected Poems*, 1971, fill 624 pages. Schuyler ("To Frank O'Hara") responded enthusiastically:

And now people you never met will meet
and talk about your work.
So witty, so sad,
so you: even your lines have
a broken nose.

For the beginner the tome may be daunting. I traded in my copy for the *Selected Poems* so as not to be buried in the avalanche of words. O'Hara pushes the boundaries of what we define as poetry. In his tongue-in-cheek essay "Personism: A Manifesto," included in the *Selected Poems*, he writes, "I don't believe in god, so I don't have to make elaborately sounded structures. I hate Vachel Lindsay, always have; I don't even like rhythm, assonance, all that stuff. You just go on your nerve.... As for measure and other technical apparatus, that's just common sense: if you're going to buy a pair of pants you want them to be tight enough so everyone will want to go to bed with you."

Until I read straight through the selected poems, I had not realized how sexual his work is. He describes step by step, albeit in metaphorical language, a blow job he performed on an African American in a porn cinema ("In the Movies"). He records ("Une Journée de Juillet") how "I suck off / every man in the Manhattan Storage & / Warehouse Co. Then, refreshed, again / to the streets!" But much as he loved cruising and casual hookups—and continued having them all his life—O'Hara, LeSueur tells us, was always seeking love. LeSueur obviously hoped he was the chosen one. But O'Hara moved on to Vincent Warren and Bill Berkson, whose names pop up in the later poems. O'Hara and LeSueur never lost their connection; even as they were drifting apart he immortalizes "Joe's seersucker jacket," which "has protected me and kept me here on / many occasions as a symbol does when the heart is full and risks no speech." But "You Are Gorgeous and I'm Coming" is an acrostic spelling out Warren's name. And either Warren or Berkson is being alluded to in the lines in "Steps":

> oh god it's wonderful
> to get out of bed
> and drink too much coffee
> and smoke too many cigarettes
> and love you so much.

O'Hara promises, "you can't plan on the heart, but / the better part of it, my poetry, is open" (My Heart). One can only guess what might have been had he not been killed at age forty.

·⁕·

TEXT: Frank O'Hara, *Selected Poems*, ed. Mark Ford (Knopf, 2011). REFERENCES: Brad Gooch, *City Poet: The Life and Times of Frank O'Hara* (Knopf, 1993). Joe LeSueur, *Digressions on Some Poems by Frank O'Hara* (Farrar, Straus & Giroux, 2003). Jenni Quilter, *New York School Painters & Poets: Neon in Daylight* (Rizzoli, 2014).

Orlando Paris: 69 Flights of Fancy (English)

Having found gay pulp novels just as I was turning thirty, that somehow crucial year, and discovering within their pages the kind of self-acceptance I saw nowhere else, I remain irritated by the cavalier fashion such pulps are too often dismissed. Paul O. Welles (1926–1981) is almost forgotten. He was born in Scranton, Penn., and attended Yale. After serving in the Navy, he worked for the State Department. His 1979 dystopian novel *Project Lambda* is occasionally still mentioned. In it the U.S. government, led by a closeted senator, begins rounding up gays and sending them to a concentration camp in the west. But Welles's writings as Orlando Paris have been largely ignored. He reviewed books for both *Queen's Quarterly* and *Drummer*. Only Gavin Dillard and David Laurents have anthologized his poetry. Not that I would make any great claims about the quality of Paris's verse. *The Short Happy Sex Life of Stud Sorell and 69 Other Flights of Fancy*, 1968, is undoubtedly a bit too clever, too fond of an O. Henry-like twist at the end. But it is entertaining. At times it can be poignant. And it is a cultural milestone in its own way, an American's belated answer to Verlaine's *Hombres*. We owe more to Greenleaf Classics than we usually accord them as publishers. The seventy free-verse poems are all narratives of a sort. They chronicle moments in the lives of ordinary gays, often with humor, more often with irony, and sometimes with muted rage at the ways gays are mistreated.

The twenty-page title poem recounts events that begin on Stud Sorell's seventeenth birthday. Cruised in a movie theater by Jimmy Moran, the captain of the school football team, he has his first sexual experience. Desolated when he finds that Jimmy is supposedly dating a girl, he allows himself to be picked up by another teen and taken to an improbable school fraternity orgy. Jimmy turns out to be the star participant, and the two reconnect. The police stage a raid; Stud is badly beaten by the other boys, who suspect that he has somehow ratted to his father, the local police chief. The homophobic father ships Stud off to a military school, where he hangs himself. Filled with clichés, it is the weakest part of the volume. The other poems rarely are more than a page in length. They cover a variety of topics, sometimes in terms that now date them. Several continue the theme of police entrapment (though in one, "Cop-Tease," a motorcycle officer propositions a man baiting him). Two describe hate crimes ("Town Meeting"; the graphic "Braggin' Dirt"); one concerns teenage bullying ("Horse Play"). Gays put down each other, making fun of a little-dicked leatherman, twinks, and screaming queens. "Old Love" laments the loss of a boyfriend to marriage and the man's subsequent hypocrisy (his using homosexual slurs in public, visiting bathhouses for quickies). In several we find out who the speaker's partner is only at the end in an O. Henry twist: a teenager's basketball coach ("Gaudeamus Igitur"), an altar boy's priest ("In the Beginning"), a son's father ("Sadist"). In one we discover that the man is married and only dreaming about being used by other men ("Masochist"). "President of the P.T.A." is the strangest poem. A boy describes his own mother's teaching him how to be a good cocksucker, then blaming the school when he is caught "doing guys / At school in the locker room." This large number of poems describing negative situations reflect the homophobic spirit of the time.

But there are also positive poems. The male body is celebrated often. Sometimes we look directly at another's body; other times we see the body via the description of a drawing or a photograph of it. In a rare rhyming poem, "Down with Jockey Shorts!," the poet begs guys to show off their baskets:

Let the world see how you're hung:
The shape of your balls, the length of your cock,
Be it hanging down soft or up hard as a rock,
It's like a song that needs to be sung.

But he also reminds us of the old adage:

It's not so much
How much
You have: it's
What you do
With it
That counts.

The poems embrace all kinds of homosexuality. They celebrate fellatio, sixty-nining, the glory of glory holes, the excitement of sex in movie theater balconies and bars' backrooms, and the thrill of cruising at the YMCA, as well as masturbatory fantasies. In "Prejudice" the poet remembers how he never liked uncircumcised men until he met his new lover: "Now, however, that I've fallen / In love with you, I'm quickly / Acquiring a zesty taste for cheese." "A la Carte" fits in with the roughest of Verlaine's poems, extolling scat and water sports; the paired poems "The Gentle Prince" (describing the flaccid penis) and "The Commanding King" (the erect penis) resemble the French poet's similar tributes to our genitals.

The couple in "Strangers No More" have an open relationship, with the result that they often end up four in a bed. The poet remarks of their tricks (in a quatrain that brings back memories of pre-plague days),

It's surprising how many
Turn halfway, embrace
Each other, and kiss at climax
And become great friends.

Some poems do chronicle disconcerting moments, such as meeting your new lover's former boyfriend, or worse, discovering your mate has lied to you when you catch him with another man at the baths (where presumably you are not supposed to be either). But many of the couple poems are quite tender. "Aftermath" lingers in my mind. A soldier, perhaps in the States, jacks off to an imaginary scene with his lover. It concludes poignantly:

When it is over and I lay spent,
I cry again, a little,
As when I first heard that
You had been killed in Viet Nam.

There are portraits of a sailor with a snake tattooed on his penis ready "to spit venom down my throat," an aroused horseman dismounting in a hidden place to jack off, a bullfighter in his tight-fitting uniform whom the poet prays for as he faces the bull, a mute who sucks off another guy, a joyful orgy at the beach. Even if the volume is not a must-read, it is valuable as a pre-liberation homophile document.

TEXT: Orlando Paris, *The Short Happy Sex Life of Stud Sorell and 69 Other Flights of Fancy* (Greenleaf Classics, 1968).

Jean Sénac: Corpoèmes (French)

In his mini-biography of Jean Sénac (1926–1973), Robert Aldrich (389) stresses the importance of "the links between his private life, his literary creativity and his politics." Or, as he quotes a friend of the poet: "Erotics, poetics, politics." Born Jean Comma—illegitimate, a French citizen of Spanish descent but an Algerian nationalist who never learned Arabic and was denied citizenship once the country became independent even though he worked for the government, openly gay—Sénac was the consummate outsider. He spent the war years in Paris, befriended by another *pied-noir*, Albert Camus, and saw his first volume of poems through the press. Attracted always to young men, *ephebes*, he had various lovers. The most important was Jacques Miel. Though Miel was basically straight, later marrying, they had a brief sexual liaison and Sénac adopted him as his son in order to establish a legal relationship. Miel often appears in Sénac's poems. He says of him, "But you Jacques, you spoke of light to me in words that were not prisons." His collected poems fill a volume of some 800 pages. *Selected Poems* is the only volume to appear so far in English. The earliest part of this selection is mostly political polemics, but beginning with "Words with Walt Whitman" (dedicated to Miel) through "Citizens of Monstrosity," his roles as "this nation's bastard / The fag the foreigner the poor man the / Ferment of discord and subversion" dominate. Aldrich (388) writes: "His distilled anecdotes—of cruising, meeting partners, having sex, sometimes falling in love, juggling lust and love, facing deception and depression—foreshadowed, then coincided with, a newly uncloseted sort of gay literature.

Despite the poet's celebration of sex, in these poems at least the mood is generally somber, disillusioned, mildly angry. "The Race," collected posthumously in the volume *Le Mythe du sperme – Méditerranée*, illustrates the complex structure of a Sénac poem. A would-be lover speaks of love, but it is an abstraction, a word only. The poet evokes the narcissistic but more concrete image of "the pain of balls mirrored / So they can be drained." The other speaks of blonds, of civilized chests; the poet counters with "pricks that run on empty. / Enormous adolescent motorcycles that skid / Across thighs." He cries out to different Arab boys, begging them to fuck him. He announces that he has engaged in blasphemous fellatio: "I have sucked your race / As far as the Koran." The youth on the beach enters the "hour glass," the sands of time as he ejaculates. Talk of love is countered by the raw need for orgasm, of "The Void but not the Hole." Algiers of the past is gone; only the landscape remains, and it has created the unicorn. The race has led to exile. In "AAAAAAA..." the poet laments, "Cocks! Cocks! I found cocks and more cocks / But where is the man?" In "Fantastic Fuck-Ups" he accuses the present state of Algeria of being a place of "Only happy assholes plugged with pretty morals." On the most elemental level in "Black Is Black" he decries the Algerian youths who "will screw me in the halls, or between the rocks" on the beach, but who then "will deny that you ever knew me":

> Who are you?
> Yes, Who am I?
> And who ARE WE
> Having only shared our gism and shit?

In "Against," with more than a touch of misogyny, he accuses Algeria of being a "pussy society."

Aldrich (386) writes, "Frenzied quests for sex, despair at politics, self-questioning about the writer's craft and a growing blackness are only occasionally relieved by sun-drenched happiness." Such occurs in "Torrid," in which the poet speaks ecstatically of the relationship between sex and language, a trope that permeates many of these poems:

> Make me drink up the sea, make me
> Drink your body against the rocks. Make me
> Drink the syllables that set me back on my ankles.
> I am so tired of words that deny
> My shame.

The long poem "Figuier's Laurels," from *Dérisions et Vertiges*, compares a memorable fuck to the discovery of America: "I sail on your hips, Columbus, towards fabulous lands." He begs,

> Raise yourself up, Aztec column, blaze of joy, of whom the caravel
> Sings! Battle of feathers, radiant
> Jets, my whole body closes over you.
> Anatonaut!
> The sea gulls already are circling your Speedo.
> Take it off! There are the Indies! Oh
> My love!

This is a "*corpoème*," a neologism Sénac created to name a poem that unabashedly celebrates the body (*corps*). In writing such works the poet was quite conscious of his gay heritage. In addition to Whitman, he addresses Rimbaud, Wilde, Lorca, Cernuda, and Ginsberg (whom he met). Much as Jean Cocteau incorporated a star into his signature, Sénac introduced a sun: a small circle with five rays, resembling a stylized anus more than a celestial body.

After an initial period of euphoria about independent Algeria, Sénac became increasingly disenchanted with the increasingly puritanical government; he was dismissed from his post at Radio Alger in 1971. Two years later, almost destitute, he was found murdered, stabbed to death, in his shabby apartment. A youth with whom he had had an affair was arrested, but the theory that it was a political assassination floated at once. Abdelkrim Bahloul's film *The Sun Assassinated*, 2004, is a dramatized account of Sénac's final years, leading up to his death. In several of his poems Sénac seemed to foresee his end. In "Hyperprism BSM" he says, "The clawed sun lasts no longer / Than a drop of semen on my chin." In "Wilde, Lorca and Then..." he equates himself with these two poets and concludes:

> The time has come for you to slaughter me, to kill
> > In me your own liberty, to deny
> > The celebration [that] obsessed you. The stricken sun, years of devastation
> > Will lift up
> > My BODY.

The circumstances of Lorca's death and Sénac's are indeed striking, but even more are the similarities between his and that of his Italian contemporary Pier Paolo Pasolini. He was every bit as engaged in the language of poetry, leftish politics, and the thrill of the chase after ephebes. Both fell deeply in love with a youth who was essentially straight (Ninetto Davoli, in Pasolini's case). The circumstances of Pasolini's death are as mysterious as those of Sénac's (a trick gone wrong or a political assassination?). But while Pasolini's poetry is relatively decorous (so unlike his later films), Sénac's is vulgar, visceral, and more immediately accessible.

TEXT: Jean Sénac, *The Selected Poems*, trans. Katia Sainson & David Bergman (Sheep Meadow, 2010). REFERENCE: Robert Aldrich, *Colonialism and Homosexuality* (Routledge, 2003), 375–96.

Jaime Gil de Biedma: *Longing* (Spanish)

Jaime Gil de Biedma y Alba (1929–1990) was born into a wealthy Catalan family who owned the Philippine Tobacco Company, headquartered in Barcelona. Throughout the Franco era, he remained in Spain save for a sojourn at Oxford in 1953 and business trips to the Philippines, where he took full advantage of the availability of rent-boys. He was generally attracted to youths of humble origins, but he had a fling with James Baldwin when the latter was in Spain and even a complex relationship with a free-spirited woman, Isabel Gil Moreno de Mora. Compromising photographs forced him out of his position with the company. In 1985 the appearance of a Kaposi's sarcoma revealed that he was HIV-positive. He died in the company of the actor Josep Madern. I discovered the poet through Sigfrid Monleón's uncompromising biopic *The Consul of Sodom*, 2009, based on Miguel Dalmau's 2004 biography. It was a revelation. Here was a poet who remained fairly open about his desires despite the Spanish dictator's homophobia. Throughout the film the director made Gil de Biedma's poems an integral part of the narrative. I bought *Longing*, the only translation of the poet's work available in English. It deserves a place not only on every gay bookshelf but on that of every poetry lover. Clear, direct, though necessarily a little cagy about gender, the poetry poses few of the interpretative problems that the works of earlier gay Spanish poets do, and the language is every bit as moving. The poems are highly personal, but I found myself constantly highlighting lines that seemed right out of my own life.

He published three volumes, 1959–68, all in Spanish (not Catalan), and then turned almost exclusively to reviewing and maintaining his more revealing diaries. His collected poems appeared in 1975, the year Franco died; the final 1993 edition is only 175 pages long. They are generally considered the finest produced by the Generation of '50. Alberto Mira writes, "The 'invention' of identity is a recurring topic in his writings, and the poetic voice he created in his work is typically distant, lucid and not too emotional. In the repressive times of Francoism, when sex was mostly taboo, he sketches some scenes in an almost Cavafy-like style, featuring raw sex that may be emotionally rewarding but certainly has nothing to do with love…. Given the harshness of the times, ambiguity is central to his expression, and the gender of the object of desire is kept in the dark when possible" (Aldrich, *Contemporary*, 159). Even in those poems, however, where he took advantage of the fact that Spanish possessive pronouns bear the gender of the object possessed, not that of the possessor as in English, the poet snuck in coded references, such as an allusion to Antinous, to leave no doubt of the sex involved. The poet was also sensitive to his place among other gay writers. *Longing* includes poems dedicated to Luis Cernuda, Juan Goytisolo, whom he knew personally, and the deeply closeted Vicente Aleixandre. He also dropped references to Eliot and Auden, both importance influences on his work.

Nolan offers the poems in roughly the order they appeared. Leafing through the volume, searching out specifically gay references, I keep getting stopped by other observations. There are poems about Spain, memories of the Civil War, his childhood, writing poetry. I force myself to focus. In "Paris: Postcard from Heaven" the poet remembers picking up an American there one August night (a poem I can especially identify with). "Yesterday Morning, Today," describes a naked lover looking out the window at the ocean one morning. "Days in Pagsanjan" recalls swimming with a lover at night in the city "famous" (Nolan [113] tells us) "for its waterfall and male prostitution." "Queen" rather puts down an effeminate pick-up, his not having found a partner more to his taste. "Tale of a Poor Young Man" depicts an aimless Filipino youth, probably a hustler when need be. "Anniversary Song" is a tribute to a lover the poet has been with for six years.

And thus I arrive to "Pandemic and Celeste." The title, Nolan (113) annotates, "refers to the two Aphrodites mentioned in the *Symposium*, symbolizing promiscuous and monogamous love." The poem opens with a man-to-man conversation in which the poet promises, "What I'm going to show you is a heart, / an unfaithful one / naked from the waist down." These lines are followed immediately by that from Baudelaire quoted by Eliot: "hypocrite reader—*mon semblable—mon frère!*" The poet insists it is not only cruising for sex, preferably with young males, that drives him, but "I also stalk sweet love, / the tender kind to sleep at my side / and make my bed a joy to wake up in." Still, he contends,

> To know love, to learn about it,
> it's necessary to have been alone.
> And it's necessary to have made love
> on four hundred nights—with four hundred
> different bodies. Its mysteries,

as the poet [John Donne] said, are of the soul

but a body is the book in which they are read.

He follows with a series of memories when the excitement of the body took control, the closeness that comes from being with one particular person but also "the pleasures of sleeping around." Then he returns to his earlier stance:

Not even the passion of a one-night stand

can compare with the passion

that comes from the understanding,

the years of experience

of our love.

Though we never objectively see the loved one, the poem remains one of the more beautiful tributes to the power of a long-lasting gay relationship that I know.

These poems were all included in the 1966 volume *Moralidades* (Moralities). In the strangely named *Poemas póstumos* (Posthumous Poems, 1968) the poet draws a number of ironic self-portraits. "Against Jaime Gil de Biedma" begins with what sounds like an admonishment to his lover, another man. But as you proceed through the poem, you begin to realize that the poet is taking stock of himself. It is not a flattering picture: "If only you weren't such a little whore! / And if I didn't know, as I have for years, / that you take over when I give in." (This duality, duplicity, whatever you wish to label it, is beautifully captured visually in the film.) "Nostalgie de la Boue" resurrects Baudelaire's term to explore

New inclinations of the night,

lewd exercises by rote, lessons in lust

that I mastered, pirate,

O young blue-eyed pirate.

The title of "A Body Is a Man's Best Friend" sums up only one aspect of the poem; as important is the poet's awareness of time and age, a theme explored further in "I Shall Never Be Young Again." "After the Death of Jaime Gil de Biedma" recreates a party held one August in his home: the poolside filled with friends, an evening spent putting on an impromptu play. The poem is addressed to someone probably well-known in the poet's circle (Nolan does not identify the person). The poet credits him with introducing "the muted romanticism pulsing in poems / of mine I like best, like 'Pandemic and Celeste.'" Nolan's selection ends with three poems that strike an even deeper note of melancholy. One longs to have the complete poems translated.

TEXT: Jaime Gil de Biedma, *Longing: Selected Poems*, trans. James Nolan (City Lights, 1993).

Thom Gunn: *Boss Cupid*; Earlier Poems (English)

Thomson William Gunn (1929–2004) met the American student Mike Kitay at Cambridge in 1952. When Kitay returned to the U.S. in 1954 to serve in the military, Gunn followed, first to Stanford, California, and then to San Antonio, Texas, where Kitay was stationed. In 1957 they returned to Palo Alto. By then Gunn had published two collections. Seen as a British poet (in fact, he never took American citizenship), he was grouped with other poets of the time who worked in established verse forms. In 1960 the couple moved to San Francisco, the city with which Gunn was associated for the rest of his life. He knew all the important poets, but maintained his own individuality. He did begin to loosen form and to experiment more with his next volume, *My Sad Captains*, 1961, but he continued to demonstrate his mastery of rhyme and both the metered and the syllabic line. Whereas the sex of the lover had been left indefinite in the earlier volumes, even in the poems inspired by Kitay, he now began to edge out of the closet with the new collection to record the ordinary life of a gay man in the city.

In 1969 he invited Bill Schuessler to move in with them; Schuessler fell in love with Kitay, and the three established a kind of commune in which other friends and lovers came and went across the years. Early on he had been attracted to the leather crowd. As he aged skateboarders and surfers show up in his poetry. Increasingly Gunn fell in with the San Francisco drug crowd. He escaped HIV, but the loss of friends devastated him. For many his most powerful volume is *The Man with Night Sweats*, 1992, the last part of which is a series of elegies. These are not so much poems about being gay as poems about a community faced with one of the worst plagues of the twentieth century having to cope largely on its own. Still, Gunn refused to give up his unsafe life style, and it probably killed him.

There have been two *Selected Poems* since his death, one American, the other British. Neither serves the gay reader well; over fifty of the poems that trace Gunn's conception of himself as a gay man are missing entirely from both volumes. One really has to buy the *Collected Poems*, 1994, and its subsequent volume *Boss Cupid*, 2000. Gunn is worth reading in his entirety anyway.

Leafing through the *Collected Poems*, dedicated to Kitay, one finds some ten individual tributes to Kitay (from "Without a Counterpart" through "The Hug"), though they are not identified by name or, in the earlier poems, even by sex. There are self-reflections ("Behind the Mirror") and portraits of various friends, including Schuessler ("Selves") and Christopher Isherwood. Gunn recalls stray sexual conversations ("The Miracle"). He loves various San Francisco scenes where gay men concentrate ("At the Barriers"). He depicts hustlers ("Market at Turk," "San Francisco Streets"). There are poems about cruising—both his own ("Modes of Pleasure," "Punch Rubicundus") and others' ("Fever," "Bally *Power Play*"). There are poems about encounters in backrooms ("The Feel of Hands"), an orgy ("Saturnalia"), a drug party ("Another All-Night Party"). In the first of two poems entitled "Modes of Pleasure," with uncanny prescience, he foresees his own future as an aging gay man. Later he records how right he was ("Lines for My 55th Birthday").

I grin as I read his poem about adolescent masturbation, "Courage, a Tale." Not necessarily gay, it is the story of a boy who has been told "that if you masturbate 100 times / it kills you." And so he slows down. But inevitably he arrives at the 99th time:

And then he thought
Fuck it
   it's worth dying for,
and half an hour later
the score rose from 99 to 105.

These themes continue in his final, otherwise uncollected volume. *Boss Cupid*, 2000, provides a good introduction for a newcomer to Gunn. The volume opens with a tribute to Robert Duncan. Later there comes a wonderful and honest vision of Rimbaud ("Shit"). There are AIDS poems. Most poignant is the portrait of a young writer who lost his lover the same week his first novel was published: "He lost the wrestler with the smile / Who pinned him to the mat of love for ever, / He'd hoped." A dead friend's memory is evoked by the sight "In the Post Office" of someone who resembles him. Besides Kitay, Gunn thinks about other past lovers. In "The Problem," a "Boss Cupid" moment occurs abed with someone in New York in 1961 in which

> ...feeling turned so self-delighting
> That hurry soon gave way
> To give-and-take,
> Till each contested, for the other's sake,
> To end up not in winning and defeat
> But in a draw.

He recalls other past pleasures. In "Saturday Nights" he unapologetically resurrects in memory the Barracks in 1975, a bath house in whose action he takes comfort that

> If, furthermore,
> Our Dionysian experiment
>   To build a city never dared before
> Dies without reaching to its full extent,
>   At least in the endeavor we translate
> Our common ecstasy to a brief ascent
>   Of the complete, grasped, paradisal state
> Against the wisdom pointing us away;

He recreates bars and cafés and the people one meets and muses on the role of drugs. In "American Boy" he describes the consequences of aging in the gay world. The most controversial poems are a series of "songs for Jeffrey Dahmer," the cannibal who picked up and killed gay men. Early in the volume Gunn gets up the courage finally to confront his mother's suicide. Late in the volume he reflects for a final time on his life with Kitay and the flings that he has had on his own.

Thom Gunn and I do not come from the same family. He was born in England of Scottish descent; my English ancestors were of direct Norse descent. But there is a certain pleasure in reading a gay poet with whom I share a name. I also like the fact that he is so at ease with conventional verse forms. And I find his honest, low-keyed assessment of his life in San Francisco more appealing than that of the members of the San Francisco Renaissance.

TEXTS: Thom Gunn, *Boss Cupid* (Farrar, Straus & Giroux, 2000); *Collected Poems* (Farrar, Straus & Giroux, 1994).

Richard Howard: *Two-Part Inventions* (English)

Summing up the poetry of Richard Joseph Howard (1929– , adopted as Richard Joseph Orwitz when a baby), Trevor Sydney writes that "a sustained evocation of European American gay men's heritage is a salient feature." He goes on to say, "He recalls and celebrates that cultural legacy as a way of defining himself as an intellectually refined gay man in the postmodern world and, more specifically, as a means of locating his own political self in that grand aesthetic tradition." Sydney acknowledges that Howard's "densely allusive poetry" with its "intimate familiarity with a wide range of contemporary and classical writers, painters, dancers, sculptors, and other artists, …at times is inaccessible to most readers… outside academic circles" (Nelson, *Encyclopedia*, 318–19). Influenced by Robert Browning's dramatic monologues, Howard is given to adopting the voices of others. This strategy acts to simultaneously mask and reveal the writer. Once one grasps the key allusions, the verse is actually pretty straightforward. Even if the exact reference cannot be pinned down, the general thrust of the poem is obvious. But, to be honest, I find his coyness often annoying.

His selected poems, *Inner Voices*, provides a generous sampling of his gay poems. One of the earliest, "1889 Alassio" (first collected in *Untitled Subjects*, 1969), is illustrative of his method, including its shortcomings. The town is located on the Italian Riviera; it started attracting British visitors in droves after the opening of its railway in 1872. The poem takes the form of a letter from an unidentified writer to an otherwise unidentified Ross. Feeling threatened somehow, the letter writer begs this Ross to block Havelock Ellis's delving into sexual secrets "he knows / to be out of the common." The apparently aged writer ("Priapus withers to a mere fig-tree stump") implies he left France because of the mercenary nature of French boys; he praises the attractions of a Pippo, but moans that the boy "has left me for the last time." Now he says,

> Farce is all I have;
> and a few poems to write, calculated
>   to make even some not over-nice
> hairs stand on end, to say nothing of other
>   erections equally obvious.

But through it all, "My nature must be / at the root male and passionate."

It is a moving portrait of an expatriate whose deracination has largely isolated him so that all he has to look forward to is "Dozing in the vale of Avalon, / ...watched by weeping queens," a quotation from Tennyson's "The Passing of Arthur," with perhaps a modern pun on "queens." The problem is, by being so specific about time and place, Howard inadvertently sends us chasing after identification of the personages, at the risk of losing the poem. Who is this Ross? Who is the letter writer? Could it be John Fiske, he of Fanny and Stella fame? Or is just some generic gay man who fled the Labouchère Amendment? A simple note would allow us to concentrate on the poem itself.

These problems continue in *Two-Part Inventions*, 1974, in which three of the six poems have gay subjects. Each poem is spoken in two voices, creating a playlet that could actually be performed. In the second poem, "Wildflowers: Camden, 1882" (for me, the best: it is straightforward, for one thing), Howard imagines what might have taken place when two of the most important icons in gay history, Walt Whitman and Oscar Wilde, actually met face to face. At first the sixty-two-year-old poet hesitates to reveal too much of himself to the twenty-eight-year-old. Wilde wants to hear Whitman read a poem from Calamus, but he demurs and ominously warns Wilde, "It will not do to fly in the face of / courts and conformity; it did not do / at all well for me, Oscar." Wilde evokes Baudelaire and translates from memory "Spleen." He makes much of the titles, *Leaves of Grass* and *Fleurs du Mal*. The two men discuss masks. Warming to the brash Irishman, Whitman admits that "Without the boys—if it had not been for the boys, / I never would have had the *Leaves*." Disarmed, Wilde kneels and proclaims himself another of Walt's "boys." Whitman gives him his blessing but admonishes Wilde that he must live his own life: "Maybe yours will be an essential life— / one needing to have been lived!"

The poem is even richer than I am indicating. Thus, it is surprising to find that Howard replaced it in *Inner Voices* with a latter poem, "Infirmities," about a meeting, also real, between Whitman and another Irishman, Bram Stoker. Actually there were several meetings that Howard seems to have conflated into one. Before Stoker arrives, Whitman reads from the letter that Stoker sent him, astutely remarking that, though "Stoker thought he was writing to me...it was really to himself." Howard accepts the theory that began to float about the time he wrote his poem that

Whitman was a model for Dracula. It's a pleasant poem but less powerful than "Wildflowers."

The fourth and the fifth poems of *Two-Part Inventions* have in common that a gay fictional character confronts a historical figure and outs himself. In "The Lesson of the Master: Paris–Versailles, 1912," "Gerald Roseman," at the suggestion of Henry James, accompanies Edith Wharton to the cemetery where she intends to bury the ashes of her lover "Gerald Mackenzie." Roseman wishes to make Wharton face the fact that she never really knew Mackenzie, or at least never acknowledged that he was one of those "men who do not need women." Somehow James has masterminded the entire encounter. There is talk about the role of the writer of fiction, Jews as the Chosen People (Roseman, like Howard, is Jewish), art. All of this has something of the opacity of a Jamesian novel. It is entertaining, but I do not understand the reasons for the poet's inventions.

In "Contra Naturam, 1913." an unknown traveler encounters Auguste Rodin in a rail carriage between Aix-en-Province and Marseille. He wishes Rodin to acknowledge *"how deeply you participate in my delight, / if not my desire."* He almost flaunts how *"I go, Monsieur, to the baths, to 'haunts of vice,'/ the places where men give themselves up to each / other, where they give themselves up...Surrender."* The aged Rodin responds,

Why must you add me to your lineage?
Surely *my* line of descent is clear, from
Praxiteles to Michelangelo
and then Rodin. I have no part in yours....

Finally, they declare a truce, but on an equivocal note with the traveler declaring to the sculptor that he is uncertain *"if the miseries / of continued possession are less dreadful / than the struggles of continued exorcism."*

Three of the gay poems from his next volume, *Fellow Feelings*, 1976, are preserved in *Inner Voices*. "Decades" describes Howard's feelings for Hart Crane at five stages of his own life. In the third section he describes meeting Crane's "old friend" from the Fugitives at a Paris café; presumably this is Allen Tate, but again Howard cannot bring himself to identify the person. Whoever he is, he drops a slur against the gays passing by. Howard is repelled, feeling that in associating with the man he has "lost the pride of my 'proclivity,' / and the penalty and disgrace of losing is / to become part of your enemy." In the last section Howard asks Crane to take his hand, for "We suffer from / the same fabled disease, and only the hope / of dying of it keeps a man alive. Keeps!"

In "Howard's Way: A Letter to 102 Boulevard Haussmann," he addresses Marcel Proust, imagining what it would have been like had Proust accompanied him to a gathering at the Dakota, the New York City apartment house associated with horror films. There he witnesses a sadistic "blue movie" that forces him to question, "is art the image of life?" The host is almost certainly Charles Henri Ford; again, why this reticence to name names? In the third poem, "The Giant on Giant-Killing: Homage to the Bronze *David* of Donatello, 1430," the speaker is Goliath, but the poem is clearly the result of Howard's minute inspection of the statue and thus a loving tribute to David in overlapping voices. Howard preserves some other gay poems of an even more personal nature, but he excludes just as many from his selected poems, including the two that anthologist Timothy Liu chose to represent his work in the latter's anthology.

TEXT: Richard Howard, *Two-Part Inventions: Poems* (Atheneum, 1978).
SUPPLEMENT: Richard Howard, *Inner Voices: Selected Poems 1963–2003* (Farrar, Straus & Giroux, 2004).

Dinos Christianopoulos: *The Naked Piazza* (Greek)

Lucky enough to find for sale a copy of Nicholas Kostis's translation of Dinos Christianopoulos's *The Naked Piazza* (*Nekre piatsa*, 2000), I instantly fell in love with the volume of free verse and prose poems. So far a copy of the same translator's *Poems*, apparently verse using more conventional forms, has escaped me. Again one can only shake one's head that no collected, or even selected, edition of the poet's work is available in English. This omission is all the more curious since one of his lines has entered American LGBT consciousness, being inscribed on the sign at the St. Louis memorial garden to murdered transgender people: "They tried to bury us. They didn't know we were seeds." We must be grateful to Kimon Friar (James Merrill's mentor) for bringing us what translations have been published in the U.S. Born Constandinos Dimitriadis (1931–), the poet has spent his entire life in Thessaloniki, a port in northern Greece on the Aegean Sea. He is openly homosexual. His themes include a nostalgia for the lost past, a fetish for military uniforms, a subdued interest in S/M relationships, and a love of the more seedy aspects of urban life. He acknowledges his indebtedness to Cavafy and to the Greek painter Yannis Tsarouchis. In fact, some of his prose poems that seem to be written from experience, such as "The Photograph," turn out to be interpretations of Tsarouchis paintings.

Like gays who moan the cleanup of New York's Times Square, Christianopoulos laments the sanitization of Thessaloniki's Vardari Square, leaving only a few lost queens to frequent the area, "the remnants of a piazza decimated by prosperity." As a result, he says, "I wander about, a nightbird, / remaining alive with archaic associations." He regrets the loss of his apartment on the square and "its contribution to love." Even the military uniforms, especially the boots, that so turned him on "have survived only in the paintings of Tsarouchis. And Egnatia Street, which in the past would perk up at dusk, now sorrowfully discovers boots on the feet of arty fellows." His distaste for the present extends to language itself. In "Names" he records the changing vocabulary and the associations that went with each change: *fellatio*, associated with "European decadence," to "doing the *Turkish pipe*, which divided roles into "fags" and "studs," to just "doing the *pipe*," by which time "The hot numbers disappeared and thousands of fairies sucking one another off blurred the roles." He wonders what more forms the "debilitating progression will assume." Besides the hustlers and the cruisers, feral dogs and cats also populate his poems. Several of the poems are about his mother, her death, and his visit to the cemetery. Even there he runs into "a queen from among those whom I used to encounter for years at Vardari Square." The man accuses mothers of being "the ones who destroyed us" so that "we ended up dragging ourselves along Vardari Square." The poet responds that "those who don't hold dear their dead do not love the living" and offers the hypothesis that that "is what drove most of us to Vardari Square."

He remembers pickups he had. There were the guy who fondled his hair as he made love "beneath the waist" ("Genuflexion"); the motorcyclist with whom he "lay down on the warm cement" of a destroyed music hall where he had heard "Yiota Lydia sing 'Lawlessness'" ("At Karabournaki"); a regular who was fond of cheese tarts. Even if "the months slip by with ever diminishing hopes [and] opportunities grow desperately scarce" ("Eyes Dissolved in Tears"), he admits, "Once again a black mustache is leading me a pretty dance" ("Heartthrob"), and there are still boots at least to be glimpsed on working-class boys. As the result of an encounter with one such boy, "The poem had already begun to kick inside me" ("At the Tavern"). In other poems he likewise touches on the relationship between homosexual desire and poetry. Seeing a "hunk...blazing with youth and beauty," he asserts, "He is the poem" ("The Poem"). He admonishes a would-be poet who "gladly offered to tear apart the poet's ass if this helped him to write a poem": "You are sadly mistaken if you believe that this is how poetry is written. A poem does not emerge from the tearing apart of an ass, but from the tearing apart of the soul" ("Commentary").

Some of the same subjects return in the poems Friar has translated. In them too he laments that "beauty no longer swarms / in the town square." Urban sprawl momentarily provides hideouts for sex "amid the scaffolding and the cement" of the buildings being erected, but the finished construction "gobbled down one more place for love in the country" ("Almond Trees"). Friar provides a selection of "Small Poems." In one Christianopoulos satirizes hustlers who refuse to kiss: "only beneath your navel / are you for sale." He defends his sexual pursuits: "when an erection throbs in the brain / prostitution is better than insanity." And here he goes further in asserting that the imagination is the source of the poem: "do not unbutton your flap / the poem will fall to pieces." Some new notes are struck. Vague hints in The Naked Piazza of the political upheavals going on in Greece now form the heart of several poems. In "The Splinter" he faces his guilty conscience, that he was "mindlessly running off to make love in the meadows" the night the political activist Grigoris Lambrakis was assassinated. In another of the "Small Poems" he tries to defend himself:

> my country, i stand ashamed before you
> you drain away bit by bit
> while i play my own fiddle
> but by keeping company with your lads
> i got to know you better
> and feel your pain.

In homage to his chosen name, there now emerge poems based on parts of the New Testament. "The Centurion Cornelius," imagined from Luke 7 and Matthew 8, begs Christ to make his servant well, barely veiling his love of the man: "Anything else I might dare ask of you would be immoral." In a different tone, the unrepentant poet takes one translation of 1 Corinthians 6:9–10 that lumps "fornicators" with "informers" to mock the deity: "my God / it's dreadful of You / to place me among the stoolpigeons." Such flashes of wit and irony are common to much of his poetry.

It is past time to rescue the poet from the English-speaking oubliette into which he has been confined. His virtual oblivion stands in strong contrast to the attention another Greek poet, Yannis Ritssos (1909–1990), has received. Two fat volumes and many smaller ones of the latter's work are available in English. I do not find his poetry that exciting. Although it is populated by naked men in highly homoerotic situations, as a whole it is all rather indirect. Gregory Woods discusses him at some length (*History*, 268–73); he does not so much as mention Christianopoulos.

TEXT: Dinos Christianopoulos, *The Naked Piazza: Poems*, trans. Nicholas Kostis (Bilieto, 2000). SUPPLEMENTS: Willis Barnstone et al., eds., *Modern European Poetry* (Bantam, 1966), 265–68, trans. Kimon Friar. Dinos Christianopoulos, "A Selection," *Journal of the Hellenic Diaspora*, 6.1 (1979), 68–83, trans. Kimon Friar. Winston Leyland, ed., *Gay Roots: Twenty Years of Gay Sunshine* (Gay Sunshine, 1991), 673–75, trans. Kimon Friar. REFERENCE: John Taylor, *Into the Heart of European Poetry* (Transaction, 2008), 159–69.

Daryl Hine: *In and Out* (English)

In his introduction to *Recollected Poems*, 2007, William Daryl Hine (1936–2012) writes: "I have always returned to the metred and rhymed forms with which I am most comfortable and which themselves have provided as much inspiration and support as any content or occasion…the formalism with which I have often been taxed is not a matter of deliberate (let alone political) choice, but an involuntary and, to me, natural style of composition, as natural if not normal as my sexual predilection." Lest we miss it, he tells us that his book-length narrative poem *In and Out*, first published in a small edition in 1975, "is written in running / accentual anapaests, three / to a line." Is this "classicism" (a word often thrown out to describe his poetry) the reason for the relative neglect he has received? Or does it stem from his rootless condition? A Canadian citizen to the end, he left Canada for good when he was twenty-two and lived in the

Chicago area with his life partner for thirty of those years. As a result, despite his tenure as editor of *Poetry* magazine, he has been largely ignored by both Americans and Canadians. Yet *In and Out* is one of the great introspective autobiographies in the tradition of Byron's *Childe Harold's Pilgrimage* and Wordsworth's *The Prelude*.

It's not a perfect poem. Though, once one starts reading it, it is difficult to put down, the two middle sections seem overly stuffed and sometimes curiously detached from the opening and closing sections. Also, the purpose of the flash-forward in the last section remains unclear to me. The poem covers Hine's two years, 1955–56, at McGill University in Montreal where he was a British Columbia outsider. It records his falling, fumblingly, in love with a youth named Mark, the hapless son of a domineering mother who seems to foster the relationship. Then another student, Theodora, disrupts their intimacy. First, she seduces Daryl and then, definitively, Mark: "Biological / urges at my age resisted / denial in ways pretty hard / to ignore."

Having lost his "erstwhile *eromenos*," the Protestant lad impulsively turns to the Catholic confessional for succor. Instead, the priest "denounced my offence as the grossest / of bestial crimes." The poet is taken aback: "Such animal / lust I discovered, excited / more righteous disgust than ingratitude, / cruelty, murder or fraud." He muses,

......If a common
and perfectly natural act
which was nobody's business but mine
had offended our heavenly father
as much as it seemed to affront
my confessor, I marvelled that God
was so easily shocked....

Nevertheless, he plows on, volunteering to help at a shelter for the homeless. The priest associated with the charitable facility more sensibly advised "me not only, to go, sin no more, / but to go and think less about sin." Not yet facing reality, Daryl requests permission to join a Benedictine monastery in Vermont.

This section of the poem, the longest, is the richest, playing with religious and philosophical thought, musing on literature and translation (a task he is given, which will become one of Hine's lifelong pursuits), the nature of brotherhood, and the like. It also slows the poem's forward thrust, even if it is relevant to the growth of this poet's mind. It is only from a later time that he gains the insight, in looking back, that "My besetting shortcoming, / not yet diagnosed, was—and is— / a refusal, or failure, to dwell / in the present instead of the past / and the future." The head of the order denies his request to become a novice and insists he return to McGill. Back in Montreal he finally encounters Mark's friend Hyacinth Star, son of a converted Catholic psychiatrist much praised by all the clergy Daryl has encountered. The sexual dance is played out again. But then they foolishly "write a joint letter / announcing our intimacy / indiscreetly, for like all clandestine / but foolhardy lovers, we had / to tell someone."

To pursue the narrative line further is to introduce huge spoilers. And anyway, my relying upon the narrative thread so much to describe the poem has already done it a disservice. The story is what we remember, but the poet's internal musings are what provide the reading pleasure. As a gay document, Hine lifts from Horace what he himself takes as the poem's moral: "Although / you may drive away nature by means / of a pitchfork, she never the less / will return all the way." Patrick Holland sums up, "*In and Out* is both witty and painfully moving, and clarifies how Hine's intellectual engagement with both classicism and Catholicism provided the confused young poet with a way of articulating homosexual experience and a way of coming out" (Summers, 365). Hine is also a translator of Theocritus's *Idylls and Epigrams*, 1982, and Book 12 of *The Greek Anthology*, 2001 (see Strato above).

TEXT: Daryl Hine, *In and Out: A Confessional Poem* (Knopf, 1989). SUPPLEMENT: Daryl Hine, *Recollected Poems, 1951–2004* (Fitzhenry & Whiteside, 2007).

E. A. Lacey: *Path of Snow* (English)

Fraser Sutherland edited *The Collected Poems and Translations of E. A. Lacey*, 2000, and wrote a biography of the poet, *Lost Passport*, 2011. Both are difficult to find and exorbitantly expensive when they do show up for sale. The same is true of the poet's first volume, *The Forms of Loss*, 1965, often cited as the first openly gay book of poetry to be published in Can-

ada. *Path of Snow*, 1974, and its follow-up, *Later*, 1978, are more readily available. The former reads much like an impressionistic autobiography recording Edward Allan Lacey's (1937–1995) sexual awakening and subsequent adventures. It opens in Lindsay, Ontario, where his memories
>Bring back my blue and silent nights
>Of masturbatory delights
>Under the warm white covering guilt
>Within the house that winter built!

He had his first sexual experience with another male at age fourteen in Montreal as the result of a student exchange program: "Québec and Ontario, *graine* and cock; one, heavy and vulgar, one, small and circumcised" ("Les Visites Interprovinciales"). He traces his adolescent restlessness ("Si le grain ne meurt"), then leaps ahead to his arrest at the U.S.–Mexican border for possession of marijuana. At the time he was enrolled in linguistics at the University of Texas, where he was roommates with the budding activist Randy Wicker, but the sentence that Judge Ben Connally imposed had the consequences of "a career broken, / future cut off, / a life of wandering, / a useless life." Thus began his life of exile.

Poems in *Path* give glimpses of his sojourns in Mexico, Trinidad, and Brazil, with visits elsewhere in Spanish America and northern Africa. In Brazil he was tutor to the former president and founder of Brasilia, Juscelino Kubitschek, but mostly he records encounters with poorer people and young hustlers. Lacey, however, is a poet of landscapes even more than of people and bodies. Poem after poem attests to his sharp eye for detail and his ability to catch the atmosphere of place. His two suites of nine poems, "Mexico North" and "Mexico South," I can vouch for, none more so than his almost perfect evocation of "San Cristobal de las Casas." Even his one-sided descriptions of his hated native land bring parts of Canada vividly to life. Still, for him it is always a winter landscape inhabited by "a Puritan people without sense of sin" for whom "there shall be no joy in aught they do" ("Canadian Sonnets"), a country created by "snow-white people" who "indoctrinated me with snowness" ("Under the Sun") from which he perpetually flees. Estranged from his family, he does not go home for his mother's death and funeral ("Stroke"), though he does mourn the passing of his father ("ATL"). He has escaped his natal country bodily, but its hold on him is firm: the volume's title, *Path of Snow*, is justified even if the majority of the poems are set in tropical climes. Sutherland in his introduction to the collected poems (online) writes that Lacey "hated Canada so corrosively that it amounted to love." And Lacey feels compelled to admit that "every country was always strange to me" ("101") and always "I hear the snow-country calling" ("Saudade").

By all accounts, despite his charm and ability to make friends, Lacey did not lead a happy life. Sutherland says he was "a binge-drinker whose nearly exclusive sexual focus was on teenage rough trade." In "Night Thoughts" he compares himself to a rooster out to crow over the boys he picks up (and pays). These include the poverty-stricken Quico Lopez, who for "a few pesos" yields "his 'manhood'—all there was left to take"; Ramon, a sailor at the railway station in Buenos Aires, who wanted more than a one-night stand; two boys he engaged for a threeway in the city's suburbs ("Cat Poem"); Fedal, an Arab in Tetouan, Morocco; and a whole catalogue of conquests in different countries described in "Poème des amours fugitifs." Of them he says, speaking for all, "you will not age, you will not die; / my mind will keep you always young, / brown-skinned and eager and well-hung." But he admits that their "bodies mate but do not meet" ("Veracruz"). He goes on, "Make friends with them. Make promises to them. Fuck or be fucked by them," but at best, "We co-exist...but do not...interpenetrate" ("San Cristobal de las Casas"). He also records his fascination with the nineteen-year-old Argentine serial killer Robledo Puch, confessing, "I cannot / cannot suppress the urge toward masturbation / when his face from the tabloids stares out at me" ("Carlos Eduardo Robledo Puch").

Later Sutherland describes as "in some ways a postscript to *Path of Snow*." It includes the ultimate putdown of Canada. One comes to what first appears to be an almost blank page with the heading "A Canadian Childhood: I." Then you see at the very, very bottom of the page two words: "Nothing happened." When one arrives further on at the page headed "A Canadian Childhood: II," one is ready. This time the two words at the bottom are "It snowed." The volume has an even greater air of melancholy about it. In "Meditation One" he reflects on the seeming meaninglessness of the life he is leading, his failure to have achieved anything of note despite all his promise: "So many chances missed, never to return." True, here he is speaking of his specific failure to find a loving partner, but it applies to his whole existence. The volume which begins with something of the same sense of unity and structure as *Path of Snow* peters out in a series of unconnected valedictions. It is perhaps significant that no "Meditation Two" occurs. The "vagrant homosexual pushing forty" identifies with the failure that Jack Kerouac turned into by the time he died ("Variations on a Theme from Henry Adams"). Sutherland sums up, "Yet, no matter how lost or deracinated he felt himself to be, he still wrote poems—until injuries to his body and brain made the process psychologically impossible." Passed out drunk in Bangkok in 1991, he was run over and severely injured. Repatriated to Canada, he died there of a heart attack. Curiously, Sutherland is ambivalent about the worth of Lacey's poetry. For my part, I read *Path of Snow* from cover to cover the way I would a work of fiction, and when I return to individual poems, I continue to find great pleasure in them, perhaps because the life they describe is so different from my more timid excursions to some of the same settings. You have to like and trust a poet who can write so candidly of a traveler's woe in Mexico: "Disease even love cannot forgive. Or share. / A man with diarrhea has no sex" ("Dysentery").

TEXT: E. A. Lacey, *Path of Snow: Poems 1951–1973* (Catalyst, 1974). SUPPLEMENT: E. A. Lacey, *Later: Poems 1973–1978* (Catalyst, 1978).

Mutsuo Takahashi: *Ode* (Japanese)

Mutsuo Takahashi (1937– ; the name is given in the Western order) was born in Yahata, Kyushu, soon after the beginning of the Second Sino-Japanese War. In 1959 he was diagnosed with tuberculosis and spent nearly two years in a sanatorium. There he came under the influence of a Catholic brother and read widely and deeply in both Christian and Greek literatures. He also met several important Japanese literary innovators, including Taruho Inagaki and Yukio Mishima. Jeffrey Angles writes, "Both Mishima and Inagaki had explored the philosophical ramifications of homosexuality in their works, and both provided intellectual and literary support to Takahashi in his fledgling years as a poet." Angles goes on to explain, "Much of Takahashi's earliest poetry consists of rhapsodies for other men and supplications to potential lovers" (Pendergast, 346). By then, Takahashi had completed his university education and moved to Tokyo.

Ode (*Homeuta*) is the culmination of his early quest to unite the various strains of his interests. It opens with an invocation, "In the name of / man, member, / and the holy fluid, / AMEN." One may take the words as a blasphemous reference to the Trinity or as a simple acknowledgment that in Judeo-Christian thought Man is made in the image of God. He compares the prick to "A newborn lamb, its name: Innocento / Or Emmanuel, or again Salvador," and personalizes it as "An infant king who is offered tribute and felicitation." Angles sums up the basic movement of the forty-plus page work: "The poem, which often verges on the symbolist or surreal, depicts a man who fellates strangers through glory-holes in bath-houses, porno theaters, and restrooms, all the while searching for a connection with the divine" (*ibid.*). It is structured by the free association of ideas, images, and action rather than by any true arc. Digressions include a "ballad for the long-dead boys" inspired by François Villon. In language much less decorous than Angles's, the poet rhapsodizes about groin odor, the prick, foreskin, cock cheese, balls, pubic hair, groping, pre-cum, and cum—these words serving as a kind of gloss down the margins. The heroic quest is narrowed to an encounter at a glory-hole.

In an afterword, Takahashi explains: "The glory-hole is a *hole*, a void. Here, however, void is, to paraphrase Lao Tzu, 'that which is useful for *what is there* (= substance) by not being there.' Without this void, reality, or substance, cannot enter." Thus it is filled with the penis, or the spirit of God. The cocksucker himself in his loneliness also represents a self-contradictory void, "the most void part of the void human being…[being his] oral cavity." Takahashi then reminds us, "the food for spirit, i.e., the sacred body of Christ, enters from the mouth, and the food for flesh, i.e., bread, water, and fish, also enters from the mouth." Thus the cocksucker, "who crouches on a toilet floor, eagerly waits for the penis that visits from the hole on the wall, and fills his oral cavity with it, is typical of the human being who 'is there because he is void,' 'aims to be there because he is void,' and 'tries to be active in the passivity of waiting.'"

And yet, as Angles sums up (*ibid.*), "Though sex has the ability to bring one closer to the divine, the connection cannot be sustained. Rising to meet the divine inevitably ends with a fall back into the mundane":

Soon the taut flesh bursts, melts away
And the visitor from the other side, a god, dies
Now the one on this side stirs
Becomes a god, visits beyond the hole the wet hot darkness

Becomes wrapped by the darkness, squeezed and rubbed by the
   darkness, climbs to the top
And the god this side, too, has at once a headlong fall
Two columns of deity leave each other, and only the hole remains, black
Verily, praise be to the hole into which one peers, which is peered into—
Though the hole that makes two solitudes one
   Two shitting places one....

The original 1971 version was translated for the first selection of Takahashi's poems published in English, *Poems of a Penisist*, 1975. The volume's title comes from the afterword to *Ode*, where the poet explains, "The penis-sucker, just like Eros in one of the stories in Greek mythology, yearns for the penis, i.e., substance, because he is void. In this sense, he ought to be called a 'phallus worshipper,' or a *penisist.*" The 1980 revised *Ode* was translated for *A Bunch of Keys*. This volume also contains yet other gay poems, many as occult (in several senses of the word) as *Ode*. Others are very direct, such as "Myself with a Motorcycle." It finishes,

   I touch the motorcycle, particularly that part of its seat which was just
      glued to the ass of my god,
   still retaining the ass's warmth.
   My god eats Kentucky fried chicken, drinks Coca-Cola,
   and from the dawn-colored slit of his beautiful ass he ejects shit.

After these poems Takahashi turned more to writing fiction, plays, his memoirs, literary criticism, and traditional Japanese verse. The several volumes of poetry that have subsequently been translated into English that I have read have none of the exuberant mingling of the crude and the sublime found in the earlier poems.

TEXT: Mutsuo Takahashi, *A Bunch of Keys: Selected Poems*, trans. Hiroaki Sato (Crossing Press, 1984).

Joe Brainard: *I Remember* (English)

While still only eighteen, Joe Howard Brainard (1942–1994) fled Tulsa, Oklahoma, with two of his friends to make his fortune in New York City. He threw himself into the overlapping sexual and cultural scenes of the

New York School and had soon scored with O'Hara, LeSueur, and poet Tony Towle. He was enough of a presence by 1964 to be included in Wynn Chamberlain's twin paintings of O'Hara, LeSueur, and Lima clothed and unclothed. By then Brainard had fallen in love with poet and librettist Kenward Elmslie (1929–). In his elegy to Brainard, "Bare Bones" (*Routine Disruptions*), Elmslie remembers, "It was love at first sight, on the Staten Island ferry." The two moved in together in the penthouse that Elmslie had inherited from his former lover, librettist John Latouche, along with a rural retreat in Calais, Vermont. Brainard did not give up his basic promiscuity. It would eventually cause problems between him and Elmslie, who was looking for a more stable, monogamous relationship, but the two remained a couple until Brainard's death from AIDS.

Brainard himself was an artist, more than a writer. Thus the success of his first collection *I Remember*, 1970, was unexpected. It was followed by three more volumes before the whole was assembled in 1975. I remember the delight I felt when I found the book in 1976 in Washington, D.C., while introducing Jacques to the capital (and its bookstores). Brainard and I were born only two and a half years apart, so we share memories:

> I remember zipper notebooks. I remember that girls hugged them to their breasts and that boys carried them loosely at one side....
> I remember reading somewhere that the average cock is from six to eight inches when erect, and grabbing for the nearest ruler....
> I remember how many other magazines I had to buy in order to buy one physique magazine.

He also includes glimpses of the New York scene:

> I remember the first time I met Frank O'Hara. He was walking down Second Avenue. It was a cool early Spring evening but he was wearing only a white shirt with the sleeves rolled up to his elbows. And blue jeans. And moccasins. I remember than he seemed very sissy to me. Very theatrical. Decadent. I remember that I liked him instantly.

Brainard's success inspired Elmslie to try his own hand at the form, but Elmslie's series basically illuminates the superiority of Brainard's collection. More vital is Elmslie's "26 Remembers of Frank O'Hara" (*Blast*). These include glimpses of Ashbery, Latouche, LeSueur, Vincent Warren, Bill Berkson, LeRoi Jones, and Langston Hughes, the only allusion I have seen a New York School poet make to someone who was part of the Harlem Renaissance. He captures something of the excitement of the time in a brief tableau:

I Remember playing bridge with Frank and the Two Joes—Joe LeSueur and Joe Brainard. Poetry scuttlebutt and art world scandal made it just about impossible to focus on the cards.

As Elmslie and Brainard drifted apart sexually, Brainard became actor Keith McDermott's lover. Elmslie summed up his and Brainard's complicated understanding in his elegy:

Four months together in Vermont.
June to October.
Rest of the year, delicate but tenacious bonds.
We cohere, summer to summer,
Despite cæsuras, rifts and dumpings,
Once each, luckily staggered.
In hosp, he mentions we've lasted thirty-one years.
In hosp, he says he thinks of us as married.

Hardly a famous pair, they, nevertheless, represent the rare occasion of two artists of equal status forging an enduring relationship. The much younger Brainard also provided a link between the first and third generations of New York School poets.

TEXT: Joe Brainard, *The Collected Writings*, ed. Ron Padgett (Library of America, 2012), 3–134. SUPPLEMENTS: Kenward Elmslie, *Blast from the Past* (Skanky Possum, 2000); *Routine Disruptions: Selected Poems & Lyrics 1960–1998*, ed. W. C. Bamberger (Coffee House, 1998).

Jean-Paul Daoust: *Blue Ashes* (French)

Jean-Paul Daoust (1946–) was born in Salaberry-de-Valleyfield, Quebec, but has lived at various times in the U.S. and travels often. *Blue Ashes* (*Les cendres bleues*, 1990) is undeniably a homosexual poem, or at least a poem about homosexuality. But can it be considered a gay poem, or a poem about being gay? It is the story of a sexual relationship between a twenty-plus-year-old man and a six-and-a-half-year-old boy, told from the latter's grownup perspective.

I loved him
And he loved me

> He was risking his life
> I didn't realize
> How could I understand at six and a half
> He asked me for nothing
> Except my love.

Fifty-two pages long, the incantatory narrative is impossible to put down until one reaches the end.

It is set in Salaberry-de-Valleyfield. The now some forty-year-old narrator looks back on his love for a young wood-chopper, a neighbor. They would meet in his woodshed:

> I was a child drugged on the penis
> Especially on his
> Not understanding a thing
> But a willing participant
> Curious about our curious happiness.

On almost every page the disparity between their ages is stressed, there occurring some variation of a refrain "A love story / But I was only six and a half / He was in his twenties." Their guarding their secret well, no one—not the boy's parents or his teachers, not the neighbors—suspected a thing. There are hints early on, however, that the relationship was not idyllic, so unthreatening as the boy-become-man says. At one point he declares, "I was a child sacrificed / In the arms of a loving Moloch." And soon we find that the roles were reversed, the man sacrificed in the fiery furnace—hence the poem's title. Two-fifths of the way through the narrator suddenly blurts out, "I know / That I killed you." He explains, "You were found / Your head in the wood stove / Burnt to ashes." Variations on these lines become another repetitive element in the chant. Later he adds,

> But how could anyone suspect me
> Of hitting him over the head
> With one of our logs
> Of pushing him headfirst into the stove.

Is this a real or an imagined act? Almost immediately he adds, "But who burned that day / If it wasn't the two of us." A possible motive is given, almost as a throwaway line:

> But when I caught you
> With another
> A young neighbor boy

I swore you would die

As he explains, "I thought the two of us were sacred." Perhaps the translator, Daniel Sloate, makes an extravagant claim in his back-cover blurb—"Gay literature will never be the same after this book"—but certainly the poem is unlike anything else I have encountered.

The rest of the poems that Sloate has chosen to include grew out of the poet's sojourn in New York City: *111, Wooster Street*, 1996. These return to traditional gay subjects such as accounts of sexual encounters, the results of meetings in bars, on an abandoned pier, in the streets, at a porn theater. The specter of AIDS makes its appearance, somewhat to the poet's bewilderment when he hears two doomed lovers receiving comfort from the idea that they will "manage to die together" and both their bodies will be cremated ("Live Epitaph"). In several of the poems he suggests that lovers "are the poems of the day" ("The Pier"). The volume's epilogue, "The Week THEY Vanished," strikes a totally different note. The poet imagines what would happen if every gay suddenly disappeared, even historic figures (no Sistine Chapel ceiling). Optimistically he thinks that "everyone [would come] to the same conclusion / Living was impossible without them."

TEXT: Jean-Paul Daoust, *Blue Ashes: Selected Poems 1982–1998*, trans. Daniel Sloate (Guernica, 1999).

Jaime Manrique: *My Body*; *Tarzan* (Spanish, English)

Though Jaime Manrique Ardila (1949–) has lived in the U.S. since he was a teenager, his cultural roots remain Spanish. True, he has an intense admiration for the film critic Pauline Kael, and he references Hart Crane. He says, "I would have given myself / to Cavafis, Barba-Jacob, Rimbaud, Melville / and, most of all, Walt Whitman" ("My Autobiography"). But, more than the Colombian poet Porfirio Barba-Jacob, his major literary heroes are the Spaniards Lorca and Cernuda, the Cuban Reinaldo Arenas, and the Argentine Manual Puig. In "Learning English, 1967" (written in English) he remembers,
   ......I discovered, in Spanish,

> Manuel Puig's *Betrayed by Rita Hayworth*.
> I read this book at night
> and during breaks at the factory:
> a novel with a homosexual boy hero.

Later, at Columbia University he enrolled in a seminar conducted by Puig, and the two remained friends until the novelist's death. Manrique has translated Arenas's poetry, and Arenas wrote the introduction to his long poem *Christopher Columbus: Reflections on His Deathbed (A Collage)*, not published until after Arenas's death. "My Night with Federico García Lorca" appears with the note "as told by Edouard Roditi," the American poet associated with the French Surrealists. One senses that Manrique wishes he could be the one recounting the evening. His 1999 memoir is titled *Eminent Maricones: Arenas, Lorca, Puig, and Me*. While teaching at Mount Holyoke College, he thinks of Cernuda's tenure there and identifies with the older poet's desire to escape "the frigid winter / nights of South Hadley" to return "to the sun, / to the color of Mexico," where,

> ...in his autumn years,
>   for a brief but eternal
> instant, he found
> love for the first time,
> he wrote his best poems of passion
> and he died the triumphal
>   death of great poets.

Manrique is quite open about his sexual life but relatively closed about his love life. He met the painter and publisher Bill Sullivan in 1977 and remained in a relationship with him until Sullivan's death in 2010. He accompanied Sullivan on the latter's painting expeditions to Colombia and Ecuador to follow the footsteps of the American artist Frederic Edwin Church. Manrique wrote the catalog for the 2006 *Autobiography of Bill Sullivan* exhibition in Albany, N.Y. But nowhere does Sullivan's name appear in the poems collected so far in English. His poem "Contemplating a Landscape by Frederic Edwin Church" evokes a memory of the poet's childhood, not a portrait of the artist presumably beside him. Sullivan may lie behind the four love poems addressed to "you" (*tu*) that open *My Body* (*Mi cuerpo*, 1999). In "Calls That Never Come" he asserts, "I have wanted / to make you immortal with my poems / so that history would remember you," then provides no clue whatsoever to the person's identity.

In contrast, Al in "Al Was from Alabama" is described concretely: he is a public librarian from Brooklyn whom the speaker meets in a Greenwich Village bar, who shares Manrique's love for Kael, and who dies of AIDS, "transformed into a radiant, pure flame." Did he and Sullivan have an open relationship? In "Travel," a poem set in Colombia, he talks not of Sullivan but of "Michael, the man / I love," who "is HIV / positive" so that "I have a relationship with him / and with his virus— / this millennium's triangle." In "Nocturne: Greenwich Village" he reveals his knowledge of cruising the New York piers. The poet stands even more nakedly before us in two English poems set in Colombia before his emigration. In "Tarzan" he recalls his fear that the openly gay title character " would expose me / for what I was— / someone like him, someone / who craved the touch of men." He goes further in "1963." The year is branded in his memory as the year "I started / getting up / at night / to play with my uncle / Giovanni's cock." Finally he gets up the courage to suck off the twenty-four-year-old man—"and when I heard him sigh / the terror of that 13th year / of my life lifted." He basks in the fact that "I felt peaceful / and unafraid / for the first time."

The poet seems curiously sealed off from the gay world around him; he rarely comments on AIDS. However, one of his most moving poems, perhaps his most beautiful, is "Poem for Matthew Shepard." In thirty-seven lines he captures the horror and then transcends it: the broken body becomes a saintly gift to God. I would need to quote the entire poem to do justice to its greatness. Manrique is probably better known as a novelist. He has written six, all in English. But Spanish is his preferred language for poetry, only those included in *Tarzan* having been composed in English. *El libro de los muertos: Poemas selectas 1973–2015* appeared in 2016. Once it is translated the English-only reader will undoubtedly be able to evaluate his contribution to gay poetry more confidently.

TEXT: Jaime Manrique, *Tarzan, My Body, Christopher Columbus*, trans. Margaret Sayers Peden & Edith Grossman (Painted Leaf, 2001). SUPPLEMENT: Jaime Manrique, *My Night with Federico García Lorca*, trans. Edith Grossman & Eugene Richie (Wisconsin, 1997).

Tim Dlugos: *A Fast Life* / David Trinidad: *Notes on a Past Life* (English)

Like the New York School of poets' first generation, the younger gay generation were in and out of each other's lives and beds. The Massachusetts-born Francis Timothy Dlugos (1950–1990) arrived in the city in 1976. He rented the top floor of Kenward Elmslie's townhouse in the Village. Dlugos concludes his poem "A Fast Life": "I wanted to be living in / New York, near all the famous poets I admired / I wanted to be famous myself [space] and still do." He threw himself full-heartedly into the scene. Poet and novelist Dennis Cooper in his introduction to *Powerless: Selected Poems 1973–1990*, 1996, recalls (xi), "One was always trailing after Tim as he flew between cocktail parties, poetry readings, art openings, the baths, services at his local church, and elsewhere, often over the course of a single evening. When he wasn't around, one traded stories about him. He was a star in a way poets almost never are." Dlugos wrote of himself, "You made pissing away / your gifts look like an art form" ("No Voice"). Jim Cory summarizes the influences of the older members of the New York School on Dlugos: "From Schuyler, the method of journal-to-poem transcription. From O'Hara, the notion of literature as an interesting personality transferred intact to the page. From Ashbery, the cluster bomb of puns exploding in mid-poem...showering the reader with images" (Nelson, *Contemporary*, 115). He stands apart from most of the New York School, however, in his religious devotion: he early joined the Christian Brothers in Virginia, to leave it after Stonewall; when diagnosed HIV-positive he began studying for the Episcopalian priesthood in Connecticut.

After his death Dlugos's close friend David Trinidad edited *Powerless*, but in his desire to illustrate the range of Dlugos's work, many gay poems were omitted. Thus one must turn to the collected poems for a more complete view. Of the 534 poems there, over seventy could be considered gay. Throughout his career Dlugos commanded a wide range of forms, from prose poems to traditional stanzaic patterns, including using full and slant rhyme. The early poems evoke the giddiness of his first sexual experiences, including the sequence "A Fast Life" about gay life in the early 1970s. His first sexual encounter was with "Rob," last name never known. He recalls, "that was the first time / I was really 'in love' with another human / being [space] I was very fond of the idea of being / 'in love in New York,' too." He recounts stories of other lovers and mentions his first case of crab lice.

Gradually Dlugos focuses on gay cultural heroes, particularly those who were part of the New York scene. His fascination with pop culture extends to television as much as to film. In his last poems AIDS becomes the dominate trope. At the opposite end of the giddy sexual escapades described in the earlier poems are the somber realities of the AIDS ward at New York's Roosevelt Hospital depicted in "G–9," 1989. He pauses to say, "Thank God I read so much / Calvin last spring." Trinidad, in one of his own poems, "Driving Back from New Haven," records Dlugos raging, "I resent that we do not know how to die." But "G–9" ends with a friend asking Dlugos "what were the best / times of my New York years," to receive the answer, "I said 'Today,' and meant it." Dlugos spent his last four and a half years in the company of Christopher Wiss, whom he named his literary executor. The poet Reginald Shepherd writes, "Dlugos's poems are often strongly grounded in specific places and times, but they constantly remind us that this moment's present is yesterday's future and tomorrow's past: by being fully here now, one can be anywhere at any time. Any moment, any place, can become luminous, numinous even, if experienced in a properly receptive state of mind. Grace abounds in these poems, inhering in the smallest and the largest things" (Nelson, *Encyclopedia*, 182).

The California-born David Trinidad (1953–) met Dlugos in the early 1980s through Cooper, whom he echoes: "Wherever Tim Dlugos goes, I follow— / dazzled, never quite able to catch my breath" ("Lost Illusions"). He shared Dlugos's feelings about New York: "I marvel / that I'm here, among the literati— / the New York School poets— / that I so admire." He was likewise friends with Brainard and Schuyler, and like them (following O'Hara's lead), he was soon dropping names into his poetry. His relationship with Ashbery was frostier; in "Lost Illusions" he recalls a party at which Ashbery turned viciously on him, with Schuyler's trying to amend matters by claiming, "John was drunk." In "Poets" he alludes to Ashbery's sneering at Schuyler's lack of a Harvard education.

Had I undertaken this survey two years ago and had thus encountered only his selected poems, *Dear Prudence*, Trinidad would not be present in these pages. That volume has to be one of the worst introductions to a poet's work I have encountered. Arranged chronologically rather than thematically, it forces the reader to engage with the poet's obsessions with Sylvia Plath, Barbie dolls, and old television programs before arriving at the meatier confessional poetry. A poem almost at the end of the volume, "A Poem under the Influence," written 2004–05, serves as a prelude to his latest volume, *Notes on a Past Life*. For me that is, as of now, his masterwork. The first time I read it I was turning the pages as if I were reading a novel. The title is literal. Although each poem is satisfying in itself, the whole volume—this one arranged thematically—provides the raw materials to reconstruct the significant points of Trinidad's life. They include, prior to his arrival in the city, his rape at age eighteen, soon after he had moved out of his parents' home, and his surviving a car accident that killed his poet friend Rachel Sherwood, leaving him with survivor guilt. He did not arrive in New York until 1988. He seldom refers to the plague:

> Thinking back on it, I see how
> deeply into myself I had retreated.
> People were dying and no one seemed
> to be talking about what mattered.

Of his years in the city he sums up, "There would be love for me in New York, / as well as deep disappointment and grief" ("Elaine").

If his observations are accurate, the younger generation of poets were more acrimonious, even cut-throat, than the first generation. In his "Ode to Frank O'Hara" he writes, "It was your New York I wanted, / but I came twenty years too late. / Careerism had, by the eighties, / taken hold of bohemia." He recalls his own fallings-out with other poets. Still, he notes, "How smitten I was (and still am) with / the mundaneness of the moment. So New York School" ("Elaine"). He pays tribute to Brainard, with whom he "once almost had sex" ("Joe"). Schuyler had a great effect on him. Of Ginsberg he notes "Allen was not the best teacher." About a fifth of the way through the collection he introduces "a handsome, dark-haired man," Ira Silverberg, a Grove Press editor. From then on we get glimpses of their ten years together and their continuing friendship after their breakup (albeit one strained by competition over their dog Byron and tensions created by Silverberg's new boyfriend). "The Breakup Poem" is raw. Trinidad stayed on in the same apartment building as Silverberg, facing the World Trade Towers. He moved to Chicago after 9/11. *Notes on a Past Life* ends on a muted up beat. Trinidad gets Byron after he "took / a nip" at Silverberg's latest boyfriend. One past rift remains unhealed when he leaves, but he floods the pages with memories of other, more happier times. The very last lines of the volume recall his buying Schuyler a vase: "Jimmy, who / freely spoke / the language / of flowers, / didn't own / a vase" ("Snow on the Ground Outside").

Upon finishing *Notes,* one can then turn profitably to some poems in *Dear Prudence* for clarification of situations described in *Notes.* "A Poem under the Influence" describes bits of his life before and his early years in New York, including the circumstances of his being raped (also mentioned in "Eighteen to Twenty-One"). "A Poet's Death" goes into some detail about Sherwood's death. "Every Night, Byron!" describes Trinidad and Silverberg's relationship as seen through the dog's eyes. And poems such as "Love Poem," "Last Night," and "Sunday Evening" record tender moments he and Ira had together. *Dear Prudence* also makes clearer why he felt such an affinity to Dlugos. Both were enamored of pop culture. Both had drinking problems. Both were in awe of established poets, though Dlugos was more brash at introducing himself to them, while Trinidad was more judgmental. Both worked in a variety of poetic forms. I sometimes feel that one could switch some poems between them without anyone catching on to the deception. If I gravitate more to Trinidad, it is because I feel his life has been richer and his emotions less guarded.

TEXTS: Tim Dlugos, *A Fast Life: The Collected Poems,* ed. David Trinidad (Nightboat, 2011). David Trinidad, *Notes on a Past Life: Poems* (Blazevox, 2016). SUPPLEMENT: David Trinidad, *Dear Prudence: New and Selected Poems* (Turtle Point, 2011).

Vikram Seth: *The Golden Gate* (English)

The University of North Carolina was a democratic society: students were invited to join teachers in the little snack bar in the building next to Bingham Hall. I remember one afternoon getting very angry with Max Steele, the creative writing teacher. A student had written a gay love story for his class. Max tried to persuade the student that it was not commercial and besides that there was nothing in the story that would not work equally well with a heterosexual couple. I thought that was the point, but in those days I was timid (i.e., in the closet), so I kept my mouth shut. But it made me start wondering if there could be an incident that would make sense only in a gay situation. Vikram Seth (1952–) provided me with a perfect example in *The Golden Gate*, 1986. Therein, Ed Dorati drops by his sister's house after having had sex with Phil Weiss:

> Liz smiles at Ed; then, startled, showing
> Signs first of shock, then bafflement,
> Thinks, 'Sure there's some accident....
> How can...and yet, what other meaning...? (6.49)

She later informs Phil that she knows about the two. When questioned whether "Ed spilled the beans," she answers, "You did, as well. Though fairly sedulous, / Sunday before the equinox / You both wore the same mismatched socks" (9.21).

The Golden Gate is a novel, but a novel written entirely using the Onegin stanza devised by Alexander Pushkin: fourteen lines of iambic tetrameter with alternate feminine and masculine rhyme (*AbAbCCddEffEgg*, the capital letters denoting the feminine rhymes). Even the acknowledgments, dedication, contents, and biography follow the Onegin pattern. The story is set in the San Francisco Bay area 1980–83. The central character is John Brown, a computer programmer and rigid workaholic. Phil, a divorced single parent, is his best friend from college. Phil used to work for the Department of Defense but is now an organizer of anti-nuclear protests. Unbeknownst to John, Phil is bisexual. John meets Liz Dorati via a dating website. And thus Ed and Phil come to meet each other. Both relationships are replete with problems. Ed has been imbued with the writings of the early Church fathers; as a result, he lives in a tension between his physical desires and his spiritual aspirations. The "Bible bilge" (8.22) he periodically spouts is more than Phil can take: "One day we're lovers, and the next / I'm gagged with sacramental text" (8.31). He questions Ed why God would create such desires in him and then damn them. He argues, "Love's whole / Or else it's nothing" (8.34). Adding to the tensions, when Phil comes out to John about the relationship, John turns his back on him. His rejection of his friend is only one example of John's narrowness, Liz comes to realize. She leaves him. After a physical fight, Ed and Phil split.

In an audacious move, Phil and Liz marry. They do not love each other, but they like each other. Phil holds

> That love's a pretty poor forecaster.
> I loved a woman—and was dropped.
> I loved a man—and that too flopped.

Passion's a prelude to disaster.
It's something else that makes me sure
Our bond can last five decades more. (11.20)

Meanwhile, the protest march occurs; the Dorati vineyard is harvested; people die; an orphan is taken in; a baby is born; Ed continues to struggle to make sense of his life; and John is given a second chance. A prayer is offered to St. Francis. And always "the golden span / Hangs for the world to hymn and scan" (9.32)—a Western response to Crane's Brooklyn Bridge.

The work is a *tour de force*, with all the exuberance of youth coupled with the wisdom of a far older poet. One would swear it was written by an American—save what American poet could sustain such witty rhyming over the course of 593 stanzas? Seth was born in West Bengal. He received degrees from Oxford and Stanford Universities. He maintains homes in both India and England, but he has been an incessant traveler. His sojourn in China, Tibet, and Nepal led to a travel memoir. His family saga set in India, *A Suitable Boy*, conventional in form, met great success. For eleven years he was the partner of the French violinist Philippe Honoré. Curiously Seth's sexuality plays only a small part in his short lyrics. "Guest" portrays a young man falling for a guy who cannot accept the fact. In "Dubious" he questions his bisexual status "In the strict ranks / of Gay and Straight." Both are in his first collection, *Mappings*, 1980. In others addressed to "you," one may infer a same-sex relationship. "Through Love's Great Power," his angry response to the Indian Supreme Court's recriminalization of homosexuality (also denounced by his mother, who is the first female Chief Justice of the Delhi High Court), has yet to be collected but is readily available on the internet. It ends with an indictment that can unfortunately be aimed at many an American politician and court justice today:

To undo justice, and to seek
To quash the rights that guard the weak—
To sneer at love, and wrench apart
The bonds of body, mind and heart
With specious reason and no rhyme:
This is the true unnatural crime.

TEXT: Vikram Seth, *The Golden Gate: A Novel in Verse* (Random House, 1986).

Mark Doty: *Fire to Fire* (English)

As soon as I read "Theory of Beauty (Grackles on Montrose)," I fell in love with Mark Doty (1953–). Has anyone else written so movingly about these much maligned birds? Yes, he ignores the abundant droppings they leave behind, causing many to detest them, but he captures perfectly their raucous song. Much of Doty's poetry is about urban nature. He normally focuses on the particular animal or plant, rather than its setting, with an intensity that makes the reader feel he is sharing the experience. His many poems about dogs intensify the affection I feel for his work. He captures the joy of the dog's world, and also its poignancy. "The Stairs" describes a pet's determination to follow his humans upstairs even as he is losing his ability to manage the narrow steps. "Shelter" vividly depicts the hopefulness of dogs who have been abandoned or who had to be given up: "they've lost habitations // and, some of them, names, / though most carry forward / a single word— // Tahoe, Dakota, Jack— / all of the past they're allowed to keep." Doty explicitly compares the dogs' reaching out to shelter visitors to humans reaching out for love, but it is not hard to make an analogy also with all the throwaway children in our culture.

The greater part of his selected poems *Fire to Fire* could be classified as examples of the urban pastoral. But Doty's personal life is the main subject of his poems. He became a gay bard by a tortuous route. At age eighteen he married his teacher, Ruth Dawson, twenty years his senior. They divorced in 1978 (she kept his name the rest of her life), and he moved to New York. Her name occurs nowhere in the selected poems. He shed his past and began life anew, even to the point of renouncing his earlier publications. "Days of 1981" records his first meaningful gay encounter with all the uncertain emotions that surge forth when one finally embraces his sexuality. Many of the poems in *Fire to Fire* regard aspects of gay life. With varying emotions he describes the cruising that went on at the "Adonis Theatre," the lure of the bathhouses ("Homo Will Not Inherit"), a threesome ("Double Embrace"), a drag queen in San Francisco ("*Esta Noche*"). Some of the poems address homophobia. The murder of a Maine youth in 1984 ("Charlie Howard's Descent") failed to elicit the sense of outrage in those dark years that Matthew Shepard's did fourteen years later. In "Turtle, Swan," he writes of the advent of AIDS:

> ......I read
> every week of some man's lover showing
> the first symptoms, the night sweat
> or casual flu, and then the wasting begins
> and the disappearance a day at a time.

He portrays the struggles, deaths, and funerals of friends and acquaintances: "Tiara," "Brilliance," "*Grosse Fuge*," "Lost in the Stars."

In 1982 he met Wally Roberts, a window designer for department stores, two years older than he. They lived together happily. Then the reality of AIDS catches up with them. "Turtle, Swan" ends with Doty's cry, "I do not want you ever to die." But "Fog" describes the moment their world split in two: in 1989 the two men took the HIV test. The results were returned: "*M. has immunity. W. has.* / And that was all." In "Atlantis" he writes, raw nerves just below the surface,

> ......It's been six months,
> almost exactly, since the doctor wrote
> not even a real word
> but an acronym, a vacant
> four-letter cipher
> that draws meaning into itself,
> reconstitutes the world.
> We tried to say it was just
> a word; we tried to admit
> it had real power and thus to nullify it
> by means on our acknowledgment.

He admits wryly, "I didn't know who I was trying to protect."

Roberts died in 1994. In "Where You Are" Doty describes scattering his ashes in the ocean. But his memory continues to haunt him. Roberts is the subject of the poems "White Kimono" and "The Embrace" and a memoir, *Heaven's Coast*, 1996. In 1995 Doty began life with the novelist Paul Lisicky, six years his junior. While reading *Fire to Fire* the first time, I relished the portrait of the two writers sharing a life after so much hurt. I was unaware of what lay ahead, just as Doty was when he wrote in "Mercy on Broadway,"

> I've been lucky; I've got a man
> in my head who's spirit and ash
> and flecks of bone now, and a live one
> whose skin is inches from mine.

> I've been granted this reprieve.

Now with hindsight I can see the basic unfairness to Lisicky of these lines. It is not clear whether the beautifully erotic poem "Lilacs in NYC" describes the two of them or is another memory of life with Roberts. The reminder of Whitman's elegiac lilacs and the reference to Macy's make me fear that it is Roberts's ghost that dominates. The most touching poem about the new relationship is "Heaven for Paul." The two men are on a flight that has to make an emergency landing. Doty describes their fears, their acknowledgment of "a fine few years" together. Then, while he himself falls apart, he records that Lisicky, "who of the two of us is the more nervous, / the less steadily grounded in his own body, / became completely calm." *Fire to Fire* is dedicated to him. It served as a wedding present, for the same year, 2008, the two were married. I closed the volume with the warm glow of having encountered two men who seemed so attuned to each other.

Thus, it came as a shock to discover that five years later they were divorced and Doty was living with a new man, Alexander Hadel, to whom he would dedicate his next volume of poems (the vastly inferior *Deep Lane*, with its irresponsible poem "Crystal"). He and Hadel were married in 2015. Lisicky has published a memoir, *The Narrow Door*, 2016—really an elegy about two deaths, that of a woman friend and that of his marriage to "M." The two men always had an open relationship, but in that monumental year 2008, we learn, Doty became seriously involved with someone Lisicky calls "S." Lisicky also indicates (13) the pain of living with someone who never let go of his dead partner. Doty's memoir about Roberts indicates pretty clearly that he never realized the pain he might be inflicting. But Lisicky never seems to consider how his devotion to his own dead friend may have created tensions within the marriage. In spite of my romantic sadness about the next chapter to be played out in their lives, *Fire to Fire* remains one of my favorite volumes of contemporary poems.

TEXT: Mark Doty, *Fire to Fire: New and Selected Poems* (Harper Perennial, 2009). SUPPLEMENTS: Mark Doty, *Heaven's Coast: A Memoir* (HarperCollins, 1997). Paul Lisicky, *The Narrow Door: A Memoir of Friendship* (Greywolf, 2016).

Essex Hemphill: *Ceremonies* (English)

> I'm an oversexed
> well-hung
> Black Queen
> influenced
> by phrases like
> 'I am the love that dare not
> speak its name.'
> And you want me to sing
> 'We Shall Overcome'?

In *Ceremonies*, his collection of forty-two poems and nine essays published two years before his death from AIDS complications, Essex Hemphill (1957–1995), a gay activist and longtime resident of the nation's capital, is pulled in various directions by race, sexuality, nationality, and disease (both *de-zeaze* and *dis-eaze*). It is troubling that the collection remains so relevant more than two decades after it was published, as Trumpery sets out to destroy everything that was achieved in a time of healing balm. Terry Rowden writes, "Perhaps more than any other black gay writer of his generation, Hemphill was committed to interrogating and complicating received ideas about both homosexuality and blackness as experience[d] by African American men. Keenly sensitive to the dynamics and positionality of black gay men in relation to the black family and, by extension, the black community, as well as to the white gay community, Hemphill explores the problematics of these issues with an explicitness and level of self-disclosure unprecedented in African American literature" (Haggerty, 434).

"Heavy Breathing," the second poem in the collection, unites many of Hemphill's topics. Apparently a post-coital reflection, a free-wheeling stream of associations, the poem asserts, "I harbor no shame. / I solicit no pity. / I celebrate my natural tendencies." He observes, "Nationalism disillusioned me," and ponders his origins, his pre-American past, "the authenticity / of my Negritude." He describes the tensions between the inchoate struggles to define black gayness and its place in the larger Black Rights movement as well as its relationship to the Gay Liberation movement. He tries, unsuccessfully, to define the role of the "drag queen." He alludes indirectly to AIDS, but "Silence = death" in this context takes on multiple meanings. He describes a visit to a bathhouse and wonders at a black man who rejects black partners, wanting to take only "milk-toned creatures to bed." He despairs that "a nigga fantasy" of a new world has been betrayed as much by blacks guilty of "scandal-infested leadership" as by whites in power. He decries the distorted world of the black ghetto in which no one raised a finger to save the life of "a Black mother murdered / in an alley near home." Religious worshipers are scorned: "The dream of King / is incomplete." Langston Hughes's "dream deferred" is a museum piece.

It seems somewhat strange that he is not more angry about the ravages of AIDS. Rather he displaces such anger onto the government's Tuskegee Syphilis Experiment, 1932–72, in which a black nurse was a prominent participant ("Civil Servant"). The tone of "When My Brother Fell" is muted: "I realize sewing quilts / will not bring you back / nor save us." In "Cordon Negro" he lumps the fact that "My love life can kill me" in with the statistics that African American males "between eighteen and thirty-five" have a disproportionately high death rate. The most references occur in poems published in the mid-1980s, included at the end of this collection. In "Under Certain Circumstances" he equals the onslaught of the virus with war: "Romance is a foxhole." In "Now We Think" he fears even protected sex: "There might be / a pin-sized hole / in the condom. / A lethal leak."

Hemphill is a major figure in Marlon Riggs's documentary *Tongues Untied: Black Men Loving Black Men*, 1989, which ends with obituaries of AIDS victims, archival footage of the civil rights movement, and shots of black men marching in a Gay Pride parade. Hemphill reads his own poetry in Isaac Julien's *Looking for Langston*, 1989. He narrated a short AIDS documentary, *Out of the Shadows*, 1990. And he appears in Marlon Riggs's *Black Is...Black Ain't*, 1994. He was also an important anthologist of gay black literature.

TEXT: Essex Hemphill, *Ceremonies: Prose and Poetry* (Plume, 1992).

Brane Mozetič: *Banalities* (Slovene)

Brane Mozetič (1958–) is a native of Ljubljana, the capital of Slovenia—"the pathetic nation / to which I belong" (Poem 5), the poet calls it. Despite the relatively negligible position that his country occupies in world culture, he has become an international figure. He has published more than ten volumes of poetry, two novels (*Lost Story* is available in English) and a collection of short stories (*Passion*), as well as translated French authors into Slovene and edited Slovenian-language anthologies of GLBT literature. He notes with amusement that "American poets are envious of my position, not being / one of many. Slovenians are embarrassed, stuffy, / preferring to keep quiet" (Poem 45). *Banalities* (*Še banalije*, 2005) has been Mozetič's most successful volume to date. It consists of fifty independent poems, arranged, so far as I can see, in no particular order. Each is between twenty and thirty lines in length. Unfortunately, the English translation comes with no editorial apparatus to orient the reader. Nor are the original texts provided; on the evidence of the translations, it would appear that Mozetič appears to favor formal patterns.

The poems are largely about sexual encounters. He often describes the act itself in sensual detail, pornographic in its explicitness. But then he undercuts the pornography by recording how detached the sex seems from all else. He assesses the gay world in which he finds himself as he enters middle age and finds it lacking: "Something must be wrong with us. I'm / forty-five years old and I have no one / to think of lovingly." He is not unusual in his detached loneliness: "people talk without / touching, or they fuck in the darkness / of the back rooms without speaking." He concludes with a significant change in pronoun: "there's something wrong with me" (Poem 16). Further on, he admits (Poem 21),

> I retreat to an obsession with sex
> or something like that, I'm not sure what to call it,
> because it's all becoming more abstract. It hasn't become
> so bad that I'd spend hours and hours on the internet
> for pleasure, but it is disturbing.

In poem after poem he describes stoned evenings with men and teenage boys to whom he is attracted only for the sexual release. But even sex can finally become inconsequential (Poem 8):

> You're stoned and drunk

and you drive from club to club. You barely know
who you've been kissing, the faces
foggy. You're tempted to take someone
home, but then you forget.

When he fails to pick up "a fucking sexy Puerto Rican," he confesses, "I return alone and I'm relieved" (Poem 17). A death wish runs through much of the poetry: *eros* and *thanatos* both coupled and in conflict. In contrast to this emotionally vacant world he evokes the erst innocence and purity of his encounters with a neighbor in a barn when they were both boys (Poem 19). The volume ends with his anti-*I Remember*. He wants "To forget"—to forget bad memories: an abusive grandfather, an ambiguous stepfather, troubled childhood encounters with other boys, a flasher, an attempt at a conventional marriage—"Ah, Joe Brainard, better to forget" (Poem 50).

Mozetič's version of the succession of the ages of man goes thus: "After the court poets came the wise poets, then the scholarly ones, / the poet seers and then the insane poets. What has now / evolved from all of this are stoned poets." Announcing that what he has written "is definitely not poetry," he leaves his latest partner in bed, after a drug-fueled blow job, and wryly comments, "the life of a stoned poet isn't an easy one" (Poem 13). In spite of the sadness, amounting to despair, and the generally negative assessment of the current gay scene, the punk sensibility sweeps one along. The imagery is vivid, and the brief stories resonate in the memory. A second volume of Mozetič's poems, *Butterflies*, was translated in 2004. It consists of ninety-five poems of four lines each plus an unnumbered coda of thirty-six lines describing the capital city. Despite the volume's title the poems present a nightmarish phantasmagoria, the content at odds with the prettiness of the fragile-looking quatrains. Again there is no help from the translator, neither an introduction nor notes.

TEXT: Brane Mozetič, *Banalities*, trans. Elizabeta Žargi & Timothy Liu (Midsummer Night's, 2008). SUPPLEMENT: Brane Mozetič, *Butterflies*, trans. Ana Jelnikar (Meeting Eyes, 2004).

Jonathan Kemp: *26* (English)

Jonathan Kemp's (1967–) *26* resembles a lyrical and philosophical version of Renaud Camus's *Tricks*. Kemp does not mention Camus in an interview for *Polari Magazine* (Dec. 3, 2011), but he acknowledges the influence of other French writers and thinkers—Georges Bataille, Jean Genet, Michel Foucault, Jacques Derrida—as well as the punk American writer Kathy Acker on the composition of the prose poems, one for each letter of the alphabet. In each he ponders the relationship between the need for the primal act of sex and the equal need to encapsulate every experience into the artifice of language. The opening poem, "Aa," sets the program. The poet describes picking up a deaf-mute in a bar, a man linguistically dependent on the medium of "handwritten notes." Taking him back to his flat, the poet is "not prepared at all for the sounds that rip out of you when you come." He thinks,

> Trained in silence, locked in speechlessness, you are unschooled, untamed, letting go of sounds as you let go of your orgasm, in violent bursts that tear like an incision in flesh. Then you sink back into a big-grinning muteness that says everything there is to say about what we have just shared.

The poet envies the mute's naturalness: "I too want to tear myself open and release something monstrous and wild, something from the other side of language, where reason lies comatose and pointless."

There follow his descriptions of a variety of sexual encounters between men (and one non-op transwoman): pickups in gay cruising places, arranged rendezvouses, visits to sex clubs, casual flings with friends, even sexual dreams. Other poems are solo depictions: for example, a man alone, training himself to be fist-fucked by inserting progressively larger dildos up his rectum. The trainee rhapsodizes, "I am dominating myself, sodomising myself, raping my body's own desire for unity, storming the citadel of my sovereignty with the battering ram of madness" ("Hh"). The final poem, "Zz," forms a pair with the first. The poet is sucked off through a glory hole. Unlike with the deaf-mute, his partner is invisible, a human reduced to a mouth. Now it is the poet who is reduced to inarticulate sound: "I made so much noise when I came that you asked if I was all right."

Because the writer must have recourse to language to communicate experiences, the poems exist in a tension between the attempt to engage the reader viscerally in the sexual act and the barrier that the written word inevitably creates. Lyricism is a futile attempt to bridge the disjuncture. He reflects repeatedly on this gulf: "My body is a book overflowing with stories that can't be read without your hands roaming the Braille of my sensations" ("Dd"). If sexuality has a voice it has yet to find it" ("Oo"), for "the nocturnal language of lovers…is not written down" ("Ww"). Fucked by two Italians in a vacant lot, their sharing no common language, "I am merely a sensation suspended between them, an excuse for a commonality each, perhaps, in his own silent way, craves—but could never, except now, with my flesh shared like a meal between them, even begin to articulate" ("Mm"). The poet begs, "Give me words with substance, words that taste of skin and smell like a well-fucked man. Give me a new alphabet, a new vocabulary of sliding verbs and solid nouns" ("Qq"). In "Zz," he asserts, "We need a thinking that does not fall apart in the face of pleasure, a self-consciousness that does not steal way when it is time to explore possibility to the limit."

Ruby, aka Rudy, recounts a comical encounter with trade. As the poet gazes on her camp transformation, "a cock in a frock," he muses, "It is thus not a question of language or the body, but language *and* the body as an interface of matter itself." In such reflections the volume serves as an adjunct to the writer's doctoral thesis, *The Penetrated Male*, 2013, an interrogation of modernist texts from Baudelaire to Genet about the desire for and fear of the male body, most particularly the anus. Kemp is also a writer of fiction (*London Triptych*, 2010) and a DJ at a London club. He misguidedly publicized 26 as a short story collection. An Amazon reviewer was far more astute in seeing at once that it is a collection of prose poems.

TEXT: Jonathan Kemp, *26* (Myriad, 2011).

Justin Chin: Poems Selected by Friends (English)

Shortly after his death from AIDS complications, ten of Justin Chin's (1969–2015) friends assembled a selection of his poems, essays, and performance pieces—*Justin Chin: Selected Works*—each person writing a brief tribute about one of the works. I am grateful for their dedication to his memory and wish I had discovered him before he died. Chin was born in Malaysia of Chinese ancestry, grew up in Singapore, where his father had a medical practice, and came to San Francisco by way of Hawaii. He published his first collection in 1997. Despite the fact that he combined poetry and performance art with in-your-face aggressiveness, all his friends attest to his great personal charm. Beth Lisick (81), who joined Chin on a reading tour across the South, praises his "ability to fuse dark truths and unpleasantness with humor; to lay down something taboo and chase it with a dirty joke or some pop culture reference he knew way too much about. He could write a mean one-two punch that took you from something heavy to something funny (and by funny, I mean it could be gross, dark, weird, or stupid, or all of these at once)." Timothy Liu (45) as a fellow Chinese American raises the question, "Beyond institutionalized racism, sexism and homophobia, what are the alternatives [for an Asian American man] to being seen as a merely exotic submissive sex object or an emasculated butt of tiny penis jokes?" In answering that question, Liu notes almost sarcastically, "Justin Chin's streetwise and subversively bossy top-to-bottom poetics flew under the radar of the Pink Literary Mafia (McClatchy & Co.)."

Much of Chin's poetry is angry: "Lick my butt / cos I'm an angry ethnic fag," he writes (note the aggressive "lick my butt," not the dismissive "kiss my ass"). With timeless irony he plays up the fact that the graffiti-covered walls of "The Men's Restroom at the INS Building" enclose the sole space "in this cold / building where anyone in those endless / lines can regain a sense of significance, / to hold heads up" in a "country / protecting its land from sea to shining sea, // bilingualism / defeated and failed, fear / and incomprehension taking over." Even in the performance piece "Chinese Restaurant," one of the most comical pieces in the collection, an undercurrent of anger pulses beneath the humor, climaxing with the cry, "I find no simple gesture can erase it all. I find a border that I cross each day for a decent wage of self-deception: call it optimism, call it a punch fuck, fist-fucking the ass of the quality of life (and it's a tight one too, baby)." The most poignant outburst occurs in "Refuging." He describes a San Francisco man trying to get his lover to the emergency room when he collapses. But no taxi will stop for "two Asian men / unsure on their legs," and when they get to St. Mark's hospital, the "moonly white" receptionist says curtly, "You have to take him to St. Luke's / we don't speak your language here." Chin writes in his essay "What I Did Last Summer," "the country is still 80 percent white, which is a heck of a lot of white, though probably not enough for some folks." Such outbursts remind us that we need his vibrant voice even more than before as xenophobia has its day under our current president.

Chin is surprisingly less angry about AIDS, more resigned. In lines that anyone who has had or is undergoing a body-threatening illness can relate to, he writes ("Undetectable"),

> There is a battle in my body. Every day
> a small chunk of me is given up in this
> microscopic war. Small flecks of cells,
> shreds of tissue, muscle, skin, bone
> disintegrate, turn to junk, float
> through my body and are pissed out.

This sense of sadness pervades almost all the poems dealing with his illness. He writes, "Happiness is never overrated."

Nowhere in this selection does he voice any regrets: certainly not about his sexuality or the choices that he made, whether right or wrong. In his essay "Hid and Found" he tells us that he started having sex with men when he was thirteen. He goes on to describe his aloofness from "the queens at school because I did not want any of the teasing and bullying they endured to be redirected toward me." But then he "started hanging around the people in the local theatre scene" and that gave him the courage to "overcome my own hang-ups" and feel "comfortable around even the screamingest queens." He himself may be a "Faggot Dinosaur," his invention in another very comical poem, but he asserts (in an excerpt from "Q-Punk Grammar") that even in the face of all adversity, "we are not vanishing. Call it sheer luck, call it divine intervention, call it tenacity."

TEXT: Justin Chin, *Selected Works*, ed. Jennifer Joseph (Manic D, 2016).

Hal Duncan: Poems of a Sodomite (English)

Hal Duncan is best known as a writer of sci fi and fantasy—what he himself prefers to call weird fiction—the creator of the novels *Vellum* and *Ink* and the short story collection *Scruffians! Stories of Better Sodomites*, among others. He has long been working on a novel based on the Gilgamesh tablets. He has also written two musicals, one based on the Earl of Rochester's closet drama *Sodom*. Born Alasdair Duncan (1971–) in Ayrshire, Scotland, he attended the University of Glasgow and has made that city his permanent home. Open about his sexuality and outspoken in his political and religious views, he has reclaimed "sodomite" as his preferred label. His poetry generally employs established forms using rhyme (or near rhyme); the Shakespearean sonnet is a preferred vehicle. Six cycles, each composed of twelve sonnets, are collected in *Songs for the Devil and Death*, 2011.

"Sonnets for Orpheus," 2006, celebrates the mythical gay singer in a vigorous protest against the present day, beginning with an attack on the
> Westboro Baptists with their leather book
> skinned from lamented Tammuz, lit with stolen fire[.]
> Go on! Wash in His blood, you bleating servants of the Crook;
> the Shepard bound to split-rail fence is my messiah.

In Sonnet 2 he addresses the muses, asking their help to "sing the new reign of Orpheus Rex // Give this poor faggot your bright flames to feed." Sonnet 3 proclaims Orpheus his "Marlowe, Lorca, harrower of Hell." In Sonnet 4 he thinks briefly of all those poets lost in World War II, and warns, in Sonnet 5, "We must learn lessons from the past, my gays, gypsies and Jews." In view of what Christianity has wrought, he looks with nostalgia on the days of Pan and Apollo, and asks who else should modern gays resurrect "from sleep amongst the hyacinths and narcissi of lost days? / What other queers and heroes, gods and gays?" (Sonnet 9). Seeming to equate Christ with a cheapened Dionysus, if I am reading the poet correctly, he begs the god to "reclaim your place," "Reclaim that golden apple / for forbidden Adams who would fuck an Yves" (Sonnet 10). In Sonnet 11 he images, with glee, the ensuing "panic of popes and priests." (In the non-cycle Sonnet 15 he vigorously attacks Pope Benedict XVI.) He leaves us, declaring that his verse is "a song more holy and more pure

/ than any cant of righteous zeal." It is a "song bound only by the lover's rhythm and the poet's rhyme."

He returns to the mythological world in his cycle "Sonnets for Kouroi Old and New," using *kouroi* in its original sense as "youths" rather than its later meaning of "free-standing sculptures." The cycle combines mythological seductions with his imagined seduction of a present-day youth. He begins by calling on Phoebus Apollo, begging him to "make me your new *eromenos*; give me your pearls [semen] to swallow." Then, "with your taste upon my tongue / to flavour, salt and sweet," he plans "to lure new kouroi to your marble and my mortal arms":

>   ....I'll bring
> a young buck to an ithyphallic herm, where I will sing
> how Hermes loved Antheus, Krokus, yes, and Therses,
> how he lay with Amphion, and Perseus, and Khryses,
> sing of Gilgamesh in mourning for Enkidu's death
>   ....
> I'll sing how even Set and Horus had their fun,
> Set eyeing Horus up across the room: nice buns!
> And if he laughs, I'll smile and, with a silence, hold his eyes,
> lean in to let him taste you in my kiss, a sweet and salt surprise.

Sonnets 3 through 6 are more of the same, evoking along the way Achilles and Patroclus and David and Jonathan as well as the singer Thamyris.

But now images of a present-day seduction end each new sonnet. In Sonnet 6 he imagines being sucked off by his *kouros*, their sixty-nining in Sonnet 7. In Sonnet 8 he remarks that, of all the Greek gods, Hades was the only one "not set on some young lad's seduction," as he thinks how he will "slip from your perineum in, to liberate a moan." In Sonnet 9, just before entering his *kouros*, he rebuts the claim that the Greeks engaged only in intercrural sex:

> I say the warrior, the hero, lay upon his back,
> resisting the full filling of his arse till he relaxed
> in sudden ease, at last ungrasped, surrendered to a slide
> of inches into him, gasping submission to the glide.

Sonnets 10 and 11 are songs of their joint ecstasy. He ends, Sonnet 12, with his gay heritage:

> Perhaps it's all just poets' dreams from Horace and Catullus
> down to Whitman, Allan Ginsberg, William Burroughs,
> just the appetence of an Omar Khayyam, the leer of an Abu Nuwas,

less Alexander and Hephaestion, more Rimbaud lusting after Verlaine's
ass.
Perhaps we Michelangelos and Da Vincis
paint the gods more queer, with just a little extra kinky;
but this art, this secret language, has a magic we can use,
the sensual power of our Apollo to enchant, the kouros as our muse.

 A second collection, *Sodom / New Sodom*, 2017, is even angrier, more political, responding heavily to the current American scene (attacking Mike Pence more vigorously than it does D. J. Trump). "Sodom" reads like a belated British response to Ginsberg's *Howl*. "New Sodom" is his contemporary call to fight back against the new forces of oppression. The ten poems between these two end pieces seem padding, stuff pulled out of the drawer. *"Nec Spe Nec Metu,"* for example, is a rather pointless gay takeoff on Owen's *"Dulce et Decorum Est."* The best is "Your Nick Cave Break Up Song." The wittiest may be his attack on Trump's nonexistent "inaugural poet," Joseph Charles MacKenzie ("From Scotland with Love").

TEXT: Hal Duncan, *Songs for the Devil and Death* (Papaveria, 2011). SUPPLEMENT: Hal Duncan, *Sodom / New Sodom* (New Sodom, 2017).

Slava Mogutin: *Food Chain* (Russian)

Food Chain could easily have been just the collected writings of Yaroslav Yurievich Mogutin (1974–). Instead, perhaps with the help of his partner, the painter Brian Kenny, it became a collage, composed out of a variety of written and visual works, that deconstructs the traditional boundaries of what we mean by *a poem*. Mogutin is a multi-talented artist. Born in Siberia, he moved to Moscow while a teenager. His outspoken views as well as his open relationship with the American artist Robert Filippini brought him into conflict with the government. Threatened with arrest and prison, he sought asylum in the U.S. in 1995. Here he began to build a new reputation as a multimedia artist and a photographer. He has exhibited his work widely and has published three collections of his photographs. For a while he flirted with a film career. Generously endowed and anally receptive, in 1999, under the pseudonym Tom International, he played a bisexual role in Canadian film-maker Bruce LaBruce's agit-prop porn film *Skin Gang*; he wrote three prose poems (included in *Food Chain*) for the softcore version, *Skin Flick*. He also appeared in four of his fellow Russian émigré Michael Lucas's hardcore loops, 2000–02. Under his own name he played a Russian-born security guard in Laura Colella's independent film *Stay until Tomorrow*, 2004. He has translated Ginsberg, Burroughs, and Dennis Cooper into Russian. He was one of Ginsberg's friends during the Beat poet's last years. Mogutin continues to write in Russian but now uses English also.

His territory is that of the lost, the expendable, the degraded, the sadistic, the sordid, the politically incorrect: "my soul is like a burned-down vacant lot or a noxious waste dump covered in snow" ("Dreams Come True: Porn"). Two of the poems written for *Skin Gang* depict the opposing viewpoints of a slave used as a living toilet and the master using that slave. Sex is not a shared emotion in this punk world. The cock is the symbol of power. It can also transform mysteriously into the eucharist. Slava taunts Anton with a monstrous imported cucumber: but "then we just ate it / in the kitchen beneath the Russian Orthodox cross" ("The Fuck Millennium"). The poet confesses, "I like it in general when people scream in pain / it always excites me it's my fucked up nature." But he can also howl with laughter when a cocksucker throws up all over him and the bed ("The Belly of an Architect"). The anus and the mouth serve as commodities: when "the Prague pussyboys sell their bowels at every corner,"

> The jism hasn't dried on their lips but they already run again
> to the train station luring in their clients with their blue-eyed
> pimpliness and blond homelessness
> for 15 bucks you can come in their mouths and for 30 do
> whatever you want with them.

Throughout the volume are scattered the author's photographs, collages (thirteen created with Kenny), and experiments with typography. (One of the collages takes an amusing swipe at Fox News.) The book ends with a memoir to a friend murdered in a Russian prison and two impressionistic autobiographical pieces. It is notable that friendship counts high in these pages; love not at all. Nor for that matter does AIDS appear often. One of the typographical pages ($oviet $lave $lut") comes close to encapsulating the volume's basic attitude: "EX / AID / O / le$bian$ / $&M

/ $ALO / $LAVA." The work is raw and transgressive; it is also exciting in its audacities.

TEXT: Slava Mogutin, *Food Chain*, trans. Vitaly Chernetsky, Margarita Shalina, Dmitry Gelfand, & Alex Cigale (Itna, 2014).

Stephen S. Mills: Two Collections (English)

We do not end our quest so much as pause. It's been a long way since *Gilgamesh*, and Stephen S. Mills (1982–) seems a far different poet from Sîn-lēqi-unninni. But looking back I sense more harmony than disjuncture among the poets in these pages. They speak to each other face to face and across the ages. Since we read the past from the perspective of the present, it seems as appropriate to speak of Mills's influence on the Akkadian as to speak of Eliot's influence on Shakespeare. Mills's poetry brought into focus for me other aspects of my personal taste. If I prefer formal pattern and some sense of narrative, I find I also like transgressive poetry of a confessional nature. Mills offers all four in spades.

True, the narrative must be extracted from various poems, but the details are there, the names and sometimes the dates given. The red-headed poet was born in Richmond, Indiana (the county seat of *Wayne* County, I might note). At age twenty-one he fell in love with eighteen-year-old Dustin Carter. Mills's parents were accepting; Carter's apparently not. One does wonder how both sets feel upon reading a poem such as "Holding Hands Outside a Pro-Family Rally with My Seed Inside You" and the information that he doubts that the protestors

> …know how long you can hold it
> within you, or how long you can still
> feel my cock hours after we've fucked.
> I doubt they would call this love,
> though I can't think of any other way
> to define it as I stand here
> with my hand in your hand knowing
> pieces of me are still inside you.

"Fisting You for the First Time on the Day 'Don't Ask, Don't Tell' Is Repealed" describes just that. Such blatant directness justifies Mills's lines in "An Experiment in How to Become Someone Else...":

> I know it can be hard to love a poet.
> To take him in your bed each night,
> knowing whatever you do might end up
> in his next verse....

The pair remain together, first registering as a domestic couple in Florida and officially marrying in New York in 2015. They and their dog currently live in Harlem, perhaps drawn there by Mills's interest in the Harlem Renaissance. After four years being miserable in a teaching job at a for-profit school in Orlando, Mills now works as an HIV/STI health educator at Mount Sinai, while Carter apparently serves as a paramedic with the New York fire department. In the title poem of his first collection he sums up, "There's something about two men together— / an understanding that is ours to have, to hold on to."

This collection was the aptly-named *He Do the Gay Man in Different Voices*, its title a reference to Eliot's original title for *The Waste Land* ("He Do the Police in Different Voices"). It is divided into three parts. The first is personal. Mills recounts his youthful sexual experiences and gives us glimpses of his life with Carter. He references television programs and movies he's watched. One of his observations about gay American films perfectly sums up one of the reasons I tend to watch only gay European and Canadian movies. He asks, "Who, after fucking, wraps the whole sheet from / the bed around them? Don't you normally just stand / in all your glory? Piss bare-assed, dick out?" He sums up America, past and present: "We like / to hide the good parts. The 'dirty' parts. A culture / obsessed with sex, yet so afraid of it."

The second section mingles the personal with the poet's fascination with Jeffrey Dahmer, whose first two victims were both named Steven, with a *v*. Mills ponders, "How many strangers' houses have I entered / looking for a hot fuck? / How many times have I survived?" In the last section he discloses a pen-pal association he had with porn star Nickolay Petrov (born Edmon Vardanyan), convicted for attempted murder of an elderly couple. Mills holds, "Danger runs in our gay blood," and cites the cases of Matthew Shepard getting in the truck with his murderers and Truman Capote's obsession with Perry Smith.

The second, even finer collection, *A History of the Unmarried*, goes into more detail about Mills and Carter's life together. No other poet I know has described so well in such a few lines what it means to be a long-term couple as Mills does in "A History of Marriage." Such a simple image as "Our clothes mixing / in the open closet" ("When the Indian Guy Cried During Sex") brings back memories. Confident in the protection of condoms the way I never was and pledging "full disclosure" (as we did too), the couple rejects monogamy, finding it doubly exciting to experience threesomes together and to describe to each other one-night stands ("We've Done This All Backwards"). On dropping ecstasy for the first time, he sighs: "Sometimes it feels / like I'm living in reverse. / Somehow more responsible at 20 than at 30."

Mixed in with these wry confessions are poems reflecting on marriage that move from "No / legal document ties my body to yours" ("Seeing a Dead Lizard after Reading Mark Doty's 'Turtle, Swan'") to

>...what does it mean to know
>that if we ever want to leave
>each other
>it will have to be official?
>Paperwork goes both ways.

I am in love with Mills's voice. I hope he is wrong when he wrote in the poem "After Watching *Capote* I Decide Not to Send These Poems to Edmon,"

>He doesn't know that poets can't become famous
>anymore, that only a handful of people will ever read
>   these, some to get off on them, others to point
>out the academic in me: the techniques, references, style.
>   Others will hate me for writing such trashy poems,
>for discussing porn, cum, hard-ons, and for constantly
>   writing about writing poems in the poems.

·|||·

TEXTS: Stephen S. Mills, *He Do the Gay Man in Different Voices* (Sibling Rivalry, 2012); *A History of the Unmarried* (Sibling Rivalry, 2014).

·|||·

Some Last Thoughts

◀||||▶

Gilgamesh and Enkidu, David and Jonathan, Achilles and Patroclus, Corydon and Alexis, Nisus and Euryalus, Rumi and Shams, Michelangelo and Cavalieri, Hobbinol and Colin, Edward and Gaveston, Daphnis and Ganymede, Shakespeare and Will, Byron and Edleston, von Platen and Schmidtlein, Tennyson and Hallam, Whitman and his lads, Symonds and Fusato, Verlaine and Rimbaud, Housman and Jackson, Wilde and Douglas, Kuzmin and Sudeikin, Eliot and Verdenal, Owen and Sassoon, Lorca and Ramírez, Crane and Opffer, Cernuda and Alighieri, Villaurrutia and Lazo, Auden and Kallman, Genet and Sénémaud, Williams and Merlo, Broughton and Singer, Duncan and Jess, Ginsberg and Orlovsky, O'Hara and all, Merrill and Jackson, Elmslie and Brainard, Gunn and Kitay, Manrique and Sullivan, Dlugos and Wiss, Trinidad and Silverberg, Phil and Ed, Doty and Lisicky, Mogutin and Kenny, Mills and Carter—couples of all kinds with all kinds of destinies, very few with happy ones I now observe.

But these are poems about connecting, about trying to maintain relationships, about supporting each other. There are expressions of tender moments; there are angry outbursts. They often snigger; they sometimes deliberately shock (*épater la bourgeoisie*). They laugh; they weep. (The classical elegy expresses the love, whether sexual or not, of one man for another.) They plead; they renounce. There are religious poems, philosophical poems, but, curiously, very few political poems . Poems explore the poet's psychology: his thoughts, his emotions, his desires. The question of Nature v. Nurture, Inheritance v. Choice, shows up in unexpected places. The poems also explore the poet's body. Some are apologetic; some are defiant. Quite a number are hedonistic. If they differ from heterosexual love poems, it is, above all, because they are about love between *equals* with all the ramifications the word conveys. Nevertheless, they speak to the *human* condition. Whether that is enough to allow them to speak to everyone, only a straight reader, a lesbian reader, a transgender reader can answer. For a gay reader, though, there is gracious plenty among them to provide those props that Faulkner spoke of, those sources of strength that kept the POW going.

A Note on Translation

Traduttore = traditore. A translator is a traitor. Thus Italian plays on the similarity between the two words. Or if you prefer: *tradurre = tradire*, to translate is to betray the original. The equation is witty enough to make us consider the nature of translation. James Merrill's biographer (Hammer, 414) quotes him as saying, "Poetry...is what is gained in translation." The translator must consider several options. Does he try to capture the spirit, the tone of the original as best he can in English, even if it means going sometimes afield to do so? Or does he try to approximate the original language phrase by phrase, image by image, verb by verb as best he can? The decisions the translator takes become all the more complicated when the culture and the emotions that produced the work recede further from our own in time, space, or degree. Conveying the comic provides a particularly knotty problem. If the translator remains faithful to the language, he may mystify his readers: why has such-and-such a work received so much acclaim? Yet if he tries to time-machine the work into our present era, he may mislead the reader about the culture that produced it.

Take Catullus's Poem 56. It presents all kinds of problems. It was written more than two thousand years ago for a culture based on a totally different class system with quite different social and sexual mores from our own. It is facetious about a subject that shocks us today. Our satirists often use rhyme to convey wit; the Romans used meter. And there's the matter of an allusion to the relatively forgotten Dione, the mother of Aphrodite. So how does the modern translator create the same spirit? The complete poem follows:

    O rem ridiculam, Cato, et iocosam,
    dignamque auribus et tuo cachinno!
    ride quidquid amas, Cato, Catullum:
    res est ridicula et nimis iocosa.
    deprendi modo pupulum puellae

trusantem; hunc ego, si placet Dionae,
protelo rigida mea cecidi.

James Michie translates the last three lines thus:

I caught a tender little lover
Bottom up, rogering his bird,
And, brandishing my own erection
(Venus forgive me!), made a third.

Here is James Wilhelm's version in *Gay and Lesbian Poetry* (98) of the same three lines:

I just caught this little kid
Heaving it into a girl. And by Venus I swear,
Instead of using a paddle, to the same timing
I whipped him half-dead with my rod.

This is the joint effort of Frederic Raphael and Kenneth McLeish (*Poems*, 63):

I surprised a lad bent on shafting his girl
And promptly rammed home my advantage.
Grateful thanks to the mother of Venus,
I found myself tailor-made for the job.

Guy Lee goes at it thus (*Complete Poems*, 55):

I late caught the girl's boy pet
Wanking, and (so please Dione!)
Banged him in tandem with my hand.

Here's Jacob Rabinowitz (*Complete Poetic Works*, 20):

Just now in the alley I surprised a little boy shoving it to a girl—
and, may it please Venus! quick as a pistol I shot up his ass.

And, finally, here's Peter Green as anthologized in Thomas Hubbard's *Homosexuality in Greece and Rome* (330):

I just caught my girlfriend's little slave boy
Getting it up for her, and (Venus love me!)
Split *him*, tandem-fashion, with my banger.

One finds the same gamut of approaches with the other Greek / Latin satirists: Strato, Martial, *et al*.

In translating modern poems, there is a tendency to seek out more exact correspondence between the original and the target language. Such attempt at some degree of fidelity drives home, even more than the above examples, the fact that translation must go hand in hand with interpretation. The passage from Villaurrutia's "Rose Nocturne" that troubles me provides an excellent example. The original reads:

> Es la rosa encarnada de la boca, / la rosa que habla despierta / como si estuviera dormida. / Es la rosa entreeabierta / de la que mana sombra, / la rosa entraña / que se pliega y expande / evocada, invocada, abocada, / es la rosa labial, / la rosa herida.

Weinberger translates it:

> It is the incarnate rose of the mouth, / the rose awake that speaks / as though it were asleep. / It is the half-open rose / from which the shadows rise, / the rose of entrails / that unfold and expand, / evoked, invoked, unyoked, / it is the labial rose, / the wounded rose.

Here is Stroud:

> It is the rose incarnate of the mouth, / the rose that talks awake / as if it were asleep. / It is the semi-opened rose / of one demanding shadows, / the entranced rose / that folds, expands / evoked, invoked, and advocated, / it is the labial rose, the wounded one.

And here is a translation by Michael Smith that I found on the web:

> It is the flesh rose of the mouth, / the rose that speaks awake / as if it were asleep. / It is the half-opened rose / from which shadow rises, / the intimate rose / that folds up and expands / evoked, invoked, seized in the mouth, / it is the labial rose, / the wounded rose.

Note that small divergences begin with the fifth line about the shadows. Then *entraña* obviously poses real problems: "entrails" or "entranced" or "intimate"? None seems quite correct, though Smith seems closer. Next comes *se pliega*. Weinberger goes for "unfold," Stroud for "fold," and Smith for "folds up." Yet "yields," "submits," or "gives way" would seem more in keeping. The next problem arises with *abocada*. Weinberger preserves sound by using "unyoked." Stroud bizarrely tries "advocated." (Did he misread the word as *abogada*?) Smith is more daring and sexual with "seized in the mouth." But here is more the sense of "directed" or "channeled." Finally, despite their agreement on the final two lines, I wonder if they could not be rendered better. That grows out of my suspicion that none of the three (unless maybe Smith) realized that Villaurrutia has segued into a description of anal intercourse.

Even the form the translator chooses to use can be significant. Both Di Piero and Scrivani open their volumes of Sandro Penna's poetry with a translation of the same lyric:

> La vita…è ricordarsi di un risveglio

triste in un treno all'alba: aver veduto
fuori la luce incerta: aver sentito
nel corpo rotto la malinconia
vergine e aspra dell'aria pungente.

Ma ricordarsi la liberazione
improvvisa è più dolce: a me vicino
un marinaio giovane: l'azzurro
e il bianco della sua divisa, e fuori
un mare tutto fresco di colore.

In translating the poem they use much the same wording. But the effect is different. Di Piero chose to maintain the form of the original.

Life…is remembering a sad
waking in a train at dawn, seeing
the tentative light outside, feeling
in the broken body the bitter virgin
sorrow of the piercing air.

But remembering the sudden release
is sweeter, a young sailor
beside me, the blue and white
of his uniform, and outside
a sea all crisp with color.

Scrivani chose to project a different feeling by playing with typography. (I have corrected the misspelling *bitting*.)

Life…is to remember
waking up sad
in a train at dawn,
the dim light outside,
a melancholy feeling
in your aching body—
virgin, bitter
in the biting air.

But to remember
the unexpected liberation
is sweeter:
beside me a young sailor,

the blue and white
of his uniform,
and outside
a sea wide with color.

Which works better for the English-reading/hearing eye and ear: the stanzaic or the free verse form? There are too subtle differences in word choice and placement. Di Piero is clearer about the fact that "virgin" modifies "sorrow," not "body," but then Scrivani's "melancholy feeling" seems a better translation than "sorrow." And though "broken body" is literal, surely "aching body" fits the general sense better. As for the difference between "sudden release" and "unexpected liberation," both are accurate, with Scrivani's choice a cognate with the Italian. But the basic question is which alternative goes best with what has passed between the poet and the sailor? Is it physical, spiritual, or both?

Traduttore = traditore is witty and contains a modicum of truth. But we could also create another, far less witty equation but one that might express greater truth: *Traduttore = amatore.*

General References

Adams, Donald M., ed. *The New American Poetry*. Grove, 1960.
Aldrich, Robert. *The Seduction of the Mediterranean: Writing, Art, and Homosexual Fantasy*. Routledge, 1993.
——— & Garry Wotherspoon, eds. *Who's Who in Contemporary Gay and Lesbian History from World War II to the Present Day*. 2nd ed. Routledge, 2002.
———, eds. *Who's Who in Gay and Lesbian History from Antiquity to World War II*. 2nd ed. Routledge, 2001.
Arberry, A. J., trans. *Moorish Poetry: A Translation of* The Pennants, *an Anthology Compiled in 1243 by the Andalusian Ibn Sa'id*. Cambridge, 1953.
Barton, John, & Billeh Nickerson, eds. *Seminal: The Anthology of Canada's Gay Male Poets*. Arsenal Pulp, 2007.
Boswell, John. *Christianity, Social Tolerance, and Homosexuality: Gay People in Western Europe from the Beginning of the Christian Era to the Fourteenth Century*. Chicago, 1980.
Carpenter, Edward, ed. *Ioläus: An Anthology of Friendship*. Cosimo Classics, 2012.
Coote, Stephen, ed. *The Penguin Book of Homosexual Verse*. 2nd ed. Penguin, 1986.
Crompton, Louis. *Homosexuality & Civilization*. Harvard, 2003.
Dessaix, Robert, ed. *Australian Gay and Lesbian Writing: An Anthology*. Oxford, 1993.
Diggory, Terence. *Encyclopedia of the New York School Poets*. New York: Facts on File, 2009.
Dillard, Gavin Geoffrey, ed. *A Day for a Lay: A Century of Gay Poetry*. Barricade Books, 1999.
d'Arch Smith, Timothy. *Love in Earnest: Some Notes on the Lives and Writings of English 'Uranian' Poets from 1889 to 1930*. Routledge & Kegan Paul, 1970.

Dynes, Wayne R., ed. *Encyclopedia of Homosexuality*. 2 vols. Garland, 1990.

Elledge, Jim, ed. *Masquerade: Queer Poetry in America to the End of World War II*. Indiana, 2004.

Fone, Byrne R. S., ed. *The Columbia Anthology of Gay Literature: Readings from Western Antiquity to the Present Day*. Columbia, 1998.

Foster, David William, ed. *Latin American Writers on Gay and Lesbian Themes: A Bio-Critical Sourcebook*. Greenwood, 1994.

Gifford, James J., ed. *Glances Backward: An Anthology of American Homosexual Writing 1830–1920*. Broadview, 2006.

Greenberg, David F. *The Construction of Homosexuality*. Chicago, 1988.

Greene, Roland, et al., eds. *The Princeton Encyclopedia of Poetry and Poetics*. 4th ed. Princeton, 2012.

Haggerty, George E., ed. *Gay Histories and Cultures: An Encyclopedia*. Garland, 2000.

Hammond, Paul. *Figuring Sex between Men from Shakespeare to Rochester*. Clarendon, 2002.

———. *Love between Men in English Literature*. St. Martin's, 1996.

Howley, John C., ed. *LGBTQ American Today: An Encyclopedia*. 3 vols. Greenwood, 2009.

Hubbard, Thomas K., ed. *Homosexuality in Greece and Rome: A Sourcebook of Basic Documents*. California, 2003.

Kaylor, Michael Matthew, ed. *Lad's Love: An Anthology of Uranian Poetry and Prose*. 2 vols. Valancourt, 2010. [not seen]

Knobel, Paul. *A World Overview of Male Homosexual Poetry*. 2nd ed., 2009. Available online.

Laurents, David, ed. *The Badboy Book of Erotic Poetry*. Masquerade, 1995.

Leyland, Winston, ed. *Gay Roots: Twenty Years of Gay Sunshine: An Anthology of Gay History, Sex, Politics, and Culture*. Gay Sunshine, 1991.

———, ed. *Now the Volcano: An Anthology of Latin American Gay Literature*. Gay Sunshine, 1979.

———, ed. *Orgasms of Light: The Gay Sunshine Anthology: Poetry, Short Fiction, Graphics*. Gay Sunshine, 1977.

Liu, Timothy, ed. *Word of Mouth: An Anthology of Gay American Poetry*. Talisman House, 2000.

Malinowski, Sharon, ed. *Gay & Lesbian Literature*. St. James, 1994.

Martin, Robert K. *The Homosexual Tradition in American Poetry*. Texas, 1979.
McCallum, E. L., & Mikko Tuhkanen, eds. *The Cambridge History of Gay and Lesbian Literature*. Cambridge, 2014.
Merchant, Hoshang, ed. *Yaraana: Gay Writing from South Asia*. Penguin, 2010.
Miller, Stephen D. ed. *Partings at Dawn: An Anthology of Japanese Gay Literature*. Gay Sunshine, 1996.
Moss, Kevin, ed. *Out of the Blue: Russia's Hidden Gay Literature: An Anthology*. Gay Sunshine, 1997.
Nelson, Emmanuel S., ed. *Contemporary Gay American Poets and Playwrights: An A–to–Z Guide*. Greenwood, 2003.
———, ed. *Encyclopedia of Contemporary LGBTQ Literature of the United States*. 2 vols. Greenwood, 2009.
Norton, Rictor. *The Homosexual Literary Tradition: An Interpretation*. Revisionist, 1974.
Pendergast, Tom, & Sara Pendergast, eds. *Gay & Lesbian Literature*, Vol. 2. St. James, 1998.
Reade, Brian, ed. *Sexual Heretics: Male Homosexuality in English Literature from 1850 to 1900*. Routledge & Kegan Paul, 1970.
Robb, Graham. *Strangers: Homosexual Love in the Nineteenth Century*. Norton, 2003.
Rayter, Scott, et al. *Queer CanLit: Canadian Lesbian, Gay, Bisexual, and Transgender (LGBT) Literature in English*. Thomas Fisher Rare Book Library, 2008.
Stehling, Thomas, ed. *Medieval Latin Poems of Male Love and Friendship*. Garland, 1984.
Studer, Wayne. *Rock on the Wild Side: Gay Male Images in Popular Music of the Rock Era*. Leyland, 1994.
Summers, Claude J., ed. *The Gay and Lesbian Literary Heritage: A Reader's Companion to the Writers and Their Works from Antiquity to the Present*. Holt, 1995.
Sutherland, Alistair, & Patrick Anderson, eds. *Eros: An Anthology of Friendship*. Arno, 1975.
Tamagne, Florence. *A History of Homosexuality in Europe…Berlin, London, Paris, 1919–1939*. Trans. not given. Algora, 2006.
Vanita, Ruth, & Saleem Kidwai, eds. *Same-Sex Love in India: Readings from Literature and History*. St. Martin's, 2000.

Wells, Peter, & Rex Pilgrim, eds. *Best Mates: Gay Writing in Aotearoa New Zealand*. Reed Books, 1997.
Wilhelm, James J., ed. *Gay and Lesbian Poetry: An Anthology from Sappho to Michelangelo*. Garland, 1995.
Woods, Gregory. *Articulate Flesh: Male Homo-Eroticism and Modern Poetry*. Yale, 1987.
———. *A History of Gay Literature: The Male Tradition*. Yale, 1998.
———. *Homintern: How Gay Culture Liberated the Modern World*. Yale, 2016.
Young, Ian. *The Male Homosexual in Literature: A Bibliography*. 2nd ed. Scarecrow, 1982.

General References

Abu Nuwas 32–33, 218
The Aeneid (Virgil) 21–22, 62
The Affectionate Shepherd (Barnfield) 16, 56–67
The Album Zutique 80–81
Aleixandre, Vicente 175
Alone... (McKuen) 156–58
Arenas, Reinaldo 197–98
Auden, W. H. 131–36, 142, 147, 151, 162–63, 166, 175
Ausonius 30
Avery, Peter 40–41
Bahloul, Abdelkrim 173
Bainbrigge, Philip 109
Bankes, William 61–62, 65
Barba-Jacob, Porfirio 197
Barks, Coleman 35, 141, 146
Barnfield, Richard 16, 21, 52, 56–59
Beccadelli, Antonio 41
bissett, bill 2
Blaser, Robin 153–54
Botto, António 107–08
Brainard, Joe 193–95, 201–02, 212
The Bridge (Crane) 112, 118, 205
Broughton, James 145–48, 154
Bynner, Witter 163–64
Byron, George Gordon 21–23, 52–53, 60–67, 151, 163
Campos, Rafael 5
The Canterbury Tales (Chaucer) 41
Carpenter, Edward 23, 36, 40, 68, 70–71, 161
Casemen, Roger 90–92
Catullus 18–20, 62, 148, 218, 227–28
Cavafy, C. P. 87–90, 150, 162, 174, 184
Cernuda, Luis 119–22, 172, 175, 197, 198
The Changing Light at Sandover (Merrill) 162–64
Chaucer, Geoffrey 41
Chernetsky, Vitaly 221
Chin, Justin 215–16
Christianopoulos, Dinos 183–86
Ciardi, John 37, 39
Cigale, Alex 221
Colman, George 65
Cooke, Reginald 67–68
Cooper, Dennis 200, 202, 220
Cooper, Walter 2
Corn, Alfred 164
Crane, Hart 111–12, 116–18, 142, 144–45, 150, 182, 197
Crowley, Aleister 98–101
Cuesta, Jorge 123
Cullen, Countee 126
Dante Alighieri 4, 20, 37–39, 45, 101, 154, 162
Daoust, Jean-Paul 195–97
David, King 12–13, 15, 48, 63, 76, 94, 183, 218
"A Day for a Lay" (Auden) see *The Platonic Blow*
Dillard, Gavin Geoffrey 5
Di Piero, W. S. 129–31, 229–31
The Divine Comedy (Dante) 37–39
Dlugos, Tim 200–01, 203
Don Leon (Anonymous) 21, 65–67
Dorset, Charles Sackville, Earl of 60
Doty, Mark 206–08, 223
Douglas, Alfred 22, 90, 93–96
Drayton, Michael 49–51
Duncan, Hal 217–19
Duncan, Robert 2, 140, 152–56, 178
Eclogue 2 (Virgil) 16, 21, 29, 38, 51, 58
Edwards, Chris 153
Eliot, T. S. 37, 70, 87, 89, 101–06, 118, 131, 175, 222
Elmslie, Kenward 164, 194–95, 200
The Fairy Queen (Spenser) 46, 48
Finch, Steven 138
Fiske, John 181
FitzGerald, Edward 33, 35, 40
Friar, Kimon 164, 183, 185–86
Friend, Robert 148–50
García Lorca, Federico 111–15, 119, 151, 160, 172–73, 197–98, 217
Gardner, John 9
Gelfand, Dmitry 221
Genet, Jean 95, 136–39, 213–14
George, Stefan 93
Gil de Biedma, Jaime 174–77

Gilbert, Sky 5
Gilgamesh (Sîn-lēqi-unninni) 9–15, 217–18
Ginsberg, Allen 151, 153–54, 158–61, 165, 172, 202, 218–20
The Golden Gate (Seth) 203–05
Goodman, Paul 139–41, 151, 154
Gorostiza, José 124
Goytisolo, Juan 175
Green, Michael 98
Green, Peter 228
Grossman, Edith 199
Gunn, Drewey Wayne 78–79, 81
Gunn, Thom 177–79
Hafiz of Shiraz 33, 40–41
Harley, Marsden 118
Healey, Trebor 5
Heath-Stubbs, John 40
Hecatelegium (Massimi) 41–43
Hemphill, Essex 209–10
Hero and Leander (Marlowe) 52
Hine, Daryl 31, 164, 186–88
Hobhouse, John 62–66
Holden, Anthony 18
Hombres (Verlaine) 83–84
Homer 14–16, 21
Horace 21–23, 62, 65, 188, 218
Housman, A. E. 23, 84–87, 150
Howard, Richard 140, 164, 180–83
Howl (Ginsberg) 158–60, 219
Hughes, Langston 123, 126, 194, 210
Humphries, Rolfe 25, 112
"I Am What I Am" (Jerry Herman) 55, 73
The Iliad (Homer) 14–15, 21
Imagaki, Taruho 191
In Memoriam (Tennyson) 69–70, 82, 102
I Remember (Brainard) 194–95
Jelnikar, Ana 212
Jonas, Steve 153
Jones, Leroi (Amiri Baraka) 165, 194
Juvenal 27–29, 62, 66
Kemp, Jonathan 213–14
Kennedy, Hubert 93
Kerouac, Jack 159, 161, 191
Kessler, Stephen 121–22
Khayyam, Omar 33, 218
Kostis, Nicholas 183
Kuzmin, Mikhail 96–98
Lacey, E. A. 31–33, 188–91
LaTouche, John 164, 194
Leaves of Grass (Whitman) ix, 70–74, 181
Lee, Guy 228
Lewis, C. Day 22

Lima, Frank 165, 194
Liu, Timothy 212, 215
Mackay, John Henry 92–93
Maier, John 9–12
Manrique, Jaime ix, 197–99
Marlowe, Christopher 21, 49, 51–53, 155, 217
Martial 18–19, 25–28, 62, 228
Massimi, Pacifico 41–43
McClatchy, J. D. 5, 164, 215
McKay, Claude 125–26
McKuen, Rod 156–58
Meleager of Gadara 29
McLeish, Kenneth 228
Merrill, James 161–64, 183
Metamorphoses (Ovid) 24–25
Michelangelo Buonarroti 44–46, 69, 74, 94, 182, 219
Michie, James 20, 23, 228
Mills, Stephen S. 221–23
Mishima, Yukio 191
Mitchell, Stephen 9, 11
Mogutin, Slava 219–21
Mozetič, Brane 211–12
Murat, Jacques 78–79
Nandino, Elias 123
Nicklaus, Frederick 144
Nims, John Frederick 46
Noel, Roden 76
Nolan, James 175–77
Norse, Harold 133–34, 150–52, 166
Novo, Salvador 123, 125
Nugent, Richard Bruce 125–28
Ode (Takahashi) 192–93
Ode to Walt Whitman (García Lorca) 113
O'Hara, Frank 126, 138, 151, 164–67, 194, 200–02
Ovid 24–25, 62, 65
Owen, Wilfred 109–11, 219
Paris, Orlando 168–70
Pasolini, Pier Paolo 129, 173
Peden, Margaret Sayers 199
Pellicer, Carlos 123
Penna, Sandro 128–31, 229–31
Pessoa, Fernando 106–09
Piers Gaveston 49–51
The Platonic Blow (Auden) 134–35
Platen, August von 40, 67–68
Poliziano, Angelo 24, 45
Rabinowitz, Jacob 20, 228
Raphael, Frederic 228
Rehatsek, Edward 35–36
Richie, Eugene 199

Rimbaud, Arthur 78–84, 122, 136, 142, 172, 178, 197, 219
Ritssos, Yannis 186
Rochester, John Wilmot, Earl of 59–60, 217
Roditi, Edouard 198
The Rose Garden (Sa'di) 35–36
Rudd, Nial 29
Rumaker, Michael 78, 153
Rumi 33–35, 146
Sa'di 33, 35–36
Saba, Umberto 129
Saslow, James 44–46
Sassoon, Siegfried 109
Sato, Hiroaki 193
Savage, Tom 153
Schuyler, James 164–65, 200–03
Scott Moncrieff, Charles 109
Scrivani, George 129, 229–31
Sénac, Jean 170–73
2 Samuel 1:19–27 (King David) 12–13
Seth, Vikram 203–05
Shakespeare, William 14–16, 37, 52–56, 65, 69, 94, 103–04, 110
Shalina, Margarita 221
The Shepherds' Calendar (Spenser) 16, 46–48
A Shropshire Lad (Housman) 84–86
Shurin, Aaron 153
Shvabrin, Stanislav 98
Sîn-lēqi-unninni 9–12
Sitwell, Osbert 109
Sloate, Daniel 197
Smith, Michael 229
"Smoke, Lilies and Jade" (Nugent) 125–27
Sonnets (Shakespeare) 53–56
Sonnets of Dark Love (García Lorca) 114–15
Spender, Stephen 131
Spenser, Edmund 16, 46–49
Spicer, Jack 153–55, 166
Stanley, George 153
Strato of Sardis 29–31, 188
Stroud, D. M. 123–25, 229
Symonds, John Addington 46, 71, 74–78
Takahashi, Mutsuo 191–93
Tennyson, Alfred 4, 69–70, 82, 102, 181
Theocritus 16–18, 47
Towards Democracy (Carpenter) 71
Trinidad, David 201–03
"Two Loves" (Douglas) 22, 90, 93–94, 209
Two-Part Inventions (Howard) 181–82
Verlaine, Paul 3, 78–84, 121, 151, 168–70, 219
Villaurrutia, Xavier ix, 122–25, 229
Virgil 16, 20–22, 29, 37–38, 47, 51, 56, 58, 62–63, 101
Voyages (Crane) 117
The Waste Land (Eliot) 101–05, 118, 222
Weinberger, Eliot 123, 229
Wells, Paul O. see Orlando Paris
Whitman, Walt ix, 16, 70–74, 102, 107, 112–13, 118, 146, 159–61, 171, 181–82, 197, 208, 218
Wieners, John 153
Wilde, Oscar 16, 55, 71, 85, 94–96, 116, 150, 172–73, 181
Wilhelm, James J. 39, 42, 228
Williams, Jonathan 153
Williams, Tennessee 116, 141–45
Wills, Garry 25, 27
Žargi, Elizabeta 212

About the Author

DREWEY WAYNE GUNN grew up a farmboy in North Carolina. He received his B.A. from Wake Forest University and his M.A. and Ph.D. from the University of North Carolina at Chapel Hill. He taught for two years at Presbyterian College in Clinton, S.C. In 1968 he joined the faculty at Texas A&I University located in the heart of King Ranch country. He visited Europe for the first time in 1972 as a Fulbright teacher to Denmark. The next year he met and fell in love with Jacques Murat, a translator for Air France. He taught at the Institut Reine in Versailles and at the Université de Metz. As it became harder for Americans to hold a green card, he returned to A&I in 1977 (it became Texas A&M University–Kingsville in 1993), and he and Jacques began a long-distance marriage made bearable by the generous vacations both received and by large phone bills with AT&T. Jacques died of a heart attack in 1994, the year after he retired. Wayne retired in 2001 and was named Professor Emeritus the following year. While taking care of his mother during the last stages of her cancer, he returned to reading gay mysteries, and a whole new career was formed as he delved more deeply into his gay heritage. Two of his books were finalists for a Lambda Literary Award. The Sallie Bingham Center at Duke University archives the Drewey Wayne Gunn and Jacques Murat Collection of Gay American Pulps and the Drewey Wayne Gunn Collection of Gay Male Mysteries and Police Stories. The Kinsey Institute archives the Drewey Wayne Gunn Gay Mysteries Video Collection. The Jernigan Library at Texas A&M University–Kingsville circulates the greater part of its Drewey Wayne Gunn Collection of Gay Literature.

www.ingramcontent.com/pod-product-compliance
Lightning Source LLC
Chambersburg PA
CBHW020924090426

42736CB00010B/1032